HAGITUDE

ALSO BY SHARON BLACKIE

NONFICTION

If Women Rose Rooted: A Life-Changing Journey to Authenticity and Belonging

The Enchanted Life: Reclaiming the Magic and Wisdom of the Natural World

FICTION

The Long Delirious Burning Blue

Foxfire, Wolfskin and Other Stories of Shapeshifting Women

HAGITUDE

REIMAGINING THE SECOND HALF OF LIFE

SHARON BLACKIE

Illustrations by Natalie Eslick

New World Library
Novato, California

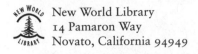 New World Library
14 Pamaron Way
Novato, California 94949

Typeset by RefineCatch Limited, www.refinecatch.com; emended for US edition by Tona Pearce Myers

Library of Congress Cataloging-in-Publication Data

Names: Blackie, Sharon, author. | Eslick, Natalie, illustrator.
Title: Hagitude : reimagining the second half of life / Sharon Blackie ; illustrations by Natalie Eslick.
Description: Novato, California : New World Library, [2022] | "First published in the United Kingdom in 2022 by September Publishing" --Title page verso. | Includes bibliographical references. | Summary: "Unearths the stories of the little-known but powerful elder women in European myth and folklore, inspiring readers to radically reimagine the last decades of their lives as the most dynamic of all" -- Provided by publisher.
Identifiers: LCCN 2022029485 (print) | LCCN 2022029486 (ebook) | ISBN 9781608688432 (paperback) | ISBN 9781608688449 (epub)
Subjects: LCSH: Older women--Social conditions. | Older women--Health and hygiene. | Menopause. | Crones.
Classification: LCC HQ1063.7 .B53 2022 (print) | LCC HQ1063.7 (ebook) | DDC 305.26/2--dc23/eng/20220629
LC record available at https://lccn.loc.gov/2022029485
LC ebook record available at https://lccn.loc.gov/2022029486

First published in the United Kingdom in 2022 by September Publishing
First New World Library printing, October 2022
ISBN 978-1-60868-843-2
Ebook ISBN 978-1-60868-844-9
Printed in Canada on 100% postconsumer-waste recycled paper

 New World Library is proud to be a Gold Certified Environmentally Responsible Publisher. Publisher certification awarded by Green Press Initiative.

10   9   8   7   6   5   4

This book is dedicated to the feisty and irrepressible old matriarchs of the far northeast of England, who enlivened my younger years and taught me never to let the illegitimi *get me down.*

CONTENTS

THE HAG'S CALL

Ceaití Ní Bheildiúin

She is the essence of weather itself.
She is the wind
tearing violently at the roof,
squealing on the old gate,
calling down the chimney.
She is my fear taking human form,
calling into me tonight —
unexpected —
seeking lodgings.
Dressed as Karalalam,
she torments me
'til, at first sight of day,
she flees.

Let me out to the wind after her,
out of my concrete skin,
out of my iron skull,
because there's a fierceness in me
that desires the edge,
the tempest,
the change.
Marrow stirs in my bones
reviving the awe of youth
in my flesh,
ending
the inertia of winter,
reopening my sword-sharp eye.[1]

HOW THE JOURNEY BEGINS

In the oldest known cosmology of my native lands, it wasn't a skybound old man with a beard who made and shaped this world. It was an old woman. A giant old woman, who has been with us down all the long ages, since the beginning of time. "When I was a young lass, the ocean was a forest, full of trees," she says, in some of the stories about her — stories that are still told today, firmly embedded in the oral tradition.

This mythology is from right here. From these islands of Britain and Ireland, strung out along the farthest western reaches of Europe where I was born, and where I live still today. In the lands where my feet are firmly planted. Although a lot of attention has been paid to the question of whether ancient European cultures honored a "Great Mother" goddess, in these islands we were actually honoring a Great Grandmother. Her name in the Gaelic languages of Scotland and Ireland is the Cailleach: literally, the Old Woman. There are traces of other divine old women scattered throughout the rest of the British Isles and Europe; they're probably the oldest deities of all.

How thoroughly we've been taught to forget. Today, we don't see these narratives as remnants of ancient belief systems — rather, they're presented to us as folktales intended

1

merely to entertain, as oddities of primitive history, the vaguely amusing relics of more superstitious times or bed-time stories for children.

Whatever we've been taught they are — they're not. They are remnants of pre-Christian cosmologies — cosmologies that are firmly embedded in the land, the sea, the sky, and the human-, animal-, and plant-populated cultures to which we belong. Cosmologies in which old women mattered.

What I love most about our Old Woman is that she clearly wasn't a character to be messed with. Take this story from the southwest of Ireland. One day, a parish priest visited the Cailleach's house to ask how old she was. He thought, as such men do, that he was a fine fellow, and very clever; he'd heard that she claimed to be as old as time, and he wanted to catch her out. Well, the old woman replied that she couldn't quite remember her exact age, but every year on her birthday, she told him, she would kill a bullock, and after she'd eaten it, she would throw one of its thigh bones into her attic. So if he wanted to, he could go up to the attic and count the bones. "For every bone you find up there in that attic," she said to him, "you can add a year of my life." Well, he counted the bones for a day and a night and still he couldn't make a dent in them. His hands, they say, were shaking as he pulled at the door handle and left.

A few years ago, on the opening night of a women's retreat I was leading on the far coastal tip of the Beara Peninsula in southwest Ireland — heartland of Cailleach folklore — I had a dream about her. I was part of a small group of resistance fighters, women and men together. We were captured by the establishment's military, then securely locked away in a prison with thick stone walls. I spoke to the leader through the bars of our cell door. "You'd better be careful," I said. "She's coming." He laughed, and shook a set of big shiny keys in my face. Just as he turned away from me, there was a rumbling outside, like thunder. A giant old woman in a black hooded cloak walked right through the prison walls as if they weren't there, and all the stones came tumbling down around her feet. The iron door to our cell crashed to the floor, and we walked right out of that prison behind her.

I'll go for that.

In 2018, in the middle of the night and in the throes of some rather cloudier dream, I woke up suddenly and proclaimed the word "hagitude" to an empty, silent room. As you do. I had no idea what it meant, or where it had come from. But, the next morning, I realized it was going to be the title of my next book. *Hagitude*: hags with attitude. Like the Cailleach, and all the other feisty, aging women of European myth and folklore who we've so thoroughly buried — just as we've relegated the aging women of contemporary life to the shadows. They're the inconvenient ones, the invisible ones. The overculture would so like to pretend they're not there.

On the threshold of elderhood, celebrating sixty years on this beautiful, troubled planet as I complete this book, I have no intention of being invisible. But I'm quite prepared to be inconvenient. As inconvenient as the Cailleach was to the Christian priests who tried to stamp out her memory — and failed. Failed, because everywhere you go in Scotland and Ireland there are stories about her. There are places in every county named after her, mountains that are believed to embody her, and ancient monuments where her presence is still honored.

But really, why should the Cailleach matter now? Why should the other fierce and shining old women of European myth and folklore who populate the pages of this book matter? Why should *any* of these old stories matter? Aren't they just ancient history? Nice to know, but irrelevant to our infinitely more sophisticated lives today? Well, they matter because the ways in which we think about aging depend on the stories we tell about it. How we think about aging women depends on the images we hold of them. And the images we hold of aging women today aren't healthy. Truth is, there is no clear image of enviable female elderhood in the contemporary cultural mythology of the West; it's not an archetype we recognize anymore. In our culture, old women are mostly ignored, encouraged to be inconspicuous, or held up as objects of derision and satire.

But our old mythology and folklore tell us something very much more interesting: that it hasn't always been so. In our more distant past, as of course in many indigenous cultures today, female elders were respected and had important and meaningful roles to play. They are the ones who hold the myths and the wisdom stories, the ones who know where the medicine plants grow and what their uses are. They serve as guides for younger adults; they're the caregivers and mentors for the community's children. They know when the community is going to the dogs, and they're not afraid to speak out and say so. When they do, they're listened to. Their focus is on giving back — on bringing out, for the sake of Earth and community, the hard-earned wisdom which they've grown within themselves.

It's not surprising that these old myths and stories of Europe that I'm offering up should be populated with European women. Although migration has been a major force throughout human history, most of these old folktales have their roots in poor, often rural communities in which travel — either in or out — was much less of an option, and in which there was much less diversity than we experience in our world today. But that doesn't mean that they exclude others. These stories offer up wisdom which is accessible and relevant to all women who are now rooted in these lands — whatever their skin color or ancestry. It's a wisdom that's accessible and relevant, in many different ways, to all those who identify as women. These old folktales are not in the business of excluding. Archetypes are, by definition, universal, and students of folklore know perfectly well that all the major themes and motifs in these stories are cross-cultural. The simplicity of the tales, and the sketchiness of their description and characterization, allows each of us to bring to them our own history, our own concerns, and our own interpretations. We draw from them what we need, and they give to all of us with equal generosity.

Myths and stories such as these help us not only to understand life as it is, or was, but to dream life as it ought to be. We perceive, explain, and make sense of the world through stories. They are the stars we navigate by, and that's why storytelling is a universal human phenomenon, a vital aspect of communal life across all cultures and throughout the entirety of our known history. Stories teach us everything we know, and their lessons are deep and rich. Stories can reveal to us longings that we never knew we had, fire us up with new ideas and insights, and inspire us to grow and change. The characters in stories are great teachers too: they are role models for our development, helping us to reimagine ourselves. Helping us to unravel who we are and to work out who we want to become.

It's always been that way for me. Since I was a small child discovering fairy tales for the first time, my favorite characters have always been iterations of the dangerous, ambiguous, but infinitely wise old woman in the woods. I didn't ever relate to beautiful princesses with wide blue eyes and golden locks, no matter how abandoned or down on their luck. Their experience was so far from my own, growing up as I did on the fringes of impoverished council estates in the far northeast of England, that I couldn't see myself in them in any way at all. But I always related to the Old Woman. The one who haunted the edgelands, the mysterious shadow in the heart of the darkwood. The exile, the rebel, the one who shrugged off the fetters of conventional society; the one who imagined and cultivated her own vision of how the world should be, thank you very much. At the earliest of ages, I already knew that was the old woman I wanted to grow into. The spirited, unpredictable, not-to-be-messed-with elder. An elder who's always ready to tell you the often-unwelcome truths about the condition of your life — leavened, of course, with compassion, and a glint of fierce humor in her eyes.

But here in the contemporary West, we don't really do elders: instead, we have "the elderly." The connotations are quite different. According to the Cambridge English Dictionary online, "elderly" is nothing more than "a polite word for 'old.'" The online Merriam-Webster Dictionary informs us that "elderly" can also mean "old-fashioned." In Lexico, the Oxford online thesaurus, the word is associated with synonyms such as "doddering," "decrepit," "in one's dotage," "past one's prime," "past it," and "over the hill."

It doesn't paint a pretty picture; these are not exactly the adjectives that most aging women would aspire to embody. But the aging woman has had a particularly troubled history in Western culture. The last convictions might have taken place in the eighteenth century, but in many ways we still haven't quite recovered from our demonization in the witch trials. Older women, when they're not rendered completely invisible, are still trivialized and marginalized, and often actively ridiculed. "Little old ladies," we call them here in Britain; "old bats" (if we think they're crazy), or "old bags" and "old trouts" (if they don't live up to our expectations that old women should rarely be seen, and certainly should never be heard). The 2019 "Ageist Britain" report, which surveyed four thousand UK adults and analyzed thousands of tweets and blogposts in the UK, found that this kind of everyday ageism is increasingly of concern to mental health experts, as evidence grows which suggests that it can impact people's physical performance, impair mental health, hasten the onset of dementia, and even shorten life expectancy.[2]

What would it mean, instead of being an elderly woman, to be an elder woman? Because to be an elder implies something rather different — it implies authority: "a leader" or "senior figure" in a tribe or other group, says Lexico. According to Merriam-Webster, a person "having authority by virtue of age and experience." The Cambridge Dictionary tells us it's "an older person, especially one with a respected position in society." So how do women transition from becoming elderly to becoming elder?

There are a lot of aging women out there. Between 1918 and 2018, average life expectancy increased by around twenty-five to thirty years in the United Kingdom, the United States, and other developed countries of the world. In most of those countries, women also live on average four or five years longer than men. The elderly — by most societal definitions, adults aged sixty and older — are now the fastest-growing segment of most Western populations, and a majority of them are women.

What should we do with those extra years of life? How should we choose to spend them, in this culture which offers few inspiring role models, and no well-trodden paths for us to follow? Because in contemporary Western society, to be old is rarely to be thought of as gifted and wise. We see old age as a time of loss, of decay; we focus on holding aging and death at bay. We find the process embarrassing, verging on distasteful. It's not something we really want to hear about, and yet the media is full of it, and all of it negative. We're constantly flooded with stories about the "burden" that old people place on health services, and with news about Alzheimer's disease, designed to strike horror into all aging hearts. There are endless exposés of appalling conditions in care homes; stories about older women being preyed upon, scammed, and even raped; stories about the impossibility of finding or even holding down a job once you're over fifty and are effectively written off by a culture which prides itself on productivity rather than quality. Where are the stories of empowered and fulfilled elders? Where are the stories of the ways in which they can bring meaning and hope into the lives of the young? Where are the still-thriving lives?

This lack of cultural recognition and support for the process of becoming elder is why so many people with aging bodies insist on trying to live as though they were still approaching midlife. It's why so few of us investigate the rich possibilities of growing older, or undertake the necessary inner work that prepares us for a passage into a more conscious and meaningful elderhood. And even if we can bring ourselves to talk about the biological and psychological dimensions of aging, more often than not we back away from discussing the existential — or spiritual — dimensions. We avoid the only question that it makes sense for us to ask now: What is all of this life *for*? Why are we still here; what do we still have to offer?

But we don't much talk about spirituality in this post-Enlightenment culture which respects and rewards only rationality. We live in a society whose power systems value only the material, and which dismiss, become vaguely embarrassed about, or actively ridicule the spiritual. Elderhood is a passage that ends in death by design, and we don't much talk about death, either. So many taboos to overcome; so many strong feelings which arise.

And yet, ever since the groundbreaking work of Carl Jung in the first half of the twentieth century, most depth psychologists have argued that the journey into elderhood is a spiritual passage above all, and that the purpose of the second half of our lives is to grow into the person that we were always meant to become. Jung believed that aging fulfilled a necessary function, saying: "A human being would certainly not grow to be seventy or eighty years old if this longevity had no meaning for the species. The afternoon of human life must also have a significance of its own..."[3] I'm a psychologist with a profound affection for Jung and his successors, and so throughout this book I'll be sharing with you some of the wisdom which this flourishing discipline offers to help us address these questions. But as a folklorist and mythologist too, I firmly believe that story is our primary inspiration — an ancient, much-neglected tool which helps us conjure up sharply honed images of who exactly it is that we might want to become if we are lucky enough to grow old. Because stories are spells; they change things. When they hook us and reel us into their magic, they change us. It's stories that will save us, in the end. Not just the stories we read or tell, or the stories we want to be in, but the ones that live inside us and the ones we live inside. The stories we invite in, those that we choose to inhabit.

As a culture, our failure to understand or embrace aging is also related to the fact that we are increasingly and profoundly cut off from nature, and thus from the natural cycles and rhythms of our human life. And yet the old women in our old stories, without exception, are forces of nature, and of the ancestral Otherworld which is so beautifully entangled with this world. There are no twice-removed, transcendental star-goddesses here; no twinkly fairy queens, reluctant to sully themselves with the dirt and mess of physical incarnation. Our old women are the dark heart of the forest, the stone womb of the mountain, immanent in the living land itself. They're elemental beings: storm hags, fire keepers, grandmothers of the sea. They show us how to live when everything we thought mattered to us has been stripped away; they teach us how to stay rooted in the face of inevitable death. They teach us how to stand firm in the face of all the culture's bullshit, and laugh.

It's interesting, nevertheless, that there are very few European folk and fairy tales with older women as their main protagonists. I have found no stories that clearly teach us how to transition into a rich and meaningful elderhood, or which hold up a mirror of clarity to the nature of our life journey at this time. But still, there exist many different kinds of archetypal old women who play pivotal roles in the stories: characters who pull the strings, weave the webs, test or advise the heroes and heroines. These elders are usually presented as wise — though they manifest their wisdom in very different ways. What, then, is the nature of an elder woman's wisdom, and how might myths and fairy tales offer us insight into the ways that each of us could uniquely embody it? That's the key question at the heart of this book: how an exploration of these wonderfully vivid and diverse archetypal characters in our fairy tales and myths might help us to recreate a map of what it is to become a good elder. How do we make the most of the fertile decades which stretch out between the first tentative buddings of menopause and the final fruits of elderhood? How can we build on those old tales and combine them with the richness of our own experience to create new elder-woman stories, and in doing so inspire the next generation? The good news is that all the archetypes in this book offer the potential to become something you couldn't have imagined before you began to grow old.

The adventure begins now.

STANDING ON THE THRESHOLD

I

THE ALCHEMY OF MENOPAUSE

The Fire and the Furies

When I look back to the early years of my menopause, what I remember most is a quality of experience that resembled British journalist Suzanne Moore's description of her own: "I don't really have the mood swings that some talk about. I have just the one mood. Rage."[4] And that fast-flowing, turbulent river of rage seething under the surface of my calm and sorted everyday persona — rage which sometimes I just couldn't find a way to contain — was more petrifying than empowering, for someone who had never been allowed to express it as a child. Whenever anything remotely resembling anger had threatened to emerge, and especially during my teenage years, my mother would clench her jaw, look me hard in the eyes, and tell me that I was "just like my father." That would be the man who had beaten her regularly throughout their (blessedly short-lived) marriage. As you can imagine, that did the job. I looked like my father; it was easy enough to believe I might unknowingly harbor some of his worse personality characteristics too.

Well, that's menopause for you: whatever else it does, it torches taboos. My inner anger-control mechanism had operated infallibly throughout my adult life, but at the age of fifty, rage seemed to have taken up residence at the back of my throat, hovering on the threshold of speech, always

ready to make a break for it. It didn't take much to trigger.
Once upon a time, in what now seems like another life, I
hiked up to the edge of the Masaya volcano in Nicaragua.
I stood there for ages, looking down into the sulfurous,
smoking hole, overawed by the melted, contorted rock of
the earth all around me. That night, I had a dream of a
woman walking out of that volcano, and everywhere her
feet touched down she set the earth alight. I felt like that
woman. I'd been storing up rage like ancient magma, and I
was all set to erupt.

Even now, from time to time, the old familial conditioning
kicks in and I look back in horror, wondering how many
situations I might have overreacted to — but I know, really,
that most of the rage I was feeling then wasn't an over-
reaction at all. I was simply reacting honestly, for once in
my life, to ideas and situations that shouldn't ever have been
tolerable in the first place. Because the rage I experienced
was rarely petty; it was well within the boundaries of
what I think of now as "righteous wrath." There are times
in our lives when it's necessary to release anger. There
are times when it's entirely appropriate for the honest,
healthy animal in us to bite. I reserved my finest vintage of
fury for the usually younger (and, frankly, almost always
less qualified or experienced) men of my acquaintance
who either patronized me, ignored my voice completely,
or kindly explained to me that I'd obviously completely
misunderstood this or that subject throughout my many
decades of relevant scholarship, training, and experience,
when they'd been so clearly capable of understanding
everything after simply reading a book or two — heavens,
some of them were clever enough to understand the entire
field of psychology and neuroscience just after skimming a
couple of nicely laid-out websites! What a pity it was that I
insisted on actual study, qualifications, insight, experience,
before expressing an opinion on complicated subjects, or

setting oneself up as an expert in them. What a pity it was that I insisted that I *knew* things, and maybe even knew more about some things than they did.

As you can see, sometimes the anger persists, even today... but all through my academic and corporate years, I'd been sidelined by men who weren't entirely sure that women should be allowed in the workplace, except of course as secretaries, tea ladies (yes, we still had them in those days, carts and all), and cleaners. I was so very tired of the patriarchy by the time menopause happened along, and a good few of the men I was responding to had made anger a feature of their public persona, a selling point. The "angry young man" archetype still has a certain romance about it, in some circles. It was okay for them to express public fury, lash out at or troll people on Twitter, but if a woman had the audacity to express a little irritation or indignation every now and again, we were hysterical harridans, or worse.

It hasn't always been so. In Classical mythology, righteous wrath was the province of old women. Three very specific old women, in fact: the Furies (or the Erinyes, in Greek). Fragments of myth featuring the Furies are found in the earliest records of ancient Greek culture. These sisters were much more ancient than any of the Olympian deities, indicating the persistence of an older, female-dominated tradition which endured here and there even when later, more patriarchal, mythologies set in. The role of the Furies was to preside over complaints brought to them by humans about behavior that was thought to be intolerable: from lesser misdemeanors such as the insolence of the young to the aged, of children to parents, of hosts to guests — to crimes that were very much worse. It was their role to punish such crimes by relentlessly hounding their perpetrators.

The Greek poet Hesiod names the three sisters as Alecto — "unceasing in anger," the punisher of moral crimes; Megaera — "jealous one," the punisher of infidelity, oath-breaking, and theft; and Tisiphone — "avenger of murder." They were, he said, the daughters of Gaea (the goddess who personified the Earth), who conceived them from the blood of her spouse, Uranus, after he had been castrated by his son, Cronos. They lived in the Underworld, and like other chthonic deities, like seeds that lie buried beneath the Earth, they were also identified with its fertility. The wrath of the Furies manifested itself in a number of ways: a tormenting madness would be inflicted on the perpetrator of a patricide or matricide; murderers usually suffered a dire disease, and nations which harbored such criminals could be stricken with famine and plague. The Furies could only be placated with ritual purification, and the completion of a task specifically assigned by them for atonement. It's important to understand that although the Furies were feared, they were also respected and perceived to be necessary: they represented justice, and were seen to be defenders of moral and legal order.

The Furies were portrayed as the foul-smelling, decidedly haggish possessors of bat-like wings, with black snakes adorning their hair, arms, and waists, and blood dripping from their eyes. And they carried brass-studded scourges in their hands. In my menopausal years, I certainly had days when I could have gone with that look.

I'm happy to admit that the existence of seriously not-to-be-messed-with elder women like the Furies in our oldest European mythology gives me great pleasure. And it's difficult not to see them as the perfect menopausal role models, because sudden upwellings of (mostly righteous) anger are a feature of many women's experience of menopause. In her passionate and meticulously argued book *The Change*, Australian feminist writer Germaine Greer suggests that society's aversion to menopausal women is, more than anything, "the result of our intolerance for the expression of female anger."[5]

But why do we find women's rage so unacceptable, so threatening? It is for sure an attitude which is deeply embedded in the culture. Several studies conducted over the past few decades have reported that men who express anger are perceived to be strong, decisive, and powerful, while women who express the same emotion are perceived to be difficult, overemotional, irrational, shrill, and unfeminine. Anger, it seems, doesn't fit at all with our cultural image of femininity, and so must be thoroughly suppressed whenever it is presumptuous enough to surface. One of the saddest findings of these studies is that this narrative is so deeply ingrained that it even exists among women — and we internalize it from an early age. Soraya Chemaly, American author of *Rage Becomes Her: The Power of Women's Anger*, writes:

> Studies show that by the time most children are toddlers they already associate angry expressions with male faces... Girls and women, on the other hand, are subtly encouraged to put anger and other "negative" emotions aside, as unfeminine. Studies show that girls are frequently discouraged from even recognising their own anger, from talking about negative feelings, or being demanding in ways that focus on their own needs.
>
> Girls are encouraged to smile more, use their "nice" voices and sublimate how they themselves may feel in deference to the comfort of others. Suppressed, repressed, diverted and ignored anger is now understood as a factor in many "women's illnesses," including various forms of disordered eating, autoimmune diseases, chronic fatigue and pain.[6]

We hide our anger by refusing even to use the word — instead of saying we're utterly furious, we talk about being "annoyed," "upset," or "irritated." We take refuge in sarcasm, we nurse grudges, or we simply withdraw. And as a consequence of these actions and attitudes, anger is an emotion that, more often than not, makes women feel powerless — not just because we've been made to feel as if we're not allowed to express it, but, accordingly, because we've never learned healthy ways to express it.

In the hot-flashed fury of my own menopause I gazed, awestruck, at a neighbor who blithely reported that she'd hurled a frying pan across the kitchen at her husband in the heat of hers. It's not that I imagined this would ever be a good thing to do — I spent the first three years of my life with a father for whom flinging fists around the room was the preferred strategy for coping with the perceived vicissitudes of his life, and it wasn't fun — but I was profoundly envious of the unstated but clearly implicit assumption that expressing anger was her right. I longed for the ability to somehow let go of my anger in simple physical expression — ideally without running the risk of injuring someone else! — because studies also show that we women often hold anger in our bodies. Unacknowledged or actively repressed, anger takes its toll on us. Numerous psychological studies have unequivocally shown that women who mask, externalize, or project their anger are at greater risk for anxiety, nervousness, tension, panic attacks, and depression. A growing number of clinical studies have linked suppressed anger to serious medical conditions such as high blood pressure, heart disease, gastrointestinal disorders, and the development of certain cancers.

There are, of course, fundamental differences between anger and aggression; the one doesn't lead inexorably to the other. Rage, properly explored, can be a great teacher. Properly expressed, it can be a great healer — because all rage hides a wound; all rage emerges from pain. My own menopausal rage, I believe, derived from the pain of being excluded, from not being allowed to have a voice, from a strong sense of exile and unbelonging which had been with me ever since I was a child. Anger, then, once examined, contains the potential for profound discovery, for a deepened knowledge of the self; working with it and through it can provide the inspiration for change. Recognized, it can be transformed, and once it's been transformed, it can be harnessed. It's a creative force. It shows us that we're still alive, still breathing, still caring, still invested in the world. Rebecca Traister, author of *Good and Mad: The Revolutionary Power of Women's Anger*, writes: "In the fury of women comes the power to change the world," and in her book she tracks the history of female anger as political fuel — from suffragettes marching on the White House, to office workers vacating their buildings in protest after Clarence Thomas was confirmed to the Supreme Court.[7] More recently, we've seen the same hunger for social transformation fueled by women's rage and given healthy expression in the #metoo movement, and three women who were furious at the violence inflicted on Black American communities by the police and others, originated the movement that is now Black Lives Matter. At its best, anger is a perfectly rational as well as an emotional response to threat, violation, and immorality of all kinds. It helps us to bridge the gap between the dreary unendurable which seems to exist now, and a more beautiful world of vivid possibility which stretches ahead of us into the future.

Men's attitudes to menopausal women have been a particular source of ire for many of us, and it's hard to countenance some of the perspectives which have been expressed over the past century or so. "It is a well-known fact, and one that has given much ground for complaint, that after women have

lost their genital function their character often undergoes
a peculiar alteration, they become quarrelsome, vexatious
and overbearing, petty and stingy, that is to say that they
exhibit typically sadistic and anal-erotic traits which they
did not possess earlier during their period of womanliness,"
Sigmund Freud declared in 1913.[8] Well, you can argue that
he was a man of his time; the first couple of decades of the
twentieth century weren't exactly known for their respect
for women's finer qualities. But unfortunately, the nonsense
didn't stop there. "The unpalatable truth must be faced
that all postmenopausal women are castrates," pronounced
American gynecologist Robert Wilson in a 1963 essay;[9]
he then elaborated fulsomely on this theme in his 1966
bestseller *Feminine Forever*.[10] This frighteningly influential
book, it later emerged, was backed by a pharmaceutical
company eager to market hormone replacement therapy.
"Once the ovaries stop, the very essence of being a woman
stops," psychiatrist David Reuben wrote in 1969 in another
bestseller, *Everything You Always Wanted to Know About
Sex but Were Afraid to Ask*.[11] The postmenopausal woman,
he added, comes "as close as she can to being a man." Or
rather, "not really a man but no longer a functional woman."

Half a century on, has anything really changed? Sadly, I
don't think so. It might not be acceptable in most circles to
write that kind of thing anymore, but menopausal women
are too often the butt of men's jokes for me really to believe
that the attitudes themselves have shifted. They've just gone
a little more underground.

So if these are the stories men are telling about us, where
are the stories we're telling about ourselves? Unfortunately,
they're not always very much more helpful. A surprising
number of self-help or quasi-medical books by female
authors toe the male line, enjoining women to try to stay
young and beautiful at all costs, and head off to their
doctor to get hormone replacement therapy to hold off the

"symptoms" of the dreaded aging "disease" for as long as possible. Their aim, it seems, is above all a suspension of the aging process, an exhortation to live in a state of suspended animation. And although more women are beginning to write about menopause as a natural and profoundly trans-formational life-passage, in the culture at large it is still primarily viewed as something to be managed, held off, even fought. Well, you can either see menopause as a possible ending or you can see it as a possible beginning. Arguably, it should be a bit of both. The ending of one phase of life, but also the beginning of a whole new journey — a challenging but ultimately fertile journey across the threshold of elderhood.

From the outside, looking at a woman objectively, there's no obvious single transition point which marks the begin-ning of this odyssey. Menarche, the first occurrence of men-struation and a gateway to adulthood, is easily identifiable; pregnancy, a gateway to motherhood, is even more visible. But the features of menopause — that final, great biological upheaval in a woman's life — aren't nearly so obvious from the outside and are often deliberately concealed.

To add to the complexity, the passage lasts for a much longer period of time. Usually, it starts during our "midlife" years. Perimenopause, sometimes called "menopause trans-ition," kicks off several years before menopause itself, and is defined as the time during which our ovaries gradually begin to make less estrogen. This usually happens in our forties, but in some instances it can begin in our thirties or, in rare cases, even earlier. During perimenopause, the ovaries are effectively winding down, and irregularities are common. Some months women continue to ovulate — sometimes even twice in the same cycle — while in other months no egg is released. Though four to six years is the average span, perimenopause can last for as little as a year or it can go on for more than ten. Menopause is usually declared after twelve months have passed without a period. In the US, the average age at which menopause is recorded is fifty-one years, though around one in a hundred women reach this point before the age of forty. Four years is the typical duration of menopause, but around one in ten women experiences physical and psychological challenges that last for up to twelve years — challenges which include depression, anxiety, insomnia, hot flashes, night sweats, and reduced libido.

Sometimes, these challenges are significant; at their most severe they can present as risks to physical or mental health, and women need help to manage them. But one of the main reasons why women fail to see menopause as part of a natural — and even desirable — life transition is that, in Western culture, it has been thoroughly and effectively medicalized. It's presented as a disability, a dysfunction in need of medication, a set of "symptoms" — rather than being imagined as a natural and necessary entry point into the next stage of life, as it once was in traditional societies, and as it still is in many indigenous cultures today.

Interestingly, menopause didn't become a matter of medical concern until the eighteenth century, when it was often referred to as the "climacteric" — a word derived from medieval theories that divided life into periods of seven to nine years that were punctuated by crises. During this period, male physicians throughout Europe began to write learned theses about the end of menstruation, suggesting that it initiated an assortment of physical and psychological diseases in women. In the early twentieth century, with the discovery of hormones and the development of the new field of endocrinology, menopause began to be viewed primarily as a deficiency of estrogen — a hormone which consequently became heavily identified with femininity. This perspective led to the development of hormone replacement therapy, and throughout the twentieth century menopause continued to be presented, in the world's leading medical journals and books, as a disease to be "cured" with medication — one which, to add insult to injury, was capable of triggering the onset of other diseases.

Everyone in Western cultures reading this book, then, young or old, will have been born into a culture which teaches us that menopause is a disease, a failure, a dysfunction. Menopause is presented to us as a *lack* — specifically, a lack of estrogen, the "femininity and fertility" hormone. And, consequently, modern conceptions of menopause encourage images of midlife women as weak, and as subject to drastic mood swings, forgetfulness, and laughable hot flashes. We ourselves tend to focus on what we've lost — dewy, unlined skin, hair color, firm muscles, the ability to give birth — and the only things we imagine we've gained in return are wrinkles, sagging backsides, painfully dry vaginas, sweat-ridden bedsheets, and osteoporosis. We're told that we should still, above all things, disguise ourselves as young women in order to be sexually attractive to prospective or existing partners at sixty. We're told that a reduction in libido at this stage in our lives is abnormal: something to panic about, to fix — again, to medicate ourselves out of, when many women are actually quite content to slip naturally into a phase of life which is much less focused on their sexuality. We think of aging as a failure, something to be fought against — rather than as a natural part of life which, like all of life, we must find a way to adapt to, and to welcome, not merely to endure.

These attitudes aside, the problems that many women face in adjusting to menopause are simply down to the fact of living in a culture that doesn't allow us to build time into our lives for key transitions. We're not permitted to take time out, so many of us try to carry on exactly as we were before. Being everything to everybody. Holding down the job, still looking after the kids, the cats, the partner. Piling on the need to care for older and ailing relatives to the backbreaking stack of existing responsibilities. Running from work to the gym to the supermarket then home to cook dinner, trying to soldier on as if nothing were happening, and medicating ourselves to cover the inevitable cracks. And then we wonder why we break. Because what we should be doing during menopause is gently and consciously letting go of one period of our lives, and slowly and mindfully easing the progression into another.

That letting go is hard — of course it is. It needs time; it needs tenderness. It can be hard to relinquish our identification with society's view of youth as the owner of beauty, hard to turn our backs on its cult of sexuality. But we must. No matter how long we try to postpone the inevitable, our body's ultimate trajectory leaves us no choice. Often, that necessary surrender to the inevitable gives rise to a time of deep grieving — and it should. Because menopause is an ending of sorts, and it is natural to mourn an ending — but it is also a new beginning. It is above all a transformation. The late author Ursula K. Le Guin expresses this idea beautifully: "The woman who is willing to make that change must become pregnant with herself, at last. She must bear herself, her third self, her old age."[12] I love this idea, because to me transformation is everything: it's the purpose of life. We women do it all the time, and often in the most cataclysmic of ways. From puberty to pregnancy... and then, just when we think it's all over, along comes menopause, to shake us to the core again. We're never done with our transformations; they just keep on coming round. We shapeshift all the way up to the end, casting off certainties like a selkie casts off her sealskin.

One aspect of menopause that is particularly difficult for many women is the need to let go of our tendency to define ourselves by our potential to birth new life — whether we have actually chosen to do so or not. Women are still, in many societies around the world, valued predominantly for their childbearing abilities. Once all that's over, so are we. We become irrelevant, inconsequential. And of course, throughout history, that was women's primary function. Until very recently, few women made it past childbearing age; most women never reached menopause at all, and hardly any passed through it into elderhood. But now that we are living longer, it's important to remember that fertility isn't actually the norm in the context of an entire lifespan. We're fertile (more or less) from approximately fifteen years old to around forty: twenty-five years out of an average, in Western countries today, of eighty.

Regardless of that, society doesn't make letting go of fertility easy for us. In 2019, a medical procedure that aims to delay menopause in women for up to twenty years was launched by ProFam — a company of IVF specialists in Britain (headed, inevitably, by a primarily male team). The procedure involves surgical removal of a fraction of ovarian tissue by laparoscopy. The tissue is sliced, then frozen at very low temperatures so the tissue and eggs can be preserved. The idea is that, if you want to become pregnant or to delay menopause at some stage in the future, the tissue will be thawed and transferred (grafted) back into your body. After that's been done, the company claims, most women gain full hormone production within four to six months. The justification for this procedure, according to the company's website, is that:

> Young women today are destined to live in the menopausal stage for 30–40 years (or more), but throughout history most women did not live much beyond their fertile period. Although modern lifestyle and medicine are ensuring we live much longer, the intrinsic nature of the ovaries has not changed, and unless we use

modern technology to preserve them, the ovaries will cease to function at around 45–50 years
of age, leaving a woman with 4 or 5 decades of
menopausal issues. Delaying menopause with
ovarian tissue cryopreservation and transplanta-
tion later in life can extend the period a woman
lives in pre-menopausal stage. Years of meticulous research has now allowed women to delay
their biological clock.[13]

Four or five decades of "menopausal issues"? Even though
some effects of estrogen depletion, such as osteoporosis,
do persist for the rest of one's life, frankly that's nonsense.
As I indicated earlier, the challenges associated with
menopause have almost always passed within a maximum
of twelve years. What the company actually appears to be
suggesting here is that fertility is normal, and infertility is
not. That there is something aberrant in the idea of women
living for decades in which they're free from the burden
of menstruation and potential pregnancy. That there is
something transgressive in the idea that we might have a
useful and meaningful life which isn't dependent upon, and
which outlasts, our fertility. This kind of attitude perpetuates
the (surely, by now, outdated) idea that women are valuable,
and can have self-worth, only in the context of that fertility.
It's enough to make you want to call in the Furies, for sure.

My own entry into menopause was hardly typical; it all
happened quite suddenly. It was less of a nice slow transition, and rather more of a car crash. I had suffered from
severe endometriosis for all of my adult life, and the only
effective way I'd ever found to manage the monthly agony
and excessive bleeding was to take the contraceptive pill to
"normalize" my cycles. But I had always planned to stop
taking the pill once I reached the age of fifty, because the

medical evidence clearly suggested that it was unlikely to be safe after that. I imagined I'd just have to deal with the ongoing pain, and hope that it would all miraculously vanish when menopause finally happened and I could kiss goodbye to menstruation forever. So, my fiftieth birthday arrived, I stopped taking the pill shortly afterward — and never had another period. Not so much as an ache or a twinge; not even the slightest spotting of blood. Menopause, it seemed, had been happening quietly in the background while I wasn't paying attention; it had been masked by the effects of the contraceptive pill.

At first, it seemed to me that all this was a very fine thing; not only had I been liberated from a lifetime of heavy and painful periods, but I hadn't even had to endure any of the menstrual irregularities most women face in the run-up to menopause. I hadn't had a perimenopause at all. But of course, there were still changes to go through — and now, they all descended on me at once. That sudden volcanic eruption of rage I've described defined my psychological experience; fire defined my physical experience too. I was burning woman; I was a walking hellfire. Some great conflagration was occurring, and I felt as if I were being consumed from the inside out.

My friend Fern, an artist, facilitator, and wilderness guide here in Wales, had the same experience. She remembers regularly going to bed wrapped in a king-size bath towel to absorb the buckets of sweat which would otherwise soak the sheets. The sweats also happened during the day. "I'd often have to do an Olympic sprint to remove at least two layers of clothing in less than three seconds flat," she laughs. "This was rather less easy if I was in company. Thirty seconds later, I'd feel chilled and have to pile it all back on again. I became magnetized by watching my body 'fire up,'" she tells me. "There was a sound I inwardly made — the mimicking of a small explosion or nuclear-fueled rocket powering itself into orbit — Pwchhhh! That's what it felt like. To so strongly and instantaneously feel my own physiology and metabolism was incredible. I started to understand that this was about accessing a new kind of power — crone power, hag power — the power of fusion or fission, if you like. It certainly felt elemental, atomic. I became fascinated by what kind of power this might potentially release in aging women if we could consciously access it."

There is power in fire, clearly, and throughout the burning times of my menopause, W. B. Yeats's beautiful poem "The Song of Wandering Aengus" was never far from my mind: "I went out to the hazel-wood / Because a fire was in my head..." And it was. I didn't experience any of the "brain fog" or forgetfulness that many women report having to deal with — quite the opposite. Now that I was no longer tied to the endless ups and downs of monthly hormonal fluctuations, and the endless seething cycles of up-and-down emotion that accompanied them, I felt not only liberated, but clarified. My thinking was sharper and more focused; I felt as if my energy was turning to things that actually mattered. It was as if a cloud had been lifted, and there followed a period of three or four years that I've always thought of, and described, as "incandescent" — a word derived originally from the Latin *incandascere*, which means to glow, to kindle from within. Because fire, kindled and properly tempered, is the element of creativity, illumination, and inspiration, of the life force that burns brightly inside each of us.

For several months I not only embodied fire, but I dreamed of it. I dreamed of firepits, of forges, of naked flames dancing around my bed; I dreamed of dragons — and I dreamed of crucibles. Crucibles: the fireproof vessels in which the first stages of alchemy occur. And that is precisely what menopause is, if we allow it: a profoundly alchemical process, designed to transform us from the inside out.

~

Cleopatra the Alchemist, who is believed to have lived in Alexandria around the third or fourth centuries CE, is one of four female alchemists who were thought to have been able to produce the rare and much-sought-after philosopher's stone. She is a foundational figure in alchemy, and made great use of original imagery which reflects conception and birth — representing the renewal and transformation of life. She also experimented with practical alchemy (the forerunner of modern chemistry) and is credited by some with having invented the alembic, an apparatus used for distillation. Her mentor was Maria the Jewess, who lived in Alexandria sometime between the first and third centuries CE; she is similarly credited with the invention of several kinds of chemical apparatuses and is considered to be the first true alchemist of the Western world. In 1964, the great surrealist artist Leonora Carrington painted Maria, depicting her as a woman-lion chimera with breasts exposed and hair wildly flailing around her, as she weaves magical gold-summoning spells.

Actually, female alchemists in Greco-Roman Egypt weren't uncommon, though they were mostly preoccupied with concocting fragrances and cosmetics. In fact, it was a collective of female alchemists in ancient Egypt who invented beer, setting up an unsurprisingly booming business by the Nile. This is all a far cry from the popular image of an alchemist: that of a lavishly dressed and usually bearded man in a medieval laboratory, bending over a fire and surrounded by all manner of arcane contraptions, trying to turn lead into gold.

However you imagine its perpetrators, alchemy is, in a nutshell, the art of transformation. It's an ancient branch of "natural philosophy," a philosophical and proto-scientific tradition which was practiced in a variety of manifestations throughout Europe, Africa, China, and Asia. Put simply, it is focused on the ways in which one thing can be changed into another, and its goal is to perfect, purify, or evolve the material in question. In Europe, alchemists with a predilection for the practical certainly spent time trying to create gold from base metals like lead, but alchemy — as Cleopatra's imagery clearly demonstrates — has always been as much about the transformation of the individual as it is about changes on the physical plane. "Perfection" of the human soul could result, it was believed, from the alchemical *magnum opus* (Great Work), and in the alchemy-inspired Western mystery traditions, the achievement of gnosis — personal knowledge and enlightenment — was a crucial part of the process.

We don't really understand exactly how alchemists accomplished their transformations; the exact sequence of the operations that were involved in the Great Work was the greatest secret of a notoriously secretive group of people. So there are no specific protocols: early alchemists referred in their writings only to key stages of their work and, in quite general terms, to the different operations that characterized each stage. The precise number varies in different alchemical traditions, but three key color-coded phases are usually agreed upon: an initial Black Phase (*Nigredo*), which gives way to an intermediary White Phase (*Albedo*) and culminates in a Red Phase (*Rubedo*). Today, in the world of Jungian and other depth psychologies, we use these same Latin terms to refer to stages of psychological transformation. The Nigredo refers to the "dark night of the soul" that we pass through when we're enduring deep changes in our lives; the Albedo represents the psychospiritual purification that results from our suffering during the Nigredo, and the Rubedo reflects the sense of completeness and possibility that results from integrating various aspects of the psyche during the final phases of transformation.

The work of the blackening, the Nigredo, was the longest and most difficult phase in alchemy, and it's this stage which seems to me to be the perfect representation of what is happening to us during menopause. During Nigredo, alchemists believed, the substance that is transforming suffers deeply, and it's forced to shed superfluities so that its true nature can be revealed. From a psychological perspective, then, the goal during this initial phase of transformation is to reduce the individual to her bare essence, to strip her down to her most essential parts. As with physical alchemy, all the dross, all the "impure" and redundant material, must be removed before she can move on to the next stages of transformation.

Alchemists called this work *mortification*: literally, "facing the dead parts." In the laboratory, mortification produces ashes, so that the characteristics of the original material are no longer recognizable. From a psychological perspective, finding the dead parts means accessing and revealing the unconscious, and confronting the Shadow that we find there — the unknown, and often darker, side of our personality. For Jung, encountering and then assimilating the Shadow were necessary steps in individuation — the process of integrating disparate and neglected parts of the psyche into a functioning whole. In psychological alchemy, mortification is accompanied by difficult emotions — shame, embarrassment, guilt, or worthlessness, for example — as we finally face up to these old issues which we've hidden away.

The first stage of mortification involves *calcination*: a process in which the transforming material is "reduced to bone by burning." In psychological terms, calcination represents the destruction of false aspects of the ego:* the ways of presenting ourselves to the world that we've constructed in response to social and personal pressures,

---

* According to Jung, the ego is "a complex of ideas which constitutes the center of my field of consciousness and appears to possess a high degree of continuity and identity." C. G. Jung. *Psychological Types. Collected Works 6.* Princeton, NJ: Princeton University Press (1971).

but which don't reflect who we really are today — or who we want to become. Personal calcination begins when we begin to understand that so much of what we've imagined to be true and important in our lives might not, as we grow older, really matter at all. And so the blackness that obscures the true light of our being must be burned away to reveal our true essence. We're required, during this process, to reevaluate our whole way of being in the world.

To be human means always to be growing, to be transforming. We're all alchemists, deep inside — it's just that women have learned that fires must be put out, not encouraged to burn. We're afraid of conflagration. We're afraid of losing control. But during menopause we generally find that we have no choice. We're not *in* the conflagration — we are the conflagration.

What is all that fire for, during menopause? As with the process of calcination, it's to burn away the dead parts of our lives so that we can reveal the buried treasure within. At this time, we need to examine the structures which have supported us up until now. Are these the structures that will carry us into a positive and meaningful elderhood, or do we need to knock some of them down? Do the behaviors and habits — emotional, as well as physical — which we've acquired in the course of our lives still serve us? Do our relationships nourish us and the work that we do? The essence of menopausal alchemy is pure Nigredo: we have to face our dead parts and reduce ourselves to the bone by burning.

During my early fifties, in those early years of menopause, many of the structures which I'd so carefully built around my life were beginning to unravel.* In 2010, when I was

---

* I wrote about this period of my life, and the events leading up to it, in my first nonfiction book, *If Women Rose Rooted* (September Publishing, 2016).

forty-nine, my husband David and I had moved to the Isle of Lewis in the Outer Hebrides. We lived in a remote croft on the fringes of a small community, at the end of what has been called "the longest cul-de-sac in Europe." We were sandwiched between mountain and sea (and in full face of all the prevailing gales that came free with the position); on a good day we could see St. Kilda from our kitchen window. We threw ourselves wholeheartedly — and neither of us had much of a history of doing anything by halves — into building up an abandoned croft and run-down house. Everything was renovated, fenced; the croft was populated with two breeds of pedigree sheep, a milk cow, geese, ducks, hens, and pigs. For a while there were turkeys, and there was always a polytunnel for the growing of vegetables. We even obtained planning permission to install a small wind turbine; we were bedding in forever and aiming for self-sufficiency.

It was hard work from which there was never any respite; there was little community support for crofting anymore, and we were also running a small literary publishing house at the time. David was struggling with who he was supposed to be, now that he'd taken early retirement after almost two and a half decades of flying fast jets in the Royal Air Force. (The ability to fly upside down at five hundred miles an hour through narrow, steep-sided valleys equips you for surprisingly few other meaningful occupations.) Although I'd always imagined myself to be a hermit at heart, I wasn't dealing well with being marooned on an island at the end of the world — especially one which still in many ways resembled a Calvinist theocracy — nor with the lack of community and dearth of kindred spirits in the particular corner of it that we occupied. Although my relationship with David had begun not only with a deep mutual attraction but with a strong sense of shared values, I had discovered through the years that we were really very different in so many ways, and our marriage began to buckle under the strain.

I think of 2013, my fifty-second year, as the year when
everything fell apart. We were knocked sideways by a chain
of deaths, as much-loved animals on the croft fell afoul of
weather or birthing or predators. Then came the first of
what would become a yearslong stream of increasingly
bizarre and overwrought accusations from a distant female
colleague I'd thought of as a friend and whose work I'd
helped promote, accompanied by the withdrawal of friendship from a small group in our community who had
succeeded finally in their conspicuous aim of turning our
tiny crofting township into a battleground. Amid all of this,
my dear old golden retriever dog died. The final straw was
the sudden blossoming of David's passion for the Scottish
Gaelic language, which led him suddenly to declare that
he'd had quite enough of crofting now, and wanted instead
to go to university on the island to study Gaelic more
intensively. And so, after three years of hard work and
major financial investment, everything we'd built up would
now have to be taken apart: there was no way that I could
manage and maintain the croft and all the animals alone.
His needs had changed and, as a result, mine had become
utterly irrelevant. There was more…but some of those
stories are not mine alone to own and so to tell.

Accompanied by an unprecedented intensity of grief, this
acute and fairly cataclysmic unraveling which was taking
place required me — whether I wanted to or not — to look
long and hard at my life, and at the situation I now found
myself in. I began to question the patterns of behavior and
the built-in assumptions about the way life should be that
had led me to this point. Through all of my life, as the
only daughter of a mostly single mother, as a friend, and
as a partner in two marriages, I had always placed more
emphasis on the needs of others than on my own. I'd done
that gladly, and without resentment or anything remotely
resembling a sense of martyrdom; I'd seen it not even as

a virtue, but as a natural, life-enhancing expression of abundance and generosity. I was strong, I believed: I could get by. Others often needed a little extra help. Well, maybe in retrospect there was a little condescension in that. Or an inflated belief in my own abilities. Or an excessive sense of responsibility. Whatever it was, it wasn't healthy, and when it came to difficult times those others didn't, it seemed, give nearly as much weight to the needs that were mine.

This time, instead of just shrugging it all off, picking up the pieces, and starting again, I got mad. The rumbling menopausal volcano inside me was in full-on erupt mode. For once in my life I decided I was focusing on my own needs, and those needs didn't include being left alone for large swaths of time on a croft at the end of the world. They didn't include being marooned in what at the time was developing into an increasingly toxic community. They didn't include staying with a husband who had absolutely no interest in what I wanted from my life, now that he was beginning finally to discover what he might possibly want from his own, and who was willing on a whim to break everything we'd built to pursue some possibly fleeting new dream.*

The hard part at first was identifying exactly what my needs actually were. But as the months passed, and the croft slowly emptied of animals, and David spent several days a week away at university in the main town on the island, I came eventually to a decision. I'd had enough. Enough of the island, enough of our intransigent local community, enough of the hard slog of running a small publishing house for no or very little profit, enough of focusing on other people's writing to the exclusion of my own. Everything had broken, and at first, as always, I'd tried so hard to hold it all

---

* It turned out not to be fleeting at all. Eight years on, David speaks Scottish Gaelic, is fluent in two dialects of modern Irish, has qualifications in Old and Middle Irish, and is now studying modern and Middle Welsh.

together — until finally I understood that I didn't actually want to put it back together again at all. I didn't want to live the way we'd been living. I wanted a more spacious life. Time to write. In a place that was softer, where people valued laughter and music and poetry. In the end, the answer was surprisingly easy to uncover: I was going back to Ireland to live — back to the country I'd loved and which had so beautifully held me in the mid-1990s, after I'd finally torn myself free from several miserable years in a corporate wasteland. So I did my own breaking now. I told David that he could come if he wanted, but that I was going with or without him. The choice was his.

The choice was, he came. We found ourselves moving to the Gaeltacht of Donegal, and three years later to another Gaeltacht in my beloved Connemara — places in which David could immerse himself in various dialects of another beautiful old Gaelic language, and where the inspiration to write descended on me like a holy dove and never went away. Through those breakings and the choices which resulted from them, both of us found what we needed, and we found it together. But that had only become possible because for once, unshackled by the ferocious cleavings of menopause, I was able to smash through a lifetime habit of insisting on piecing together what was terminally broken. I allowed the process of Nigredo to occur. I faced my dead parts, and let them burn away.

The truth is, by the time we reach menopause, we've all lived with too much loss; we've all been broken open. We've accumulated too much pain. Menopause is the time to transform it. To stop trying to stitch ourselves back together again into the same old pattern. To put away that darning needle, blunted by our persistent and insistent repair work. To step into the crucible, and let it do its work. We can't mend everything. We can't. And, sometimes, we simply shouldn't.

The period of disarray I lived through in the run-up to those choices is typical of the chaos that so often confronts women during menopause. At this time of our life, one way or another, and whether we choose eventually to go with its flow or insist on resisting its tide, chaos is going to come knocking at our door. As someone with an unreasonable need for control over my own life, I've always feared chaos; but chaos, it seems, was precisely what I needed in order to break free. Insight into the strong medicine that chaos brings comes from the word's origins: it is derived from the Greek *khaos*, referring to the void which was said to exist before the cosmos was created. Chaos, then, contains the seeds of new life, the seething potential out of which an entirely new universe might be born. As Nietzsche said, "One must have chaos in oneself to give birth to a dancing star."[14] Chaos is the beauty of uncertainty; it unbinds us so that it can create us anew. In his book *Timaeus*, Plato declared in this context that chaos also incorporates the concept of *chora*: it is "a receptacle of all becoming — its wetnurse, as it were." For me, this time was nothing if not a time of becoming. An old story had been consumed, and the ingredients for a new story were just beginning to assemble in the mixing bowl.

~

Menopause, like all times of transition, is a time between stories, when the old story fades and a new story is waiting to emerge. Its invitations are manifold. It's a liminal time, when we hover on the brink of profound transformation. During this period of intense physical change, it's also necessary to turn inward, to embark upon the inner work of elderhood — the work of reimagining and shaping who we want to be in the world, of gaining new perspectives on life, of challenging and evolving our belief systems, of exploring our calling, of uncovering meaning, and ultimately finding healing for a lifetime's accumulation of wounds. Menopause is the threshold place we occupy before that new expedition to the country of elderhood properly begins: the waiting room in which we quietly sit and meditate on the unknown that is to come. The trick to navigating that space is not to push too hard, but to let the new story emerge in its own time, and to sit with, and perhaps even learn to cherish, the uncertainty.

Uncertainty is the apprentice of mystery. It's an antidote to our desperate need to know, to predict, and therefore to control. In the old native traditions of these islands where I was born, uncertainty wasn't a threat, it was a natural condition of existence. The people we now call the Insular Celts* had a particular love of ambiguity, an explicit comfort with not-knowing. A riddle was a gateway to the Otherworld, piercing the veil between this reality and the one which envelops it; formulaic koan-like questions jolted the listener into the heart of ambiguity. First, such questions and riddles produce confusion — but then they engage the imagination. They break down the rational, overintellectualized categories we're so attached to but that limit our perception, and teach us how to break the spell of everyday reality. To learn from them, you need to have faith in enigma, be prepared to apprentice yourself to bewilderment, and so find comfort in a shadowland where all things are possible and might be, but nothing yet actually *is*. This ability to sit with mystery and explore the dark but fertile realms of infinite possibility is crucial to the work of inhabiting a meaningful life. We have to learn to stay rooted in the midst of chaotic obscurity,

---

* The British and Irish never referred to themselves as Celts, and were never referred to as Celts by others. But because we spoke languages that are now classified as Celtic, many scholars feel that the term Insular Celts is appropriate: the Celts of the islands.

in the shadow-haunted wild places of the psyche. We need these rootings more than ever during the bone-deep metamorphosis that is menopause.

Inhabiting this in-between space can be uncomfortable, especially when we've grown up in a culture which values doing so much more than it values being — and infinitely more than it values the process of apprenticeship, the time we spend learning to be. But in order to benefit fully from this time between stories, it's necessary to let go not just of action, but of attachment to outcome. The Tao Te Ching asks: "Do you have the patience to wait till your mud settles and the water becomes clear? Can you remain unmoving until the right action arises by itself?"[15] Knowing when to gather together our resources and go all-out to change a situation seems easier somehow than recognizing instead when to sit quietly and surrender to its momentum. But the best of all strategies is simply to stay present, because the only certain way through uncertainty is through it.

My dear English friend Sara is particularly good at honoring uncertainty; her elegant stillness is one of the characteristics I love most about her, and that quality came into its own during her experience of menopause. "My menopause — a decade ago now at around fifty — followed swiftly in the wake of the loss of my marriage, of a beloved place, and of cherished work," she tells me; she was living in America at the time, and running a spa-based retreat center from her home. "I had the instinct to swim for the riverbank of a forest where I went into a six-year retreat under the care of a wizard and a cat. Well, that's the romantic way of putting what was a determined attempt to recover from a violent uprooting with the help of a good friend who gave me shelter. In retrospect, I can think of no kinder way for me to have adjusted to that phase of my life. I had few challenging symptoms of menopause and perhaps being able to go at my own pace helped with that.

"I did live in an actual forest, though, and spent most of my time communing with and caring for the trees, with few demands upon me, aside from those that were self-bidden. There were scary moments along with the challenges of living in the wilds, but they suited my process well. Eventually, I had to find my way back into the wider world alone, which, incredibly, involved flying halfway around the globe to India to resume my earlier work — a form of warm water therapy — in a very different culture. I found I was still capable, resourceful, and courageous. Perhaps what I learned to honor most during my menopause was my integrity."

Menopause, at its best, is more than just a pause in our menses; it's a sacred pause in the hurtling trajectory of life. As we slowly begin to burn away those old identities and outdated structures, and as our pale, exhausted visions begin slowly to recede, we enter a state of conscious incubation in which a nascent life can be dreamed into being. These multiple acts of deconstruction and reconstruction are what menopause is for. Because menopause, as I wrote in *If Women Rose Rooted*, "is not a medical condition, it is an earthquake, shaking us to our deepest foundations, wiping out the edifices we've so carefully constructed on what we once imagined to be the solid ground of our life. Menopause hacks us open; it is the cleaving to end all cleavings. One by one, it systematically strips away all the trappings of womanhood and sexuality which we've clung to — or had foisted upon us — for the whole of our lives."[16] Menopause tells us, above all, that there are new wisdoms in which we can now immerse ourselves, new ways of being in the world to be uncovered. Life is not over; it is simply, and irrevocably, changed.

One of my favorite descriptions of menopause comes from a character played by the marvelous actress Kristin Scott Thomas in the cult BBC series *Fleabag*. Playing

Belinda, fifty-eight years old, sitting at a bar and flourishing a martini, she declares to her female companion that menopause is the "most wonderful fucking thing in the world. And yes, your entire pelvic floor crumbles and you get fucking hot and no one cares. But then — you're free! No longer a slave, no longer a machine with parts. You're just a person, in business." When Fleabag replies that she has been told the whole thing is horrendous, Belinda responds: "It is horrendous, but then it's magnificent. Something to look forward to."[17]

As Belinda suggests, menopause is a call to autonomy: a response to the need, perhaps for the first time in our lives, to define ourselves and our own path. It's a time to reclaim ourselves and tell our own story, in our own unique voice. For many women, then, menopause is a time when we pull back a little from our relationships and begin to evaluate who we imagine ourselves to be outside the frameworks set for us by others. Often, this leads to periods of intense longing for time alone. I loved my husband and valued our marriage, but throughout menopause I struggled with a serious yearning to live by myself. I couldn't seem to reconcile the two desires: to live with him and to live without him. Because I've always understood that solitude is more than just a luxury: at certain times in life it's a necessity. It's a prerequisite for deep change, for freedom of thought and imagination.

The solution to my dilemma might have been unoriginal, but nevertheless it was compelling: a room of my own. I'd been corresponding for some time by email with an older friend in Tasmania; she sent me some photographs of her solitary bedroom: a sanctuary, a pale temple, containing only what she believed to be beautiful and essential, and uncluttered by the detritus of other lives. I longed for such a space, in which the peripatetic, shifting rhythms of my sweat-soaked nights would be uninterrupted by David's need for greater warmth and his orchestral nighttime snoring performances, but our tiny old Donegal cottage offered no space for such luxuries. It was that yearning of mine, as much as any other, that led us to move to a larger house in Connemara — and there it was that I took my opportunity. The former owner, a structural engineer, had bolted onto a neglected and nondescript small 1970s Irish bungalow, an eccentric but unfinished extension with a vaulted ceiling and gallery area. We found a builder and completed the work. The downstairs area became my study, and up in the gallery space, backing on to a large moon-shaped window and overlooked by two skylights through which I could contemplate the night sky in its infinite variety, I placed my new bed.

My friend Véronique, a professional translator and raven-haired Earth Mother who lives in the Netherlands, did the same thing — though she was smart enough to manage it earlier, in her perimenopausal years. Through a series of unlikely synchronicities, on the "for sale" pages of a website through which she was searching for something completely different, she happened across a Romany wagon identical to one that she had recently seen in a dream — a wagon in which she saw herself traveling, pulled along by two mules. So, in late summer, she traveled to the opposite side of the country, and, on a whim, with the last of some money that her mother had left her when she died, she bought it.

"And then I went home," she told me, "not knowing what for. We'd said we'd pick up the wagon in September, but by September we were thinking about moving house, and the 'what for, what for' had only grown in my mind. I was wondering what I'd been thinking, so I procrastinated and said I'd pick it up next spring. Then winter came, very dark, and I had almost decided to not pick it up at all, but there was, at the heart of the cold inside my heart, this little ember still glowing. Early spring came, and I started waking up. One morning, I said to my husband, 'I think it's time to pick up this wagon. I don't know what it's for, but we have to bring it here. Then we'll know.' Two days later it arrived, and it happened to fit quite precisely through our garden gate, quite precisely under the overhanging cherry tree. I climbed on the platform, opened the little door, walked in. Sat on the bench. And didn't move for a very long time. That night I brought all my bedclothes and blankets, electronic candle and diary, tarot cards and books to the wagon. I said goodbye to the big family bed that I'd slept in for seventeen years, covered in children, and I quietly moved into my own little den. And ever since (it's been a month now), every night, I tuck my family into bed, I quietly close the door of the kitchen, and I walk out under the stars and the moon, into the night air, towards my alcove."

Like Véronique's, my new physical space soon began to shape itself to my new mental and emotional space. I don't know what it was about menopause, specifically, that caused me all of a sudden to become a gatherer of "found objects." But now, wherever I went in this bleakly untamed and often inhospitable landscape in the wild western extremes of Ireland, I seemed to hear things calling out to me. I was rooting for something — I didn't know what. For fragments of myself, perhaps; my life, my loves. For fragments which reflected something of myself back at me — whatever I might be becoming now, at this turbulent, shapeshifting time of my life. And all the fragments I seemed to need came from this new place, from the ancient, uncompromising earth around me: that land which I walked compulsively, day after day after day. I would come home from the woods reverently carrying strangely shaped sticks, from the lough with pebbles and water-bird feathers, from the beach with seashells and mermaid's purses — as if I were reassembling myself from elements of the land itself. After the deep dissolutions of menopause, I was refashioning myself from those calcinated ashes; I was growing new bones. It's something we all have to do at this time in our lives; somehow, with whatever tools are available to us, we have to begin to curate the vision of the elder we will become. It's an act of bricolage. And so now I had become like the bright-eyed, cackling magpies which regularly ransacked our garden: a collector — though not of trinkets, but of clues. I was gathering them together in the safety of my new nest. The clues were there in the pieces; those clues are threaded through this book. Scattered in shadowy corners and brightly lit windows; these objects I've selected are so much more than random gatherings of whatever it was that I happened to come across in my wanderings. They're so much more than mere clutter. They are active choices, carefully selected objects that mirror my sense of myself as a shapeshifting, storied creature. Because the clues to our re-memberings are in the stories, and the stories are always born from the land.

~

Finding our path through this time between stories that menopause represents, and feeling our way into whatever story might be offering itself to us next, is complicated by the fact that we're not educated to expect that elderhood might offer up a new story at all. If Western culture teaches us anything about elderhood, it's that it's supposed to mark the end of all meaningful stories, not the beginning of a new one. But there can be a certain perverse pleasure, as well as a sense of rightness and beauty, in insisting on flowering just when the world expects you to become quiet and diminish. Yes, elderhood begins with the often-shattering physical conflagration that is menopause, and it ends in certain death. But we each have choices about how to approach these final decades of our life. We can see them as a drawn-out process of inevitable and terminal decline, or we can see them as a time of fruition and completion.

As a fervent devourer of fiction since first I learned to read, I've always looked to novels both to illuminate the nature of the world I dwell in, and to reveal to me the purposes and possibilities of a woman's inner life. I've searched for myself, and the stories I might inhabit, in books. I've often found characters who, at least in part, reflect my own concerns or obsessions — or at least, this was true until I began to approach my middle years. It's frequently declared that there are relatively few novels about menopausal or postmenopausal women — relative, that is, to "coming of age" novels, or novels about finding love or experiencing motherhood. It's a surprising fact if it's true, since research in several countries has consistently shown that women over the age of forty-five buy more novels than any other group. And yet so few books seem to reflect the lives of women in midlife in any insightful way; instead, stereotypes of aging women and depictions of tired and clichéd lives abound.

Today, there's more awareness of this lack, and a growing number of novels are trying to cast light on the real, contemporary challenges that women face in midlife and beyond — but in my earlier years I couldn't find many that whetted my appetite for the journey ahead. Mostly, they just depressed me. When I was in my twenties, the novels of British author Anita Brookner were having a big moment, and I read several of them out of a sense of obligation to find them as subversive and luminous as the literary critics of the day did — until finally I allowed myself to decide that they were some of the most disheartening and mournful books that I'd ever inflicted upon myself.

Brookner, it seems, is a little like Jane Austen: you either love her or loathe her. I'm afraid I'm inclined to the latter perspective. Although I can recognize the genius in her subtle and meticulous portrayals of middle-aged women who are disappointed by life and have lost all hope, the predominant effect of those novels was to render me terrified of my future fate. *A Start in Life*, for example, published in 1981, depresses the reader from the very beginning with the sentence: "Dr Weiss, at 40, knew that her life had been ruined by literature," and tells the story of a lonely woman, entirely detached from the world around her, whose days seem filled with resignation.[18] As with all of Brookner's characters, there is an utter lack of joy in her life, and no prospect of anything remotely resembling joy to come. I felt suffocated by that lack of joy, by the lack of vision, the lack of transformation or transcendence — the lack of anything other than stasis, pale endurance, and renunciation. That might indeed be the plight of some middle-aged women, but it was a vision I found... well, uncompelling. I would come away from the books feeling flat at best, bleak at worst.

As an antidote, thankfully, there was always Doris Lessing — one of a handful of writers who have shaped my worldview throughout my life — to challenge and inform. In *The Summer Before the Dark*, published in 1973, Lessing's protagonist, forty-five-year-old Kate Brown, begins to question the roles of wife and mother that have defined her life for decades. The novel traces her attempts to come to terms with the idea of aging, which at first she imagines primarily in terms of decline: "What was she going to experience?... she could look forward to nothing much but a dwindling away from full household activity into getting old."[19]

At first, Kate's experience of growing older is informed by the attitudes of others toward her. The fact that her children see her as the archetypical menopausal madwoman causes her to be angered and alarmed, even when she also finds herself wondering whether she might really be slipping into some kind of madness. Increasingly, as time passes, she begins to think of her many years of devotion to her family as "a form of dementia." Heading to Spain for work (as a translator), she tries to break free of her family and their needs. She fears the loss of her sexuality, and so launches herself into an affair with Jeffrey, a younger man — but when the staff of the hotel she's staying in show their disturbance at the age imbalance in their relationship, she realizes that this is not the answer she's been looking for. As a consequence of this experience, though, she grows a new awareness of all the ways in which sexuality informs our ideas of what it is to be a woman, and how women are defined primarily in terms of their attractiveness to men. She imagines herself transforming into a sexless old person — and so no longer, by society's definition, a "proper woman."

One of the most interesting aspects of Kate's growing insight into a woman's experience of midlife is the way in which she is forced to acknowledge her own complicity in the cultural ideal of womanhood. She has, she realizes, spent years looking into mirrors, wondering "what others would judge her by," and so fashioning an identity — no matter how false — that others would be comfortable with. After her return from Spain, a three-week-long illness accentuates the changes in her aging body: she loses weight and her hair starts to return to its natural gray. Finally, she grows angry after realizing that her entire adult identity has always been a performance for the benefit of others, and so she decides to actively choose a life of "invisibility." Her most extravagant rage is reserved for men who have told her that her greatest fulfillment will come in responding to their desire: "It was a rage, it seemed to her, that she had been suppressing for a lifetime."

Kate, then, begins to refuse to conform to societal expectations about what it is to be a woman, and looks for validation in other ways. By the end of the book, she has slipped into a different way of being in the world, which is defined more by her own needs than the expectations of others. And if invisibility is an inevitable consequence of these changes, it's perfectly acceptable to her. Lessing herself has spoken often of the advantages that the invisibility of growing old brings, describing it always as a form of freedom: "You see when you're a young woman you're ALWAYS on show, always being noticed ... when you're not continually on show you can notice much more, you're much more free."[20]

It's possible, then, to find an occasional novel which reflects the profound challenges that women face on the threshold of menopause. But can the old stories also help us here?

I've not yet uncovered folk or fairy tales that overtly show us how women might neatly navigate that twisting pathway through midlife which leads us to the land of elderhood. Perhaps that's not surprising; many of these stories originate in times when fewer women made it past their childbearing years, and fewer still lived to enter the murky territory of old age. But there are plenty of stories which offer up clues by telling us how *not* to navigate that pathway: in particular, the many tales which are constructed around a mother or stepmother who is aging and losing her beauty, and so grows jealous of her daughter or stepdaughter. The wicked stepmother in "Snow White" is one of the best-known examples. In the Grimms' version of the tale, Snow White's father, a king, takes another wife when her mother dies shortly after her birth. The new queen "was a beautiful woman," the story tells us,

> but she was proud and arrogant, and she could not stand it if anyone might surpass her in beauty. She had a magic mirror. Every morning she stood before it, looked at herself, and said:
>
> > Mirror, mirror, on the wall,
> > Who in this land is fairest of all?

To this the mirror answered:

> You, my queen, are fairest of all.

Then she was satisfied, for she knew that the mirror spoke the truth.

But when, one day, the mirror declares Snow White to be the fairest of all, the queen grows frantic:

> The queen took fright and turned yellow and green with envy. From that hour on whenever she looked at Snow White her heart turned over inside her body, so great was her hatred for the girl. The envy and pride grew ever greater, like a weed in her heart, until she had no peace day and night.

We're accustomed, not least because of our exposure to the oversimplified, black-and-white "Disneyfication" of so many of our oldest fairy tales, to thinking of the stepmother in this and similar tales as straightforwardly evil. We label her simply as "bad," and don't really interrogate her choices or think more deeply about her motives. But if we apply a little more depth to our examination of her situation, we might come to understand that, although she is undoubtedly an unsympathetic and negative character, she is nevertheless a reflection of the problems that women approaching middle age face in societies which value women predominantly for their youth, beauty, and fertility. She lives in a world in which women can't afford to grow old, because those who grow old age quickly and are no longer valued. As a consequence, she is forced to compete not only with the original queen, her husband's first wife, but now with that queen's daughter — and so she becomes her adversary.

The story of Snow White has been subject to many

retellings and reimaginings over the years, in all media. Most recently, the movie *Snow White and the Huntsman* held up a mirror to these issues faced by aging women. In this and in other retellings, the queen's search for some equivalent of the "fountain of youth" is a key motif. In the film, Queen Ravenna is presented as an unequivocally evil stepmother. Despite her youthful looks, we soon learn that she is actually an old woman, and that, in the context of this story, old age signifies a loss of power. When Ravenna is about to kill Snow White, she justifies her deed by saying: "You don't even realize how lucky you are never to know what it is to grow old." Old age, then, is presented as a punishment to Ravenna, and is associated with physical affliction and powerlessness. Ravenna needs to devour young, beautiful women and suck the life force from their bodies in order to retain her own youth. And when she stabs Snow White's father on their wedding night, she displays an acute awareness of what it means for a woman to grow old. "I was ruined by a king like you once," she tells him. "I replaced his queen, an old woman. And, in time, I too would have been replaced. Men use women. They ruin us and when they are finished with us, they toss us to the dogs like scraps... When a woman stays young and beautiful forever, the world is hers." And indeed, Ravenna is defeated in the end by a triumphant Snow White, whose youthfulness is starkly contrasted with the rapid aging of the queen.

If we are paying attention and probing beneath the seemingly simple surface, these stories throw up important questions about what it is to be a woman when beauty fades, when we are no longer fertile, and when motherhood is no longer our defining role. These are the questions that women are forced to confront during menopause, and during those years I remember asking myself, again and again, what it meant now to be a woman.

As someone who didn't ever take the usual and well-trodden path into motherhood, and whose early experiences of women had been largely negative, this was a question that had preoccupied me from time to time throughout my life. Now, as the signs of my own aging grew undeniable, it made its way again to the front of my consciousness. The truth is, I think, that I found it easier then to confront this question than I had when I was younger — perhaps because, as someone who had chosen not to have children, and who had spent nine years single from her mid-thirties onward, I'd never quite felt that I slotted into the normal patterns of womanhood anyway. I'd always channeled my creativity elsewhere. But I believe that many of those of us who've never been mothers find it hard to own our own authority. Menopause requires us to break through that limitation. For some of us, it's our key, and our most challenging, task.

Well, we might not take much positive inspiration from the fairy-tale archetype of the wicked middle-aged stepmother, but there is another, more sympathetic character in the old stories who usually is presented as a woman in late midlife: the Henwife. Although she only ever makes fleeting appearances, she is one of my favorite characters, and shows up not only in the folk and fairy tales of Britain and Ireland, but much further beyond. The Henwife most often appears as an important helper to the protagonist. The fact that she also keeps hens is part and parcel of her unique character, but although the heroine of the story may approach her looking simply for eggs, she always comes away with rather more than she bargained for. The Henwife is an integrated member of the community; unlike the classic solitary witch in the woods, or the wise woman who lurks on the fringes of the village (both of whom we'll meet later), she lives right in the thick of things. Her specialty is advice in the areas of life we can think of as "women's mysteries": the mysteries of sexuality, menstruation, pregnancy, and childbirth (reflected, perhaps, in the constant fertility of her companion hens) — and, though it is never directly spoken of in the stories, of menopause.

Perhaps I'm so fond of the Henwife because of my fondness for hens. Ever since I was presented with a trio of beautiful (but profoundly lazy) Partridge Wyandottes by a kind neighbor in 2003, I've never been without them. I love their quirks, their shifting feuds and alliances, and their unique personalities; collecting the still-warm, smooth eggs from the nest boxes each day is an intensely pleasurable sensory experience. And eggshells feature prominently in my gathering of found objects. I particularly treasure the half of a blue-green heron's egg we discovered on the floor of the heronry in the woods behind our old Donegal cottage. There is a line of old, dried blood around the ragged edge where the chick broke out. It's fragile, of course, so it's not for handling, but I can't look at it without remembering how, in the mythology of my Celtic ancestors, the heron (and, more precisely, her ecological predecessor the crane) is associated with the mysteries of the haggish women into which she so often shapeshifts. She's a magical bird who is equally at home in the realms of land, water, and air; she guards the entrances to the Otherworld and embodies its wisdom. The egg itself is an ancient and ubiquitous spiritual symbol. It represents eternity and the endlessly self-perpetuating, fertile power of the universe; in many mythic traditions, the world was born from a cosmic egg. Henwife, heron-hag — there's an overlap in my own unique inner imaginarium; when I think of them I think of the wisdom of longevity, of the mysteries of creative power that are passed down through the female line.

I first became properly aware of the Henwife as a distinct and unique character when reading Sylvia Townsend Warner's novel *Lolly Willowes*.[21] In it the protagonist, Laura "Lolly" Willowes, is a middle-class Englishwoman who, after the sudden death of her father, sinks into the gray, spinsterish life of a conventional maiden aunt, living with her brother's family in London. Then, "groping after something," one day she makes a sudden, late break for freedom and takes herself off to live in Great Mop, "a secluded hamlet in the heart of the Chilterns," where she embarks on a journey of increasing subversion. She distances herself from her family, refuses to be defined by her relationships with men, and repudiates the entrenched social barriers between the ruling and the working classes. Before long, she finds herself drawn into becoming a witch. She attends witches' sabbaths and indulges in several friendly discussions with Satan — who she imagines as "a kind of black knight, wandering about and succouring decayed gentlewomen," seducing the soul of a spinster "when no one else would give a look at her body even!" Rather more mundanely, Lolly also befriends a poultry farmer, and develops a fondness for hens:

> She liked to feel their acquiescence, their dependence upon her. She felt wise and potent. She remembered the henwife in fairy tales, she understood now why kings and queens resorted to the henwife in their difficulties. The henwife held their destinies in the crook of her arm, and hatched the future in her apron. She was sister to the spaewife, and close cousin to the witch, but she practiced her art under cover of henwifery; she was not, like her sister and her cousin, a professional. She lived unassumingly at the bottom of the king's garden, wearing a large white apron and very possibly her husband's cloth cap; and when she saw the king and queen coming down the gravel path she curtseyed reverentially, and pretended it

was eggs they had come about...But though she
kept up this pretence of homeliness she was not
inferior in skill to the professionals. Even the
pretence of homeliness was not quite so homely
as it might seem.

The Henwife in fairy tales is often depicted as a rather
subversive character, subtly undermining patriarchal authority, even though she's embedded in the community and
sometimes lives in the castle grounds. In most stories, the
Henwife offers practical advice as well as performing spells.
And so, in one of my favorite Scottish fairy tales, "The Black
Bull of Norroway," three sisters, one by one, pay a visit to
the local Henwife to ask her in which of the Four Directions
they ought to go to find the best fortune. "You don't need
to go any farther than my back door, hinnie," the Henwife
tells each of them in turn — and indeed, as they peer outside the back door in question, each one of them sees her future husband traveling down the road toward her. The first
two princesses are carried off by the inevitable handsome
princes; the third finds that her fate is rather more interestingly tied up with that of an enchanted Black Bull — and a
fine and transformational quest then ensues.

In "Rashiecoats," another Scottish folktale (a version of
which, in England, is called "Catskin"), a young woman
named Morag is ordered to marry a sullen, rude boor.
She seeks the advice of the local Henwife, who tells her to
return to her father and inform him that she will consider
the marriage only if he makes her a coat of the finest gold.
When this strategy fails, she tells him she'll comply only if
he offers her a cloak and shoes made from feathers, freely
given, one from each of the birds of the air. When this also
fails, she requires of him a coat, cap, and shoes made of
rushes. Finally, when there seems to be nothing left to be
done, the Henwife advises Morag to pack up her three

coats, her two pairs of precious shoes, and her down-soft hat, and to make her way into "the land of towers" to try to find herself a new fate. And, of course, she does.

In the Irish tale "Fair, Brown, and Trembling," which in many ways is reminiscent of "Cinderella," the Henwife advises the neglected younger sister, Trembling, to go to church as her two older sisters have done, to find herself a husband. Once Trembling has decided what kind of dress she'd like to wear to church, the Henwife "puts on the cloak of darkness" and magics up some new clothes; she continues to advise Trembling until eventually she finds her prince.

It's only in the Scottish tale "Kate Crackernuts" that the Henwife appears as a rather more ambiguous character. In the story, a king has a daughter named Anne, and his second queen has a daughter named Kate, who is less beautiful. The queen is jealous of Anne, but Kate loves her. The queen consults with a Henwife, who agrees to help her to ruin Anne's beauty, and after three tries they eventually succeed in exchanging Anne's head for a sheep's head. Kate takes the sheepish Anne away, along with her original human head, and the rest of the story is about her quest to help her stepsister recover her natural form.

In all these stories, then, the Henwife is presented as the keeper of women's mysteries — an everyday wise woman with knowledge which reaches far beyond the everyday. She's a character who introduces us to the archetype of the Medial Woman — who embodies those women's mysteries more than any other.

2

SOMEDAY YOUR WITCH WILL COME

The Medial Woman

If I close my eyes, I can still smell the sea I grew up by. Not the soft salt embrace of the western shorelines I've clung to for the past couple of decades, but the cold, clear air of the far North Sea coast: invasive, pugnacious, and infinitely more in-your-face. I can feel its icy currents ravaging my shivering skin during childhood swims, taste the summer sea haar fretting its way inland on an easterly wind. The sound of foghorns still fills me with strange longings. I remember falling asleep to their mournful bass notes, droning like the voice of the sea itself, throwing out portents like prophets of doom.

I grew up in a land of clammy fog, a haunter of dune-covered beaches surrounded on their landward sides by the steel-clad troops of heavy industry. The place beyond the high-tide line of seaweed, stretching down to the ebbing water — we used to call it the Black Shore. Where my great-aunt picked cockles for a living as a young woman, and the men of her neighborhood gathered sea coal. It's a place, the stories tell us, where you can cross into the Otherworld. One of the threshold territories, liminal zones — "thin places" where two worlds collide. A selkie slips out of her sealskin there under a full moon; a mermaid reclines on a rock, brooding over her stolen comb.

I grew up in a land of betwixt and between, in the shifting borderlands between sea and shore, and my ancestors for as many centuries as we can trace inhabited the similarly shifting borderlands between the far northern countries that eventually established themselves as Scotland and England. Does that account for my comfort with ambiguity and fluctuating realities? Perhaps it explains my fascination with the Otherworld of my tradition — because in these islands, the Otherworld isn't a location: it is the shimmer of something just out of sight, seen through a glass darkly, but inextricably interwoven with this world. The veil between worlds was always thinnest in the borderlands; at any time, it might slip to one side and allow you to fumble on through. As a child I found my Otherworld on the seashore, searching for mermaids. I didn't find their physical presence there on the beaches, but I found them in my imagination. To the child I was, that was just as real a world as any other — maybe more real than all of them.

If I close my eyes, I can still smell another, more recent, sea — I suppose I should call it an ocean — and a Pacific beach at the southernmost tip of a rocky Californian peninsula that felt curiously like home. On that temperate coast, and coinciding with the early days of writing this book, I happened upon a treasure that I had been longing to find for years: an entirely undomesticated, found-in-the-wild hag stone. In fact, I'd stumbled across a whole beach full of them. I carried a pocketful home with me; they're piled up in an earth-toned pottery bowl beside my writing desk. A hag stone, you see, is a pebble with a naturally formed hole in it, and the old stories say that if you look through that hole with one eye and the other closed, you can see right through the veil and on into the Otherworld. My favorite hag stone has not just one but three holes in it, and it is made of sandstone. That feels especially appropriate, now that I live among mountains whose geological foundations are mudstone and sandstone. Especially appropriate also because these rocks contain memories of the sea; they are formed by the bits and bodies of dead aquatic organisms, suspended in water and slowly piling up over the ages, and of minerals transported by water and ice. Those ancient sediments were deposited in what was once a deep sea basin, but is now a range of mountains. Just as I do, the mountains here embody the ghosts of oceans. Nothing is ever lost; nothing is ever really gone. If we ourselves forget, the land holds the memories for us.

I think, as women grow older, that we miss mystery. We miss magic. Not the kind of magic that stems from magical thinking, but the magic that comes from wonder. The wonder of experiencing the world as still brimming with possibility, in spite of the fact that certain life paths and choices disintegrate before our eyes as we age. At sixty years old, my fleeting and not especially original childhood dream of becoming an astronaut is clearly no longer an option. But we always have the capacity to reinvent ourselves, right to the end. This world will always be disposed to transform us beyond our wildest dreams. Not in an outer sense, collecting accolades and appurtenances — but inside ourselves, as we burn away all the dross and come to embody that person we were always meant to be. The problem we face is that by the time we reach our menopause years, we've spent too many years being practical, caretaking, raising children, building security, paying the mortgage, toeing whatever white lines the culture has painted for us on the too-straight highway of our lives, our shoulders stooped under the weight of the heavy stories it requires us to bear. The enchantments of childhood and the lambent possibilities of adolescence — they seem so very long ago.

But deep down, part of us knows the mystery still exists, and that it's not out of reach. The part of us that can't sleep properly when the moon is full, that stands on the seashore at sunrise, singing to seals. The part of us that yearns to set off alone one day into the dark woods — not, as when we were young, to test ourselves against the dangerous old woman who lives there, but one day perhaps to become her. Something inside us knows that the cultural mythology which tells us what an aging woman should be is not only misguided, but pernicious. It knows that we're missing something essential; something we badly need. Something that the culture badly needs.

So then, menopause comes knocking at our door, burning us up with strange longings. Wild as the berries in the basket of the wise old woman in all the best fairy-tale forests, it comes to wake us up, to revivify the magic that was lost to most of us when we left childhood behind. Its invitation to us isn't that we should try to revert to that childhood, or allow ourselves to be enticed into the frivolous worlds of fantasy and escapism — but rather to reclaim the old potent sense of magic in the everyday, and reclothe it in all the deep, embodied, and grounded wisdom we've accrued along the way. It invites us at the same time to reimagine the female creative power that, for many of us, has formerly manifested itself in having children, and encourages us to channel that creativity elsewhere.

Indigenous cultures have always recognized the new creative power that women have access to as they pass through menopause. "As the bleeding stops, the fire goes within," Lakota elder Paula Gunn Allen says, noting also that in her tradition medicine women do not practice until they have reached their menopausal years.[22] Because, then, the menstrual blood remains inside us, and so does the creative fire. Our creativity as elder women isn't about birthing others anymore — it's about birthing our own unique wisdom, our own unique gift to the world. At the beginning of menopause, then, we are the substance on which its rough alchemy is performed. But as we pass through it and out of it, we become the Alchemist.

The Alchemist is one of those instantly and universally recognizable, irreducible characters that psychologists refer to as "archetypes." That's a word we'll encounter often in this book — so what does it actually mean? The word itself derives from the Latin noun *archetypum*, which in turn derives from the Greek adjective *archētypos*, which means "first-molded." This is a compound of *archē* — "beginning, origin" — and *týpos*, which can mean, among other things, "pattern," "model," or "type." So an archetype, essentially, is an "original pattern."

Archetypes are usually spoken of in the context of the work of Carl Jung, who proposed that there are two different levels of the human unconscious. First, he suggested, there is an upper level, which he called the "personal unconscious" and which relates specifically to the individual. But beneath this lies a much deeper "collective unconscious," universal, and which "constitutes a common psychic substrate of a suprapersonal nature that is present in every one of us."[23]

"Archetype" is the word that Jung used to refer to the contents and structures of the collective unconscious: inherited or innate potentials, forms, or ideas which are transformed into universal symbols once they enter into the conscious mind. Archetypal figures include the Great Mother, the All-Father, the Child, the Devil, the Wise Old Man, the Witch, the Trickster, the Hero; archetypal motifs include the apocalypse, the deluge, the creation; archetypal situations might include the battle between good and evil, the heroic task, the descent to the Underworld, the cycle of death and rebirth. The more specific forms in which these archetypes present themselves are shaped not only by the culture we are part of, but by our own personal history, so that they can take on particular and unique meanings and associations for each one of us. In this context, it's important to stress that we can't directly perceive the archetypes or ideas themselves — rather, what we see are the specific forms or images which derive from them. For example, the Wise Old Woman is an archetype. It's an idea that, in its essence, is recognized by all cultures. But we never engage with the archetype itself; instead, we encounter culturally specific images that derive from it. So certain Native American peoples might see the Wise Old Woman as Grandmother Spider, weaving the world into being. In the Gaelic tradition, she'd be the Cailleach: that granite-faced old woman who creates and shapes the land. In the Slavic tradition, she'd be the dangerous old woman of the woods, Baba Yaga — and so on.

The presence of archetypal characters, images, and motifs in myths and fairy tales is one of the main reasons why they're so powerful: they are bridges between the personal and the universal. They are also, in a way, like keys — capable of unlocking the imagination, opening the door to the dark, cobweb-laden room which houses the mysteries of our inner lives. In the vehicle of a fairy story, archetypes become more than mere characters: they become energies, embedded with instructions which guide us through the complexities of life and show us what we might become — or how we might participate in the becoming of the world.

The archetypal qualities of the Alchemist reveal her to be a mistress of transformation: she's not afraid to burn things back to the bare bones to expose what lies beneath. She's both a visionary and a catalyst for the irreversible changes she conjures into being; in effect, she reimagines, and so recreates, the world.

The Alchemist is one of a cluster of characters which

reflects aspects of a wider archetype known in Jungian circles as the Medial Woman. In 1956, Zurich-based analyst Toni Wolff, lover and colleague of Carl Jung, described what she believed to be four key female archetypes: the Mother, the Hetaira, the Amazon, and the Medial Woman.[24] Wolff argued that although every woman has the potential to embody all of these four archetypes at various stages of her life, one or more of them tends to be of primary importance to each of us. The woman who is most identified with the Mother, for example, finds her primary identity and fulfillment in nourishing life — usually, but not necessarily, in bearing and raising children. The word *hetaira* refers to a class of highly educated women in ancient Greece who were trained not only to provide sexual services to men, but also to provide them with long-term companionship. And so the Hetaira woman, according to Wolff, finds her primary identity and fulfillment in relationships; in some senses, she might be thought of as a muse. The Amazon is a capable, resourceful woman who finds her primary identity and fulfillment in the outer world; she excels in work and skills that are usually perceived to be the domain of men.

The Medial Woman, unlike the other three archetypes, doesn't define herself in relation to others. Instead, she finds her primary identity and fulfillment in cultivating relationship with Jung's "collective unconscious" — which is similar in many ways to the place that in many older European traditions might be called the Otherworld — and acting as a bridge between it and the human community. Medial Women are visionaries, psychics, healers, and poets. In some cultures, they might be priestesses or prophetesses, shamans or oracles. If the Medial Woman archetype is active within us, then, it launches us on a search for the kind of knowledge which we might think of as mystical. Medial Women are seekers and keepers of esoteric knowledge and wisdom, and they value gnosis — direct, personal mystical experience — over that which is passed down in the form of dogma and doctrine by existing religious hierarchies.

It's interesting, then, that right at the heart of those hierarchies, sometimes — unexpectedly — we can find the Medial Woman embodying a different way of being in the world. I'm not usually much of a fan of the Christian tradition (or any other institutionalized religion, for that matter) but the great medieval mystic Hildegard of Bingen has long been one of my heroines. Primarily, because she represented a rare, strong, and enduring female voice at the very heart of medieval patriarchy, but also because her deepest work and writing came to her in the second half of her life.

Hildegard was no ordinary nun. She was renowned as a visionary and mystic, and her correspondents and petitioners included royalty, bishops, and even popes. She was born into a noble family in 1098, in the lush, green Rhineland of Germany. She didn't choose to lead a religious life, but as the youngest of ten children she was given to the church at just eight years old. When she arrived at the convent which had been chosen for her, Hildegard was placed in the care of Jutta von Sponheim, a family friend — and an anchoress. Anchoresses were nuns who went through a ritual burial to indicate that they were "dead" to worldly things; they also took a vow which required them to confine themselves for perpetuity in a small enclosure attached to a convent or church. Jutta became Hildegard's teacher and friend, and, at some time between the ages of fourteen and sixteen, Hildegard became a nun.

In the three decades that followed, Hildegard came to be respected by her peers for her intelligence, wisdom, and spiritual insight, as well as her leadership skills. And so, after Jutta died, at thirty-eight years old Hildegard became abbess of the convent in her place. But a few years later Hildegard's health began to deteriorate significantly. One day, a vision came to her. "In the forty-third year of my passing journey," she wrote,

> when I clung to a heavenly vision with fear and trembling, I saw a very great light from which a heavenly voice spoke to me and said: "O weak person, ashes of ashes, dust of dust, speak and write what you see and hear. Because you are timid about speaking and unskilled in writing, speak and write these things as a listener understanding the words of a teacher. Give others a clear account of what you see with your inner eye, and what you hear with your inner ear. Your testimony will help them come to know me."[25]

Despite her anxiety and self-doubt, Hildegard began to write, just as she'd been instructed in her vision, and as soon as she did, her health began greatly to improve. When she was fifty years old, one of her manuscripts was taken to Pope Eugenius III, who then wrote to Hildegard giving her permission to write and to publish her visions. By the time she died in 1179, at the age of eighty-one, Hildegard had completed five books, composed seventy-seven sacred songs, and created the first-ever musical morality play. She had also corresponded with hundreds of petitioners, had publicly campaigned against church corruption and sexual misconduct by its priests, and had embarked on four speaking tours around Europe — all of this while managing and presiding over the spiritual health of the inhabitants of two convents. In her spare time, Hildegard was also an herbalist and a healer.

For a twelfth-century woman, Hildegard's accomplishments were unprecedented. Even in her early eighties, Hildegard refused to be bullied by male authority figures, either sacred or secular, and she argued vehemently against injustice where she perceived it to be present. But perhaps the most important, and groundbreaking, aspect of Hildegard's visions was her claim that the Divine was female as well as male, and that both elements were essential for wholeness. She personified the feminine divine principle as Sapientia, or Wisdom, whose role was to nurture the human soul. "Praise her!" Hildegard wrote. "She watches over all people and all things in heaven and earth. She is incomprehensible to mortals. She is with all and in all; great is her mystery."[26]

The most interesting aspect of Hildegard's mysticism for me is her passion for the natural world. She accorded great importance to our relationship with the Earth, which she saw as a living organism endowed with the same vital power that animates all life forms. "The Earth sustains humanity. It must not be injured; it must not be destroyed," she declared. And her vision, rather than being human-centric, was profoundly inclusive: "Every creature is a glittering, glistening mirror of divinity," she wrote. In Hildegard's worldview, a beam of sunlight, a flower, a bird — all were participants in the divine force which she believed animates the world. She called this force *viriditas*, the Latin word for "greenness," and taught that it continually nourishes the world and all its creatures. "The Earth sweats germinating power from its very pores," she told her nuns. Hildegard's spirituality, then, was deeply grounded; she believed that human beings are not separate from nature, or from the wider cosmos, but an intimate part of it. She told her nuns to pay close attention to the rhythms of nature, suggesting that those rhythms held the secrets both of physical well-being and of a profound and luminous inner life. She urged them to think of themselves as partners with the natural world, saying: "Humankind is called to cocreate, so that we might cultivate the earthly, and thereby create the heavenly."[27]

Hildegard of Bingen, then, displays a critical quality of the archetypal Medial Woman in the European tradition: she might be a mystic, but she is still fully present in the world. She doesn't eschew the physical for the transcendental — instead, she is profoundly connected with nature. In this sense, she perfectly reflects older European beliefs in which the Otherworld — the place where mystical visions reside and from where they arise — is not set apart from the everyday physical world (as, for example, the Christian idea of "heaven" is) but is inextricably entangled with it. The Otherworld, however, cannot be perceived with our physical senses. We can't see it or touch it; we can access it only through what we might call a psychospiritual sense: the imagination.

~

When I was a small child I lived, like most children, in a vivid imaginal world. Everything in the physical world was a metaphor for something else; what adults considered to be inanimate objects were always inhabited by some mythical character or other. Nothing possessed only one face; the world was multifaceted and multilayered. I grew up on the fringes of a council estate in a coastal town in the far northeast of England; the landscape just south of us was a curious mix of salt marsh and sand dunes (now the Teesmouth Nature Reserve) and full-on heavy industrial nightmare. The salt marshes were inhabited by all kinds of strange wights; dragons lurked in the sand dunes; the pitchfork-shaped, steam-spewing industrial structures across the River Tees were wielded by devils whose purpose I didn't then fully comprehend.

Just as many of us do, at a very early age I came to understand how profoundly we have come to devalue imagination in the West — how we think of it now as little more than fantasy, or escapism. But throughout human history, until the so-called "Enlightenment" actively disenchanted us, the Otherworld which is interwoven with this one had always been known to be just as real as any other. And acts of imagining were seen to be the only way we have of coming to know that world which lies beyond the limits of the physical world which we perceive with our physical senses.

It is imagining, then, the oldest philosophical and spiritual traditions of the West tell us, which allows us to see beyond the everyday, to understand the "Forms" or "Ideas" which Greek philosopher Plato suggested were the underlying structures of the cosmos, and which Jung (calling them archetypes) argued were also reflected in the structures of the human psyche. The Otherworld, which we might also call the "imaginal world,"* and which has sometimes been conflated with the *anima mundi*, the world soul,[28] is always in some sense the place beyond the veil. Not to know it (those older and infinitely wiser traditions tell us) is to be cut off from the source, from whatever we perceive to be the Divine: the creative force which underlies and animates the cosmos.

The idea of an Otherworld (or, perhaps, several) which runs alongside this one, which can sometimes be reached from this one, which influences this one, and which is inhabited by archetypal images and beings, is a key aspect of several mythologies and spiritualities throughout the world — especially European traditions. Belief in an Otherworld which coexists with our own has always been a defining feature of the culture and literature of Britain and

---

* It is important here to differentiate the word "imaginal" from "imaginary." "Imaginal" suggests a world that is based on the imagination, a world of images — a world that is real, whereas "imaginary" suggests a world that is made up, a fantasy.

Ireland, for example — and our Otherworld (unlike the Greek Underworld, ruled over by Hades) is not a land of the dead; it is very much a land of the living. Although it can be dangerous, it is more often than not a land of beauty and harmony; its occupants are gods and other supernatural beings; it is full of magical, archetypal creatures and objects. This belief in another, deeper level of reality is fundamental to our ancestral traditions, our native lineage. Fine modern sophisticates that we so often believe ourselves to be, we might think that as adults we're beyond such fancies; but whether we choose it or not, the veil between worlds often begins to disintegrate in menopause — and the Medial Woman archetype begins determinedly to assert itself.

My own work suggests that, particularly during our menopause years, one of our key tasks is to uncover our own unique inner Medial Woman in order to fully individuate. Individuation, Carl Jung suggested, is the process by which we grow into our own most authentic self.[29] When we're young, we're guided by norms that are imposed by family and society, striving to become what is expected of us; the result is the development of what Jung called the *persona*: the mask which we present to the world. The persona rarely reflects our true self, because over the years we compromise, we adapt; we pretend to be something that we're not — and along the way, in some fashion or other, we begin to betray our authentic nature. The process of individuation, then, is the process by which we begin to understand, in the second half of our lives, that the way we've been living is not the way that we need to live now — that we need to change, to live in a manner that is more aligned with our passions and our longings. It is the energy of individuation which hurls us headlong into the alchemical crucible and frog-marches us through the Nigredo.

During the process of individuation, we are opened up to what Jung called the *transcendent function*, as we foster wholeness through a search for meaning. In order to live a meaningful life, he argued, we need to know that we're related to something infinite, something that transcends the limitations of our individual human nature. We need to recognize "a divine life" within us, to believe that we have a place in the universe.[30] In his writings, he repeatedly lamented the loss of the spiritual — what he called *numinosity* — in the modern world. Most people today are reluctant to apprentice themselves to mystery. Caught in the toils of egohood, he suggested, we've been taught to distrust anything we can't see, touch, or quantify, and we're disoriented and dissociated because we've lost our ancient moral and spiritual traditions. And so Jung asks us — no matter how out of step with the overculture we might find ourselves as a consequence — to foster our soul growth, arguing that, unless we do, we will never achieve our full potential. "Of all those who ever consulted me who were in the second half of life," he wrote, "no one was ever cured who did not achieve a spiritual outlook on life."[31] The second half of life, then, gives us the opportunity to rediscover the parts of ourselves that we've buried, to find the path we have lost.

My tall and rather glamorous friend Martine (who, like Véronique, lives in the Netherlands) is a physician. Although there are many aspects of this work that she loves, in her early fifties, when her periods stopped, she began to feel more strongly than ever that she was in the wrong place, doing the wrong work. "I craved for nature," she wrote to me, recently. "For making myself dirty and sweaty in hard earthy labor. I craved to understand the song of the earth and the sky and the moon and the stars. Not by buying and reading books, but through being with them. I wanted to listen to the old stories of indigenous people, or to the myths of a place. I wanted to live more closely with animals and plant life and start learning what they could teach. I wanted to tell stories myself. And, perhaps most of all, I wanted to live a life that in its own small way would help bring back balance to an exhausted world, an exhausted earth. Instead, I felt part of the opposite. There was a growing and deep resistance against being in an institute, between walls and protocols and sterilized conditions. I started to feel ashamed for my power as a doctor and people surrendering to it. I didn't like quite a few of the solutions my profession had to offer. I felt like I was taking care of a health mess that, more often than not, had been created by a dysfunctional way of living that I was part of myself, and that I was sustaining through my own ambitions. I desperately longed for a different way of being."

The problem was, she told me, for a long time she didn't trust herself and her instincts. "Being a medical doctor can be a wonderful, important, and deeply satisfying and rewarding profession. Why then couldn't I go on?" But the dissatisfaction continued, even after forays into other ways of working. "So finally," she said, "in autumn 2019, I decided to quit that whole catastrophe of trying to be a doctor. I gave in my notice, both thrilled and extremely frightened, because there would be nothing left in the way of financial security. Some voice inside me said: Who are you to decide and give up such an extremely important and responsible job? It felt selfish, childish, ungrateful, cowardly, stupid. It felt very much like giving up. But on a deeper level it felt wonderfully right. I found a sense of contradictory pride and strength popping up."

The inevitable question was — what would replace her old life? "Another root was becoming stronger," she wrote. "One that had been there all the time, but that I only now took seriously. And a truth that I found myself sharing with lots of intelligent, thoughtful, and creative women, and which became recognized and somehow legitimate after reading your book, *If Women Rose Rooted*. The truth was the need to let go of a lot of the old securities that I was clinging to, and follow my path.

"So now here we are, on a real jumping-off point. Friends who live in France found a small and ancient farmhouse for my husband and me in the westernmost part of the Vosges. It's a country of hills and forest, with little population. It will give us solitude, space, and clean air. Wild animal life on our small piece of land, a narrow stream at its border. It is utterly frightening and utterly important. I hope to jump in with a great big roar and to get soaked to the bone by the story of the earth."

It's a place, she told me, where she hopes to be able to cultivate what she calls her "weirdness." She hesitated when I asked her to explain what she means by that. "Its essence, I think, is being prepared to become still, to listen. In really listening, sooner or later the question arises — are we prepared to challenge and let go of commonly held attitudes and opinions? Because they blur the capacity to be aware and awake. All that striving for 'still better,' for 'more,' for economic growth or personal comfort or status. I want to listen to something much older and more profound than that. So, being prepared to be 'weird' to me is being prepared to take a different view than the one that is usually required by the culture we live in. It's about trying to become part of a balance between all that lives.

"And so, from trying to be, or to become, something — grown-up, attractive, intelligent, successful, sensible; a good doctor, or mother, or friend, or all other things I thought I should strive for — I suddenly realized that what I needed was to give in to something that had been traveling with me from my childhood years, but that I was always a little afraid of. To give in to being able to be weird. To having an uncomfortable edge. To acting beyond logic."

These things are only "weird," of course, in a culture whose values are based on productivity and materialism, and it's only by stepping out of that cultural mythology — or being jolted out of it, by the volcanic force of menopause — that we can glimpse the beginnings of another path. "So, reluctantly I gave in to these weird qualities, after years of trying to ignore them, eradicate them, or thinking them superfluous or shameful," Martine wrote. "This confidence in who I am as a spiritual woman is only recently ripening to maturity. Now, after menopause, I find myself coming closer to others, and closer to a connection with the earth and all creatures she harbors. Is being a true hag about being able to wear the power of your weirdness comfortably? — because now you have reached an age at which you can truly ride this beautiful and unpredictable dragon. You can shake and burn away some of the too-comfortable and caging truths and cackle with laughter about them. Being sensible alone doesn't make one a hag. Nor does experience, or knowledge, or being a nature-lover, or an herbalist, or an expert in tarot. However great those gifts are. This kind of weirdness itself becomes the mature talent. Perhaps all our previous efforts and experiences — even the ones that we think of as wrong paths — are meant to lead us there."

~

Jung believed there is a dimension of the psyche beyond the ego (the conscious personality) which is the source of spiritual experiences; he called this the "self." This spiritual element of the psyche reveals itself to us in various ways — through dreams, symptoms (physical and psychological), experiences of synchronicity. It is an inner force which guides us, expressed through a symbolic life which connects us with the transpersonal, with whatever it is that we imagine to be beyond us: the Divine, the creative power of the universe, the sacred. Not everyone might relate to words like "Divine" or "sacred," of course — but I think that most of us can relate to the idea of looking for a deeper, more meaningful way of living. And whatever we consider the Divine — or that deeper meaning — to be, working with myth and archetype through exercising the imagination is a natural way to understand it. It helps us to shine a light on who we really are.

As a child, as I've described, my imagination was rooted in the landscapes I occupied. Industrial edgelands, or "natural" and wilder — it didn't matter to me at all. The land, urban or rural, was alive, permeated with the Otherworld, and inhabited by a multiplicity of archetypal beings. And this is how it was in the ancient traditions of these islands, which derive from a culture that was intensely animistic, and whose spirituality was rooted in the natural world. A well was never "just" a well; it was a conduit for Otherworldly inspiration, and therefore to be revered. A bird could be a messenger from the Otherworld, or a guardian of its gates, and when human wisdom failed, we went to the animals for theirs.

Residues of those beliefs persist today, because for all our modernity that lineage is still in us. Whether we think of it that way or not, many of us in these islands walk with one foot (at least) in the Otherworld. When we moved to Donegal in 2014, the first question our neighbor, a lifelong farmer, casually asked me on discovering I wrote books about myth, was, "So you keep the fairy faith, then?" Well, I didn't leave out saucers of milk at night for the fairies, but I believed our friend the poet when he told me never to take so much as a stick from the fairy wood down the lane, because it belonged to the "good people." I never walked in there without some kind of little offering (a sprinkling of tea leaves, a song, or a poem) to whoever might hold sway. Like much of the population of rural Ireland, I have the greatest respect for a solitary hawthorn tree as a place where the "good people" dwell; roads are still diverted around them today. Just as, in contemporary Iceland, new roads and construction projects are often delayed or rerouted to take into consideration "elf rocks": land formations that are believed to be inhabited by elves.

My own imagination, then, is intensely place-based, and I've always thought of the places I've lived (and a few I haven't lived in, but which have had great significance for me) as the biggest teachers in my life. Every place has taught me a lesson I needed to learn precisely at that time, because places, above all, reflect us back to ourselves. More than this, they teach us the many ways we might *become* in the world. Deserts, forests, coastlines, mountains, rolling green-fielded countryside, prairies; centers of human habitation from great, ancient cities to small country villages — each of them reveals something different to us about our patterns and potentials.

In *If Women Rose Rooted* I wrote about all the ways in which, around the time of my own menopause, I began to develop a deep relationship with the land we then lived in: the wild and beautiful Isle of Lewis, in the Outer Hebrides. I hope that those of you who've read that book will forgive a bit of backtracking here, so that I can update and recontextualize the story I told there.

Over the four years that we lived on the island, I came to know that land as I have never known anywhere else. I came to know which wildflowers grew where, and the names of them, and when they should appear, and whether they were late this year; I watched every spring for the oystercatchers to return, then the lapwings, and finally the whooper swans. I knew the best rock pools in which to forage for dulse and other seaweeds, and could pick my way, sure-footed, through the boggiest ground. I knew the land intensely in every season; I walked it in storms so fierce that

I could hardly stand up, and I danced barefoot on sunny summer rocks.

But more than just knowing the ecology and physical features of the place, I knew its folklore. And wherever I walked, those old stories were made visible in the permanent features of the land. I lived in a house from which, on the skyline in the mountains opposite it, the reclining figure of a woman could be recognized. There are several such locations throughout the islands and in mainland Scotland, where the shapes of specific mountains or ranges of hills represent the silhouette of the ancient goddess of the land. The best known of them all is the Isle of Lewis's "Sleeping Beauty," known rather more interestingly in Gaelic as *Cailleach na Mointeach* — "the old woman of the moors" — who can be seen at a distance from the Callanish stone circle. I looked out onto our own reclining figure every morning when I opened the bedroom curtains; she dominated the landscape when I walked or worked the land. In the islands, the stories tell of that old goddess's two aspects: the youthful Brigid (or Bride), who was associated with the summer half of the year, and the stony, blue-faced Cailleach (the Gaelic word for "old woman"), who was associated with the winter half.

The silhouette opposite our house was clearly that of a young woman rather than a hag; to me, then, she represented Brigid. I found her sister or alter ego, the Cailleach, by accident. While haunting a hidden fragment of the shoreline, I stumbled across a remarkable location which afterward I only ever called the Rocky Place. It was *my* place; I recognized it as such the first moment I saw it. Vast expanses of smooth, slabbed rock like a multicolored, layered carpet which sloped gradually at first, and then more acutely, down to a cluster of smaller rocks, coated with emerald-green algae and onto which the sea continually crashed. This undulating rock carpet was primarily made of Lewisian gneiss, one of the oldest rocks in the world;

its boundary with the grassy headland above was a long, curving, sharply chiseled cliff face, perhaps the height of two average people.

In one corner of the cliff face I saw the rough-hewn silhouette of a hag, slightly larger than human height, staring out to sea. The Cailleach. The old stories tell us that she is given to standing in such places, looking out for the return of her husband, sometimes called the Bodach (the "old man") — and sometimes identified in folklore as Manannán Mac Lir, a god who makes his home in the sea. And then, just around the corner from this Cailleach rock, I found a vast, flat stone slab wedged into an alcove up against the cliff face, which looked for all the world like a giant sofa, fit for any Flintstone. I called it the Cailleach's Bed, and one night I slept there under the late-August stars, with the Gasker light flashing slowly out to sea to the south of me, and the Flannan Isles lighthouse flashing at a quite different tempo to the north.

And so, directly out of the land and the features of the landscape, I found those old stories... or maybe they found me. They became part of my life, and my life became part of the land just as the stories were part of the land. I called it "falling into the land's dreaming." Intrinsic, inseparable: me, the land, our stories; the physical world and the imaginal, perfectly entwined. Walking the land, I had immersed myself in stories of the Cailleach, and here at the Rocky Place I became Cailleach for a time. I sat there often, cross-legged, mesmerized by crashing waves. I stood for long periods of time by the side of that silhouetted old woman and stared out to sea with her, imagining the long, lonely ages and the unyielding rock and the unforgiving power of the stormy ocean. I shared her vigil for a while and told her all of my stories; I wept by her side when, for a few months, life became unbearably hard. Leaving that place for Ireland in 2014 was one of the most difficult things I have ever done;

turning my back on that solitary old Cailleach felt like a betrayal.

The four years that we spent on Lewis were mythic years. The land spoke to us in shattered ideals and dead totem animals. We learned the lessons of our life, and each one of them arose directly out of the land. They were hard lessons, but they were lessons we needed to learn. They changed us, and they changed us in ways that we needed to change. The land taught us, and it certainly tested us. I learned about bleakness, about endurance, about making a stand, and more than I ever wanted to know about the risks of turning to stone. I learned that, as much as I love and need solitude, I need community too. I learned, more than anything, that I am not an island.

I had a dream, the night after I first stumbled across the Rocky Place. It was one of those that Jung called a "Big Dream": the kind you have just a few times in your life. The kind of dream you know is telling you something, though often enough you have no idea what, at the time. I dreamed that the Rocky Place was made from stone animals, and these animals formed the boundary cliff face as well as the surface of the ground. One was an eagle with outstretched wings, and above the Cailleach's Bed was a stalking wolf with holes for eyes where the sky shone through. In a shallow but wide channel of seawater that I would somehow have to cross if I carried on walking, was a huge whale which might act as a stepping-stone. I could sense something stirring in the air around me, and it was a sense of power and of danger. *If you tread on that sleeping whale,* the place seemed to be saying to me, *if you waken the animals, the sleeping heart of the rock; if you waken the sleeping power of this abandoned land and let loose its stories, you have no idea just what it is you are going to awaken. Will you wake them anyway? Will you do it? Will you do it, without fear of the consequences?*

I did; of course I did. And I was roused from my own sleep just as the drowsing dream-animals began to stir. I put the dream to one side; I didn't then know what it meant. But one of its many lessons which I've come to understand since is that in merging myself so deeply with that abandoned land and its stories, I woke it up. And then I left it.

Just before we moved away from the island for good, I traveled to our new cottage by the river in Ireland and spent a week there alone. I remember that I wondered which animal I would connect with there — which animal would become the one I most resonated with in that new, noncoastal landscape. Because ever since I had moved to a croft on the shore of a sea-loch on the northwest coast of Scotland back in 2003, the animals I lived with which most captured my imagination were seals. In that place, in the years before I met and married David and right up until the time we left for Lewis, I would walk down to the sea-loch early each morning and almost always there would be a solitary seal, gray head bobbing up and down in the water, watching me. I sat with it, sang to it, and it became a character in the novel I wrote in those years, *The Long Delirious Burning Blue*. If there is such a thing as a totem story, the story of the selkie, the seal-woman who lost her skin, was then mine. And when we moved to Lewis, on those long early morning walks with the dogs down by the shore, most days I would find a seal there too. A single, solitary seal with a particular penchant, it seemed, for my efforts at "Danny Boy." It sang its own mournful song back to me one morning, and I've never forgotten the chills that ran through my body, and the way my hair seemed to stand on end.

I returned to Lewis after that first week in Donegal, and found the seal dead on the beach.

After we moved permanently to Donegal, it took us eighteen months to sell our old croft. When finally we found a buyer, David returned to Lewis for a few days to gather up a few remaining possessions. I asked him while he was there to go to the Rocky Place and say hello for me, and he did. Here is what he found: the Cailleach's Bed had gone.

Yes, there are big storms in the islands, and yes, big storms can move rocks. I once was trained as a scientist; I was trained to be a skeptic. I understand that water, under great pressure, forced into gaps and crevices, can do remarkable things.

Moving an enormous, thick slab of solid, heavy Lewisian gneiss, bigger in both dimensions than a single bed? Lifting it completely out of the alcove inside which it so tightly fit, casting it aside, leaving no traces behind?

Under some circumstances, perhaps. And yet... just this one particular impossibly large and heavy rock? Which was so firmly wedged into its place?

You may wonder what I am trying to tell you here. Am I filled with delusions of grandeur? Do I imagine that because I left the land, the Rocky Place had no more need for a Cailleach's Bed and spat it out? That the land was in some way responding to me and, in particular, to my departure? Angry, perhaps, or grieving? I can't possibly be trying to tell you such a thing — surely it would be ridiculous — and yet I suppose I am. Some happenings can't so easily be dismissed. They are not mere coincidences, but rather what Jung called synchronicities: statistically improbable experiences or circumstances that appear to an individual to be meaningfully related, but which lack an obvious causal connection.

This kind of personal mystical experience or encounter hints at a world beyond the constraints of "consensus reality." Before priests and other religious officials decided that intermediaries must arbitrate between ordinary humans and the Divine, and put an end to the ancient idea of

developing a personal relationship with the sacred, encounters that we would define as mystical or visionary
were a part of everyone's life — just as they are in many
indigenous societies today. But in the world of scientistic
psychology and neuroscience that I'd previously inhabited,
they were much more likely now to be thought of as evidence
of mental illness. Now, those experiences on Lewis — the
dreams, these and other synchronicities, the recurrence of
certain animals and archetypes in the landscape — called
to a part of me that had long been suppressed. And
during those early menopausal years I broke through a
personal taboo which sprang from my early training as a
neuroscientist, and began to speak and write openly about
the ways in which the animate land we inhabit can make
itself known to us, and draw us into relationship. It's not
as radical an idea as I then believed; indigenous cultures
around the world have always held it to be so. My own
native culture once held it to be so. But it's radical enough
here in the contemporary West, where this kind of mythic
imagination is held to be the province of children or fools.

The practice of mythic imagination which I've developed
since those experiences on Lewis (and which I now teach
in workshops and courses) is premised on the fact that
each of us has our own unique inner "imaginarium." We
are each haunted by different images; we each resonate with
different myths or fairy tales, and with different archetypal
characters within them. We each resonate with different
archetypal landscapes, and with different nonhuman others
which inhabit them alongside us. And each of us identifies
with different archetypal characters, stories, and landscapes
at different times in our lives. How then do we uncover
those patterns; how do we bring those images to life and
let them work their magic on us? It's not about striving to
interpret them, because an image is like a kiss — once we

begin to dissect it, the magic is gone. It's simply about *being with* the images which call to us. It's about believing that these images hold wisdom and insight. It's about letting them slowly reveal themselves to us, 'and so revealing something of ourselves in the process. They provide clues to who we are and who we might become. They provide clues about our path in the world and about the nature of our unique calling.

As we'll see throughout this book, myths and fairy tales are particularly helpful in offering up guiding images and archetypal characters which help us to experience the imaginal world. The imaginal realms can also be experienced in other ways — for example, through dreams; when we are touched by a sense of the sacred in prayer or meditation; when we feel ourselves strongly moved by an image from a film, a book, a poem, or a work of art. Annie, a member of my online community who lives in northwest England, tells me of reading a poem by Dawna Markova, "I Will Not Die an Unlived Life."[32] She was forty-nine at the time, and on the threshold of menopause. Her daughter had just left for university, and, since Annie was a single mother, all the structures of her life, and the things she had built it around, seemed to have vanished.

"I was completely cut adrift," she says. "I'd spent years doing a job I hated to make sure I could keep a roof over our heads and pay the bills. And now the reason for that willing self-sacrifice was gone. I didn't know what to do with myself, or who I was going to be now that I was all alone. And then, on Facebook one day, I saw a post with that poem. It was as if someone had lit a candle in my soul. I loved my daughter and I had no regrets, but I'd been doing work that was completely devoid of passion and meaning for the best part of two decades. I'd been on autopilot, just chugging along — but now I needed to find a way to live on purpose. So that poem, in which she writes about not fully living because you're always afraid of catching fire, conjured up an image which changed my life. It was as if something took hold of me by the throat, shook me, and screamed, 'Wake up!' I wanted more than anything to catch fire again. I wanted to change my life. It took me a long time to figure out how, but it was the image of a burning woman that I carried with me in my imagination, and which opened me to the possibilities. I sat with that image every day. I meditated on it. I drew it. Until eventually, somehow, I became it. I found my passion after volunteering at a local wildlife trust. When a job as project officer came up, I applied for it. I was successful, and handed in my notice as administrator in an accountant's office for good. I've never looked back."

This is how the imaginal world beckons to us: when an image really stirs something in us and awakens a strong emotion: a sadness, a longing, a feeling of joy or expansiveness. And if we can learn to explore and to engage with these images, to carry them along in our hearts as we go about our lives, they will often guide us to insights that are both unexpected and mysterious. As William James, one of the founders of modern psychology, wrote:

> Our normal waking consciousness ... is but one special type of consciousness, whilst all about it, parted from it by the filmiest of screens, there lie potential forms of consciousness entirely different ... No account of the universe in its totality can be final which leaves these other forms of consciousness quite disregarded.[33]

These "potential forms of consciousness" include the mystical and visionary experiences which help us to navigate the profound transformations we undergo in the second half of our lives, and to recognize our immersion in the more-than-human world around us. It's about moving beyond the limits of our superficial ego and descending into the deepest layers of our own psyche, to understand the ways in which we are uniquely entangled with the psyche of the cosmos itself.

This is a world in which the Medial Woman is absolutely at home. The Medial Woman in her manifold forms teaches us to court the world soul, to invite the mystery in. She's prowling in the shadows at the edges of our vision; she's been waiting for years for us to notice her. So strip off your tight, laced-up shoes, and join her as she dances barefoot with the mystery.

~

The Alchemist shows us one face of the Medial Woman archetype, and Hildegard represents another, the Mystic — but perhaps better known than either of these is a third face: the compelling, iconic character of the Witch. The women we usually think of as historical witches were edge-dwellers: haunters of moonlit crossroads, inhabitants of the margins of community. They were keepers of the "old ways," we imagine — animists who thought of plants and animals not just as allies, but as kin. We see them today as healers and medicine women, shapeshifters and storykeepers. In our imaginations, they were dancers, diviners, and dreamers; they were visionaries, cavorting and consorting with the denizens of the Otherworld. They were the "fairy witches," the cunning folk, the wise women. They were executed in their millions during the main period of the witch trials in Europe, from the early fifteenth century through to the late eighteenth.

Except that they weren't. Not until we made them so, in our imaginations. But if that isn't the "true history" of the witch, what is? And how has she been reinvented over the

years? How is she relevant to us, in our menopausal years
and beyond?

One of the most often-repeated misunderstandings about
witches — and specifically, those who were prosecuted and
killed at the height of the witch trials — is the notion that
they were really nature-honoring, goddess-worshipping
herbalists and midwives, or other kinds of healers and
wise women. But there is no significant body of evidence
to suggest, and quite a bit of evidence to argue against,
the idea that communities in Europe were "goddess-
worshipping" in any organized way during the period of the
witch hunts; there is certainly no trace of it in the historical
records. The suggestion that the majority of women accused
of witchcraft during the main period of the witch trials were
midwives or herbalists is also unfounded — although, of
course, such cases did exist. Midwives, in fact, were rarely
charged. Instead, and sadly, they often worked side by side
with the prosecutors to help them identify "witch marks"
on the accused. Others practicing what was thought of as
benign magic, especially along the Celtic fringes of Britain
and in Ireland, where wise women were seen as respected
and valued members of the community, were much less
likely to be accused of witchcraft.

So if the women who were accused of being witches
were mostly not these people, who were they? In order to
understand that, it's necessary to look back at the historical
use of the term "witch." Throughout history, all the way up
to the main witch trial period and beyond, the word had
been used exclusively to refer to someone who caused harm
to others by magical means. Witchcraft has historically been
a term for evil magic and sorcery; witches were entirely
malevolent in their intent. There were others who worked
what was also labeled as magic, but which was clearly
benign — healing, for example, or divining, counteracting
the negative effects of witchcraft, tracing lost or stolen

goods, or intervening in affairs of the heart. In Britain and Ireland, such people would not have been called witches, but "cunning folk" or "wise women." Our contemporary and very much wider definition of witchcraft might now incorporate such people — but historically they were seen to be quite different. It's also worth noting that both witches and wise women were differentiated from a third group: practitioners of "high" or ceremonial magic, who were much more likely to be men, and who were almost always members of the upper echelons of society.

In Britain, the idea of the witch as a perpetrator of malevolence — someone who worked to actively harm neighbors or kin, and who sometimes worked together with others to do so, with techniques and resources which had been handed down through a particular tradition — can be traced back to Anglo-Saxon descriptions of witchcraft in clerical texts and secular law codes. *Wiccecraeft* — the ancestor of the word "witchcraft" — was practiced by the female *wicce* or male *wicca*, from which comes the modern English word "witch."

This belief in human practitioners of malevolent magic is related to another, Europe-wide, belief in supernatural females who were similarly intent on doing harm to humans. The most common label for such beings in the old texts was *haegtis* or *haegtesse* — the precursor of the word "hag" — which ultimately came, as a consequence, to refer to a malignant old woman. The most widespread of these beliefs was in terrorizing female spirits who haunted the night. The Wild Hunt, one such common folk motif, refers to a band of supernatural hunters and hounds who would fly through the night sky whipping up storms, with the howling wind as a musical accompaniment to their dastardly deeds. The hunters were thought to be either the dead, or fairies, depending on local tradition. In some parts of Europe, the leader of the Wild Hunt was believed to be an ancient goddess — the Roman Diana, or the German Perchte or Holda (a fine old woman who we will meet in a couple of later chapters). Various reasons were given for the night-roamings of these Otherworldly women: to do battle with other bands of spirits, to kill and eat humans and then restore them to life again, or to work other kinds of strange magic. Belief in these beings converged with similar beliefs in other, more benign, wandering female spirits who would visit houses at night to bless them.

These folk motifs are found across the world and have clearly fed belief in wicked, night-flying witches. But Europe was unique in that it was the only part of the world in which the idea also took hold that witchcraft represented an organized, heretical "anti-religion," dedicated to worshipping the Christian Devil and to committing acts of evil in his name. So, by the high Middle Ages, the tradition of night-roaming female spirits had come to be associated with this new, Church-inspired image of the evil, Devil-worshipping witch who stimulated the European witch trials. The ugly witch, venturing out on her broomstick at night to terrify and terrorize, became the new stereotype; we see her plainly depicted in the work of artists like Francisco Goya and Luis Ricardo Falero. Witch-hunting during the period of the witch trials, then, was primarily inspired by heretic hunting.

During the past four decades there has been a huge amount of scholarly Europe-wide research into the written records of the witch trials. This research has discovered that around forty to sixty thousand people were legally put to death for the alleged crime of witchcraft, from the early witch hunts that took place between the years 1427 and 1436 in Savoy (in the western Alps), to the execution of Anna Göldi in the Swiss canton of Glarus in 1782. These figures include proportionate estimates for cases in areas where no reliable records exist. Around 75 percent of those executed were women, and they were often women who were on the fringes of community — old, alone, or in some other way unusual or eccentric. The most intense areas of witch-hunting were Calvinist Scotland, Lutheran northern Norway, some Catholic states in western and central Germany, and the Franco-German borderland. The highest proportion of cases occurred in places where makers and enforcers of the law were embedded in the local community, and where personal or factional enmities, as well as political ambitions, came into play. But the records show that there was always and above all a genuine fear of witchcraft in the local populations in which witch hunts were instigated, undoubtedly seeded by those folk beliefs in malevolent nocturnal females which had been prevalent for so long.[34]

The popular belief that millions of women, rather than tens of thousands, were executed during the European witch trials has no basis in reality, then — but nevertheless, in the significantly less populated world of the Middle Ages, these numbers are quite high enough, and the psychological weight of the witch trials, real or imagined, remains with us today. Its main burden that we carry as women, I think, is a fear of not conforming to what society, or our narrower community, expects of us. A fear of being too different; a fear, arguably, of our own potential power. Women were affected in many different ways by the cultural repressions which were associated with the witch trials, and many of them — especially the aged, or the disabled — lived in fear. It's likely that many women modified their behaviors, and presented themselves as people they were not, to avoid being overly visible. There would also have been, entangled with all of this, a deep suspicion of other women — because the persecutors who brought cases during the witch trials were not always and only men, but women too.

What we might think of as the "witch wound" that is borne down through the generations, then, is the psychological wound in the collective consciousness of women that prevents us, even today, from fully and fearlessly embodying the person we feel ourselves really to be. The witch wound is dread at the idea of speaking out against "authority," and of being too different — "weird," to use Martine's word — because those were precisely the kinds of women, as far as we can tell, who were victims of the witch trials. The ones who didn't quite fit in. The eccentrics, the unconventional ones. The women who had the audacity to speak their minds, who refused to be complicit in the injustices of the patriarchy. The witch wound is the result of centuries of marginalization by both religious and secular authorities — centuries in which women had no power, no autonomy; in which we never felt truly safe and were constantly subject to abuse. Above all, then, the witch wound is fear.

More recently, though, we've come to think of the Witch archetype as very much more benign — an archetype that will teach us, and maybe even save us. How was it that the Witch came to be so thoroughly revisioned after the horrors of the witch trials? How was she transformed from a creature of evil and malevolence into a character that so many of us now aspire to be?

It began in the centuries following the witch trials, when a number of writers and scholars — many of them, curiously, men — began to rewrite the history of the witch. The French writer Jules Michelet was a particularly influential character in the mid-nineteenth century. Christianity itself, Michelet declared, was outdated and irrelevant and must now give way to a new religion: one more suited to what he thought of as a "new age." He suggested that such a faith would best be built around the notion of women and motherhood, and he held up the honoring of the goddess Isis in ancient Egypt as an especially good example of what he had in mind. He became interested in the witch trials and produced a book on the subject, entitled *La Sorcière*, in 1862. To Michelet, who clearly was influenced by the pan-European Romantic movement, the witch was an archetypal figure who represented spiritual freedom, as well as the rights of women and the working classes. This is the first time that such ideas had been expressed in print in Europe and widely circulated. Michelet portrayed witchcraft (entirely based on his own imagination, not from any evidence) as a surviving pagan religion which had kept the spirit of liberty alive all through the "thousand long, dreary, terrible years" of the Middle Ages. He also, strangely and apropos of nothing very much at all, proclaimed that the Renaissance had occurred when the wisdom preserved by witches came to the surface again to inspire members of the cultural elite. That wisdom, he said, was gained from a close knowledge of, and relationship with, the natural world and the universal life force, and Michelet believed that women were especially suited to such knowledge and so had always served as priestesses of the witch religion.

In Michelet's conception of it, the Witches' Sabbath — the main religious assembly, he declared, of the faith — was held on "a wide heath, often in the neighborhood of an old Celtic dolmen, or at the edge of a wood." It was largely made up of peasants. When she was not presiding over such ceremonies, the priestess would commune with animals and trees: "They awaken in her things that her mother told her, her grandmother — old, old things that for century after century have been handed on from woman to woman."[35] This theory put forward by Michelet and others — that the victims of the witch trials had been nature-loving pagans — had a huge impact throughout Europe, where it was propagated widely and eagerly taken up by writers and scholars of the day. By the early twentieth century a miscellany of people in England had come to believe that a revival of paganism, and especially a benign form of witchcraft, would be a very fine thing indeed. It was out of this impulse that modern pagan witchcraft, and in particular the new practice of Wicca, was created.

Even well into the twentieth century, Michelet's ideas were still influential; his view of witchcraft was enthusiastically espoused by American radical feminists, who wholeheartedly accepted his idea that the witch trials had represented both the suppression of an "Old Religion" and the control of women, who could now perhaps regain their long-lost power by identifying with witches. Although at first the emphasis of the feminist movement was on witchcraft as an antidote to patriarchy, it later became focused on promoting witchcraft as a religion. Many women were involved in this process through the decades, but a particularly notable figure is American writer and activist Starhawk, whose book *The Spiral Dance* (1979) was one of the main inspirations behind the Goddess movement and the expansion of Wicca and other forms of witchcraft at the time. Through her "Reclaiming" movement, Starhawk suggested that modern witches' covens could be turned into training camps in which women could be liberated, men reeducated, and new forms of human relationships explored which were free of old gender stereotypes and power structures. She reinterpreted magic in terms of psychology, as a set of practices for self-discovery, self-fulfillment, and the realization of human potential. Starhawk also suggested that a network of such covens could serve as a mechanism for the transformation of society in healthier and more sustainable ways, advocating an "eco-pagan," nature-based perspective in which the Earth is viewed as a living entity, and the environmental justice movement is a key outcome.

Starhawk was far from the first woman to associate the practice of witchcraft with honoring nature as well as courting the Otherworld; from early Classical times, literature offered up an image of the Witch, whether benign or malign, as firmly situated in the natural world. Homer's Circe, for example, lived in a forest glen, and Ovid's Medea served the goddess Hekate from a temple deep in the woods. The tools of the witch, and especially the ingredients she needed for her magic potions, came from nature and were all tied up with the cycles and seasons of the year: herbs, for example, must be gathered in specific places (such as mountaintops) and at specific times of the day or night. Witches' potions also contained parts of wild animals, and so we find Medea using the wings and flesh of screech owls, the entrails of a werewolf, the scaly skin of a snake, the liver of a stag, and the eggs and head of a crow.

Witches were closely associated with animals in many other ways, and so Homer and Ovid both tell us that Circe's house was guarded by wolves, lions, and bears. Witches would commonly transform themselves or other humans into animals: according to the Roman writer Apuleius, Thessalian witches could transform themselves into birds, dogs, mice, or flies. Some witches looked or sounded like wild animals: Horace's Canidia wore serpents in her hair, while Sagana had hair like a raging boar; Lucan's Erictho had a voice that sounded like a dog, wolf, owl, and serpent combined. Some witches behaved like wild animals, so Canidia and Sagana dug at the earth with their nails and shredded a lamb with their bare teeth; Erictho ate human corpses and tore into living flesh with her teeth and nails.

Witches could also control natural phenomena, and Ovid's version of Medea addressed the gods and spirits of nature with these words:

When my power commands, the rivers turn from their accustomed ways and roll far backward to their secret springs! I speak — and

the wild, troubled sea is calm, and I command
the waters to arise! The clouds I scatter — and I
bring the clouds; I smooth the winds and ruffle
up their rage; I weave my spells and I recite
my charms; I pluck the fangs of serpents, and
I move the living rocks and twist the rooted
oaks; I blast the forests. Mountains at my word
tremble and quake; and from her granite tombs
the liberated ghosts arise as Earth astonished
groans![36]

This connection of witches with nature undoubtedly
reflected the prevailing cultural associations of women
with the physical and with the natural world, in contrast
to male identification with reason and the intellect. But the
witch's control over nature was seen as an inversion of the
"natural" order of things — the order which, men believed,
grants control of the world to them. Classical authors,
living as they did in patriarchal societies, presented this
reversal as profoundly threatening; they suggested that it
ran contrary to all law and would lead to the destruction
not only of human culture, but of the entire world. Witches,
then, represented the ultimate fear of the chaos that would
result from the loss of men's control over the human and
the natural world.

As a result of this recent historical revisioning of the
archetype, to publicly identify as a witch today is no longer
a cause for embarrassment; indeed, it's almost mainstream.
Alice Tarbuck's 2020 book *A Spell in the Wild: A Year (and
Six Centuries) of Magic* declared on its back cover that
"witches are back.... They are here because they must be
needed...," and even received coverage in traditional print
media.[37] Witchcraft, according to Alice, is "the practice of
using our will to shape and change the world, to care for

it." I'm not entirely sure that humans haven't done enough damage to the world by imposing our will on it, but it's clear that, by the vision we might prefer to embrace today, the source of a witch's power isn't culture, dogma, and hierarchy, but nature, imagination, and grassroots. It's a power, above all, which threatens the establishment — and, especially, the patriarchy. The Witch has come to embody all of our longings for what we imagine to be the old ways of our ancestors: a reverence for the natural world and our other-than-human kin; a wild, green spirituality linking feminism with environmentalism. Not only is this Witch (like all iterations of the Medial Woman) autonomous, relying on no man for authentication, but she's a woman who's rooted in nature, finding her "power" in the land, in herbs and trees, in the wind, in the sea. The Witch archetype, then, has adapted itself admirably to what many contemporary women would like to be — because so many of us have lost a connection with our own deep knowing, with our intuition, and the natural cycles and seasons of the world we live in. Identification with the archetype of the Witch restores it to us.

On the other hand, it's also likely that the whiff of danger associated with crossing a witch in the old stories makes her all the more alluring to us. You don't mess with a witch, and women today are bone-tired of being messed with. So the idea that we might find ways to protect ourselves has its resonances too — though the new archetypal Witch possesses not only power, but a much-coveted mystery; she's not easily known and is often hard to define. She lives well outside the village — or at best, on its borders; she holds herself apart from "civilization" and chooses instead to live by her own deeper values. For those of us who have fallen out of our cultural mythology and are looking for new, more meaningful stories to live by, this quality is perhaps at the heart of the strength of the Witch archetype. It's also important to note that, for all our benign revisionings, we don't always find the Witch in the light. We find her as often as not in the shadows, in the dark places where we sometimes fear to go. But these are precisely the places we need to go in order to unveil our inner power and wisdom. They're precisely where the Witch can lead us, and where she can teach us not to be afraid.

The archetype of the Witch is complex and multifaceted, but, once upon a time, the classic fairy-tale witch was almost always portrayed as an ugly and frightening old woman. My earliest memory of such a witch is from a childhood dream in which I was cowering underneath an armchair, watching in terror as a pair of feet in shoes with stereotypically curled-up toes slowly approached. The chair was moved away to reveal me — and there she was: the vintage storybook witch, all hooked nose, gap-toothed cackling mouth, and glaring eyes. It's one of the few nightmares I can ever remember having. But in spite of that scary dream, I only ever wanted to dress up as and pretend to be the fairy-tale witch, not the princess. I understood even then that it was witches, not princesses, who held all the power. Witches got to make their own decisions. Rather than being caught up in the stories, they stood a little outside them, while still determining their trajectory, and they knew all the important and necessary secrets. They'd tell you what it is that would save your life — but only if they thought you deserved to know.

For a long time, the old beliefs about ugly, wicked witches predominated. In 1563, in his book *De Praestigiis Daemonum*, Johann Wier wrote that witches were "poor, mindless old women," "childish old hags," "old women of melancholic nature and small brains," and were to be pitied rather than feared. Reginald Scot, in *The Discoverie of Witchcraft* (1584), declared that "one sort of such as are said to be witches are women which be commonly old, lame, blear-eyed, pale, foul, and full of wrinkles." The most famous literary witches of this kind must be Shakespeare's three "weird sisters," in *Macbeth*. They are repulsive and frightening "midnight hags," with thin lips, chapped fingers, and beards. The content of their spells — eye of newt and toe of frog — are presented as equally repellent.

Those old ideas about ugly, malign witches still crop up today. In 2020, British academic and broadcaster Mary Beard wrote an article in which she declared that she is frequently called a witch on Twitter — a deliberate attempt, she believed, not just to discredit her, but older women in general. Beard, who is professor of Classics at the University of Cambridge, drew a parallel between the historic witch trials and the kind of online abuse she consistently receives today. Noting that the ancient Greeks and Romans feared that old women might be sexual predators, and that women with long gray hair seem even today to make some people anxious, she suggested that, during the witch trials, "There was a fear of female agency, a fear of women communing with a supernatural world where — perish the thought! — the patriarchy was not fully in place and, perhaps most profoundly, a fear of older women."[38]

Sometimes, though, in the guise of sorceress, the archetypal Witch was envisioned as a beautiful and seductive woman in the prime of her life. One of the most interesting examples is the woman in medieval Arthurian literature who we know as Morgan le Fay. Morgan is usually offered up as King Arthur's villainous half sister; she's known to us primarily from Sir Thomas Malory's fifteenth-century text *Le Morte d'Arthur*, in which she appears as Arthur's greatest enemy. But in older texts, such as Geoffrey of Monmouth's *Vita Merlini*, she is portrayed in a quite different way. The *Vita Merlini* makes no mention of any type of familial relationship between Arthur and Morgan; instead, she is presented as a benevolent healer, a renowned scholar of the arts and sciences, and the ruler of a magical island of women to which Arthur is taken after his final battle.

Although witches in history, and throughout folklore and literature, have usually been presented as a mature or elder woman, the contemporary cultural witch revival seems largely to be centered around teens and young adults. According to *Cosmopolitan* magazine, there is a "witch influencer" movement on Instagram that is aimed predominantly at young women and millennials; *Marie Claire* magazine refers to them as "spookily glam Insta-witches" and notes that in 2019, the tag #witchesofinstagram boasted over three million posts.[39] We're living, it seems, in the era of the digital witch, helped along by television series such as *Sabrina the Teenage Witch* (now rebooted and reimagined as *Chilling Adventures of Sabrina*) and *A Discovery of Witches*. But "witch lite" isn't what we're talking about as we pass through menopause; we've no use for "starter witch kits" complete with magic[k]al candles, "charm bags," sanitized packets of herbs, and a pretty crystal for stimulating the odd chakra. We'd rather get our hands dirty, grubbing in the woods for roots and chatting to crows along the way. We're entering a time in our lives when we have no desire to skim the surface, when what we're searching for is nothing less than an inside-out transformation not just of ourselves, but the world.

I'd say it's hard to find sympathetic depictions of a meno-pausal or postmenopausal witch in fiction, but the truth is it's hard to find them in contemporary fiction at all — though I admit to a bit of a soft spot for Minerva McGonagall, the elderly Scottish witch in J. K. Rowling's Harry Potter series who was brilliantly played by Maggie

Smith in the movies based on the books. McGonagall is head of Gryffindor House at Hogwarts, and a teacher of the art of "transfiguration." In some ways she seems to be the time-honored storybook witch, as Harry Potter's first impressions of her suggest: "The door swung open at once. A tall, black-haired witch in emerald-green robes stood there. She had a very stern face and Harry's first thought was that she was not someone to cross."[40] McGonagall, a powerful and talented woman, evokes considerable respect (and the odd soupçon of fear) in the students and staff of Hogwarts. She's accustomed to having her way, has a sharp and biting sense of humor, and doesn't suffer fools gladly.

But my first adult contemporary fiction witch-love was Janice Elliott's character Martha Price, in her 1988 novel *The Sadness of Witches*. In it, married couple Molly and Walter move from London to Poltrue, a village in Cornwall; strange things begin to happen to them when Molly starts having peculiar dreams and Walter finds himself caught in a storm from which he is rescued by Martha. Martha, a mature witch who is finding it increasingly hard to bear her solitude, is determined to make Walter her lover.

> Living alone. Bad and good. The voice furs up in the throat and comes out as a growl, a smile as a grimace, children play grandmother's footsteps in my wake; and although my ordinary need for company has atrophied I miss touch. Not merely in a sexual way — by no means — but the ordinary exchanges of the flesh. My arms are empty.

But it was Martha's words on the challenges of knowing and seeing more than others which caught my attention when I read the book, in my late twenties:

...I hear more than I can bear — the keening
of bright widows at their bridge, the death-
croak of a child in Ethiopia. Oh yes, I know,
put me on trial for the sea-widows I made
today. But remember the sadness of witches. No
wonder they are tempted by tricks — think, for
a moment, what it is to be shut out from the
warm rooms of life.

Martha is at best an ambivalent character, and I think of
her in the same way I think of the solitary old sea witch in
Hans Christian Andersen's fairy tale "The Little Mermaid."
The Disney movie based on the story inevitably (Disney
movies not generally having much truck with shades of
gray) cast her as a straightforward villain, but I have
always imagined "the sadness of witches" to be a phrase
which likely applied to her too. In Andersen's story, the
sea witch isn't evil; she simply responds to the mermaid's
request and, not unreasonably, asks for payment for the
exercise of her power. And what she most desires is the
Little Mermaid's voice. She longs to be able to sing. So I
find myself wondering, what is the sea witch's backstory,
that this should be what she most hungers for in the world?
She lives in a house built from the bones of shipwrecked
humans, in a strange underwater wasteland, where "all the
trees and bushes were polyps, half animals and half plants."
Does she live alone by choice, or simply because she isn't
as easy on the eyes as the sleekly beautiful mermaids? For
company, she has only the toad who feeds out of her mouth,
and the snakes who are clustered about "her great spongy
bosom." Like all fairy-tale witches, hers is the story we are
never told. There are too many older women whose stories
no one will ever know.

In the old stories, there are no aging mermaids: they're
forever young, forever beautiful, their hair always long and

glossy, and their voices always ringing out clear and bright over a moonlit sea. I find myself wondering what the stories of their grandmothers might be. In "The Little Mermaid" there is a grandmother, but although she's described as a "very wise woman," she is entirely defined by two domestic roles: caring for her granddaughters and keeping house for their father, the king. She is concerned mainly with rules and with tradition; she tries very hard to turn the Little Mermaid aside from her dreams of travel and adventure. *Be content with your lot* is the essence of the lessons she conveys. Don't rock the boat. Don't want more. Conform, conform, conform.

An elder mermaid should be so much more than that. Where are the mermaids with hagitude? I can imagine them more clearly when I look at the mermaid's purse that sits on the bookshelf above my desk, and which my husband brought home to me after fishing one day off a Donegal beach. If you're not familiar with the name, a mermaid's purse is actually the tough casing which protects eggs laid by some sharks and skates; the pockets are discarded after the baby fish have hatched. You can often find them washed up on beaches at the high-tide line, caught up in a tangle of seaweed. Depending on the species, they have distinctive horns or tendrils at either end which help to anchor the purse to the soft sediment of the seafloor, or which permit the laying female to attach the purse to seaweed in her chosen nursery area.

That hard, spiky casing seems so much more redolent of the older mermaid who lives in my imagination than the archetypical bulging-breasted temptress who sings ships to their doom. Like the Little Mermaid in Andersen's tale, she too might long to know what is beyond her own world and will risk everything for that knowledge — but she won't surrender her power, or sacrifice herself for a self-absorbed and uncaring prince. She's learned a few things along the way. She's lost the dewy-eyed beauty of the young mermaid whose vanity causes her to sit on a rock, combing her shiny long hair for hours. This one's hair is coarser, tangled, and white; the fish scales on her tail are a duller, more steely gray. Her eyes are sharp and bright; she is all jutting bone and very little flesh. It's a more radical kind of beauty, for sure.

3

A RADICAL BEAUTY

Kissing the Hag

Precariously perched on the boundary of field and lane near our hillside farmhouse in Wales, there is a solitary rowan tree. She captured my heart from the moment I first saw her, battered and leafless, on the cusp of a still-frosty spring. Immediately, I took to calling her the Entwife; there was something Tolkien-esque, Treebeard-esque, about the way she held herself. She was tall and thin, branches flailing in the wind like the waving arms of a drowning person, a forked lower trunk which looked for all the world like a pair of legs, and a cluster of divaricate limbs bursting out of her head like Medusa's serpents. She was more hole than tree, and her survival seemed improbable; I thought she was more dead than alive.

Then spring arrived properly, and along with spring, a miracle. From each of her many nooks and crannies, new life began to erupt. Green shoots popped up everywhere: all around her bony, multiple-toed feet, inside her many chasms and craters, from improbably contorted joints along her branches. The Hag of Winter had become the Green Woman, kicking up her bright new petticoats as she cackled her way through the summer. *Thought I was past it, did you?* she crowed, as I walked by, marveling at her unexpected transformation. *Well, there's plenty of life in me yet.* Just like all the best hags in all the best old stories, she was both ancient and young at the same time. And I understood that she was beautiful, exceptional, full of life and heart in her gloriously rickety, gnarly old way. She was the green and growing at the heart of the dormant, rebirth at the heart of death.

And so the Entwife, the Old Lady Tree, possessor of winter's bare bones and summer's green, frothy skirts, became my soul mate. In her stripped-back, broken-down beauty I saw the shadow of what my own would surely become, someday. I just didn't expect that day would come so soon.

On March 23, 2020, the same day that the first national Covid-19-related lockdown came into effect in the United Kingdom, we completed the most stressful relocation I've ever undertaken. We had moved from Connemara, on the far west coast of Ireland, to the Cambrian mountains of Mid Wales. To say that it was not the best time to be moving house, let alone moving between countries, would be a radical understatement. We'd spent three weeks tripping over ourselves trying to speed up the various transactions involved; every time we thought we were out of danger, some new national or international Covid-related crisis would loom on the horizon and off we'd have to go again, phone call after phone call, pleading and cajoling, as borders and possibilities seemed to be closing down all around us. Finally, we made it onto a strangely deserted Friday morning ferry from Dublin Port to Holyhead by the skin of our teeth, each of us with two anxious and overexcited border collies in the boot of a car, and David with the cat on his front passenger seat as well. Both cars were piled high with all the last-minute detritus that goes along with vacating a house after the removal van has departed; there's always more left behind than you've accounted for. We were also leaving a trail of gibbering solicitors, estate agents, sellers, and buyers in our wake, and we were frazzled and utterly exhausted. But we thought we were safe at last. The old house was sold and the money in the bank, and the new house purchase was due to be completed on Monday. In the meantime, we'd be camping out for the weekend in a dog-friendly Airbnb near the ferry port on Anglesey.

Our anxiety had been well founded; we had seriously run the risk of being left "between houses," caught with our old property sold but unable to complete the purchase of the new one because of stringent British lockdown rules which were now coming into full effect. Our original completion date, before we set about trying to accelerate it, would have been a full month later — and if we had stuck to it we would now have been homeless, because if you were in the middle of negotiating a house sale or purchase when that first lockdown began — tough luck. Everything was grinding to a halt; all forward motion, it seemed, was forbidden. But on that eeriest of Monday mornings, clutching a set of keys in relieved and grateful hands, we drove along deserted roads and arrived finally at our new home. We weren't exactly smug, but certainly we were brimming over with satisfaction at having managed to make everything work. Lockdown, we thought, would be easy by comparison. We'd be glad, we thought, of the chance to rest.

Our movers were due to arrive two days later, but that afternoon they sent us an email. They wouldn't be delivering our belongings as planned, they declared, because they weren't entirely sure it was allowed. Unfortunately, they couldn't possibly tell us when that situation might change. Bye.

As I read the email, my whole body began to shake. It had been a scary and exhausting three weeks. And now we had no beds, nothing on which to sit, no desks at which to work. We each had a very small bag of winter clothes, and spring was on its way. The house was old, cold, eccentric, and we didn't know how anything worked (the sellers, who we had never met, having already split up and moved away by the time it went on the market). Thankfully, we had our computers with us, but important books and documents — everything that was essential to the imminent completion of a master's degree in Old Irish that David had been immersed in at the university in Galway, and to my ongoing writing and teaching — were locked up in the back of a removal lorry, which was in turn locked up in the car park of a warehouse somewhere in the vicinity of London, which was now locked up and effectively abandoned — and for how long, no one could possibly begin to say. And didn't, frankly, much seem to care.

I've always thought of myself as a strong person, the epitome of resilience, good in a crisis, but now I was having something of a meltdown. The unrelenting weeks-long pressure of the move had been compounded by an unexpected and shattering period of unpleasantness from several of the overseas attendees of an event in Ireland which I'd organized but had been forced to cancel due to the impending lockdown, and I was at my wits' end. With all "nonessential" retail shut down, and the definition of what was and wasn't essential clearly having been concocted by someone who didn't do anything very much for themselves, there seemed to be no way of acquiring what we needed for simple day-to-day tasks like cooking, let alone getting our hands on the materials necessary to repair the rotting stoves, the dysfunctional oven, and the myriad broken gates and fences in this lovely but long-neglected old farmhouse. Kind new neighbors whose holiday lets had been closed down helped us out with mattresses and a couple of pieces of spare furniture, but it soon became apparent that the damage to my physical and mental well-being was already done.

It began, innocuously enough, with a pain in the heel of my right foot. I couldn't remember any specific event that had caused it, but I imagined that somehow, amid all the to-ing and fro-ing and packing and heaving, I'd twisted something and just hadn't realized it at the time.

A couple of weeks later, my knees were cracking when I went up and down the stairs, and the bones across the top of my feet hurt when I put pressure on them. Walking was out; I began to hobble. Shortly afterward, my wrists grew painful and weak, and I couldn't use my thumbs — couldn't write, could barely cook, couldn't lift the kettle to make a pot of tea. Within a month, every joint in my body was hurting, and within two months I was spending most of the day and all of the night in wrist braces. Some mornings, I had to ask David to put my socks on for me. Getting in and out of bed was agony — everything was agony. To add to my joy, a lump had appeared in the vicinity of my thyroid gland. I called our local medical practice, and eventually managed to speak to an abrupt and harassed senior doctor, who told me I probably had a case of strep throat and to come back in a month if it hadn't cleared up.

That was the point, I think, when I hit rock bottom and lost all hope. The National Health Service had effectively closed down to everything but Covid-19, and, like so many people with debilitating and even life-threatening other illnesses during this period, I felt both terrified and abandoned. When we moved to Wales in March I had been fit and healthy, walking miles each day. Up hills, across bogs — being out in the wilds was my sanity. It was who I was. On top of the walking, I did regular Pilates and danced like a dervish to seventies and eighties rock music two or three times a week. Now, just a couple of months later, I was shuffling around like an old woman. I didn't know where this rapid deterioration would end, but I feared it would be in a wheelchair, and soon. Life in that endless, oddly frightening first lockdown wasn't just on hold for me — it seemed as if it were over, and I couldn't get Diana Wynne Jones's novel *Howl's Moving Castle* out of my head. The book's protagonist, eighteen-year-old Sophie Hatter, is the eldest of three sisters living in the magical kingdom of Ingary, and is resigned to a dull future running the family millinery shop. But then she manages to offend the powerful Witch of the Waste, who retaliates by turning her into an old crone; she is transformed from a healthy young girl to a faltering old woman in a flash. I felt as if that had happened to me, and remembered my childhood horror at the movie version of H. Rider Haggard's novel *She* — the terror when the beautiful and immortal sorceress Ayesha (played by Ursula Andress) steps into the Pillar of Fire and, instead of being renewed, withers away in the flames, and her body wrinkles and shrinks and crumbles into ash. The sight of her sudden disintegration is so shocking that one of the onlookers dies of fright. I sympathized; I had nightmares about that scene for years.

In the middle of June, I managed finally to speak to a more sympathetic and switched-on younger doctor who ordered up a couple of tests, and in July I was diagnosed with Hashimoto's disease (an autoimmune form of hypothyroidism). But it wasn't till the beginning of September that I finally obtained an appointment to see a consultant at the nearby orthopedic hospital, who confirmed that I did indeed have some kind of radically aggressive inflammatory arthritis, which might or might not be rheumatoid arthritis — it was all, apparently, something of a mystery. Nevertheless, treatment for both conditions followed, and slowly, very slowly, I began to regain the use of my limbs. In late November of that year, at long last, I rejoiced at having managed a faltering two-mile walk along an easy, well-paved walking track. I was far from what I still thought of as my "normal" self, but it seemed that I might not imminently need a wheelchair after all.

The sudden onset and rapid deterioration had been shocking because I had always taken my strong body and good health for granted. I rarely caught so much as a bad cold, and it had been a full twenty years since I'd had anything resembling flu. The only long-term health issue I'd endured was endometriosis, and I'd managed in my thirties to bring that largely under control. I didn't think of myself as Superwoman, exactly, but I certainly believed that chronic ill health was for others.

The timing of it all was…interesting. I had initiated this relocation from Ireland back to Britain during the early stages of writing this book. I'm a national of both countries, and think of both as home. But I'd been thinking about the kind of elder I wanted to be, and where might be the best place for me to carry out that plan. Because I had a plan, of course; I had my elderhood all figured out. I would carry on exactly as I had been doing, writing and teaching at the same time, with a full schedule of travel for workshops and lectures. I'd write more books, develop more intensive online courses, push on just as I always had. I would be as lean, fit, and healthy as I always had been, and would carry that fitness well into old age. A bit of stiffness here and there would be acceptable, but I was having no truck with the age-related ailments suffered by others — including members of my own family, many of whom seemed not only to revel in the illnesses they acquired as they grew old, but to actively define themselves by them. I was the one who would be different, and the complete implosion of my immune system certainly wasn't in the cards. But the complete implosion of my immune system was precisely what I got — as another of its many unexpected "gifts" would later reveal.

We all face the loss of at least some physical function during elderhood, and many of us face life-threatening or debilitating illnesses. How do we approach these challenges? How do we learn to stay steady and grounded in an aging body which is always threatening to break, and in which we no longer feel entirely safe?

For people like me, the major challenge is a lack of preparedness. I knew perfectly well — intellectually, at least — that bodily functions deteriorate with age, but I simply didn't believe it was going to happen to me. And so I wasn't paying attention to the signs my body was sending me before it began to break. Now, I understand all too well that menopause, and the years which follow, require us to pay attention to the body, whether we want to or not. If you go through this process naturally, without the dampening influence of HRT, your metabolic rate will go to hell in a handbasket, and the hormones which have defined and dominated you for decades will set off up the proverbial creek without a paddle. Estrogen is a powerful hormone, and it's implicated in more physical functions than we generally recognize. Suddenly, at this time of life, it's in serious decline, verging on the actively extinct. We have to learn to adjust to life without it, and whatever the specific consequences might be for each of us, one thing is for certain: nothing will ever be quite the same again. Strange things will happen to your body, and you won't quite know how to inhabit it anymore. My friend Jenny told me she felt as if she'd landed on the set of *Invasion of the Body Snatchers* — her old body had been stolen, and she'd ended up in someone else's: someone who was slower, heavier, infinitely more tired, prone to temper tantrums, and possessed of an unreasonable fondness for lavishly buttered toast. Because when that menopausal storm finally settles, what's left of you isn't what it once was. Your body will have changed. It will need different things. And whether we're blessed with continuing health or struck down by illness, each of us will one day, nevertheless, have that universal experience of looking into the mirror and suddenly realizing that our faces have begun to crumble and cave in. Many of us, whether or not maintaining a comfortable weight has previously been a problem for us, will watch, aghast, as the pounds pile on for no apparent reason that we can diagnose.

Through all of our clever talk about psychological and spiritual transformation during major life transitions like menopause, this is what is so often forgotten: you can't do any of it properly if you haven't begun to come to terms with your changing body. In a sense, the journey to elderhood actually starts there, because whatever else we might or might not be, we are all embodied creatures. The body is literally the ground of our being. To ignore what is happening to it because we're horrified or afraid might be natural at first, but if that attitude doesn't shift, life soon becomes profoundly dysfunctional. This final life-passage which begins with menopause is defined by our response to the many physical changes that inevitably we must undergo — no matter how hard we might try to keep them at bay. We have to grow up before we can grow into good elders. We have to accept that we're not what we once were. We have to learn not only to accept these changes, but maybe, somehow, even to cherish them. Perhaps adopting the attitude of my friend Pat McCabe, Woman Stands Shining, an elder of the native Dine and Lakota traditions in North America, who told me, "I used to be horrified at the discovery of a whisker or a 'misplaced' eyebrow…now I can't wait for my tusks to come in!"

There is some strange beauty in examining your own aging body and beginning to become properly acquainted with it. Beginning to take it seriously — beginning to listen to it, maybe even for the first time. Illness forces that on you, when nothing else will. A profound gratitude takes hold of you, as you acknowledge all the things it's seen you through, as you begin to enumerate all the gifts it's given you. As well as a deep appreciation for the body's tenacity, coming face to face with its ultimate fragility brings a curious tenderness, and a sense of wonder and awe. Because life changes us, constantly. The transformations never end. We are shapeshifting creatures, through and through — shedding skin after skin, till finally we arrive at our essential nature: our quintessence, our bones.

The aging body is like the crumpled, much-used, lightly stained map of a life. That's what I saw when I looked in the mirror then — the faded impressions of everyone I ever thought I was, the ghostly etchings of everyone I might still become. The very occasional gray-white hair that reflected the moonlight, the fine net of lines at the corners of my eyes. Eyes still as blue as ever, still as full of humor — but maybe a little less guarded than once they were. This scar below my left eye, when I foolishly jumped off a swing I was standing on at seven years old. The small white wart on the side of my nose — evidence of impending hagitude, if evidence should ever be needed. The bony hands, the knobbly knees — the weakened body that emerged from this last brutal skin-shedding. Yes, this aging body is a story; I haven't yet come to the end of its pages.

An insistence on examining the changes we're undergoing is one of our key strategies for learning to live in this new physical space we find ourselves inhabiting; one of the best ways of coming to terms with it all. It's a good, and a necessary, start. But, as always, I found deeper answers to this new existential problem in the myths and fairy tales of my native lands. The body, in these traditions, is always something of an unstable site. Shapeshifting from one form to another is commonplace — and not just between human form and animal, but between youth and old age.

～

One of my favorite character types in our old tales is an archetype that folklorists have dubbed the Loathly Lady. There are two quite different kinds of Loathly Lady in the stories, and we'll meet one of them later: the truth-teller, most common in the complex and beautiful legends of King Arthur and the Grail. But there is another type of Loathly Lady who mostly appears in the Irish tradition: a repulsive old hag who has the capacity to transform herself at will into a beautiful young woman. She appears at her most iconic in the old Irish tale known as "Echtra Mac n-Echach Muigmedóin": "The Adventures of the Sons of Eochaid Mugmedón."

This story focuses on Niall (later called Niall of the Nine Hostages, one of the few mythical kings who is believed to have been real), who was the son of Eochaid Mugmedón, king of Ireland at that time. Niall was the son of his father's servant, and so was not in line for the throne; the succession was reserved for his four half brothers, who were born to Eochaid's queen. Well, Niall and his half brothers were out hunting one day, far from home. They gorged themselves on rich meat and grew thirsty, so they decided to go looking for water. One by one, the four "true" sons of Eochaid approached a nearby well, but they found it guarded by an ugly old hag. The story tells us:

> Thus was the hag: every joint and limb of her, from the top of her head to the earth, was as black as coal. Like the tail of a wild horse was the gray bristly mane that came through the upper part of her head-crown. The green branch of an oak in bearing would be severed by the sickle of green teeth that lay in her head and reached to her ears. Dark smoky eyes she had: a nose crooked and hollow. She had a middle fibrous, spotted with pustules, diseased, and

shins distorted and awry. Her ankles were thick,
her shoulder blades were broad, her knees were
big, and her nails were green. Loathsome in
sooth was the hag's appearance.[41]

The deliciously gruesome hag demanded of each of the
brothers that they should kiss her, in return for a jug of
water — and each of the brothers, revolted, refused. Except
for Niall, who, when asked for a kiss, roundly declared
instead: "Besides giving thee a kiss, I will lie with thee!"
Quite the lad, our Niall. And so, the story continues, "he
threw himself down upon her and gave her a kiss. But then,
when he looked at her, there was not in the world a damsel
whose figure or appearance was more lovable than hers!
Like the snow in trenches was every bit of her from head to
sole. Plump and queenly forearms she had: fingers long and
slender: calves straight and beautifully colored. Two blunt
shoes of white bronze between her little, soft-white feet and
the ground. A costly full-purple mantle she wore, with a
brooch of bright silver in the clothing of the mantle. Shining
pearly teeth she had, an eye large and queenly, and lips red
as rowanberries." Lucky old Niall. The much-transformed
hag declared herself to be "the Sovereignty of Ireland," and
told him that he would now be the rightful king of the land.
She had tested his suitability for the job, and he had passed
that test with flying colors.

Sovereignty, the story tells us, is the quality represented
by this particular shapeshifting Loathly Lady, and it's
important to understand that the Old Irish word for
sovereignty (*flaithius*) has a very specific meaning. It has
nothing to do with personal power or agency, but denotes
the power of the goddess of the land to bestow kingship
on whoever she believes will make the best ruler of it. And
the best ruler, in this old tradition, was the one who would
uphold the covenant of mutual care and respect between

people and the land. The Sovereignty goddess was the personification of the land, but she was also more than this: she came from the Otherworld, and embodied all the ways in which the two worlds were entangled. She was the spirit of the Earth itself, the *anima mundi*, a deeply ecological force. From an archetypical perspective, she can also be seen as the *puella senilis* — the "maiden of old age," perfectly uniting youth and maturity in the same body.

The young woman who represents one facet of this archetype always carries within her the strength and wisdom of age, and the old hag who represents the other always carries within her the life force of fertile youth. And as we grow older, we too carry forward with us the selves we once were; like geological strata, the layers of experience accumulate and live on in the face we present to the world. But it isn't always easy to see this as a gift. In Penelope Lively's beautiful 1987 Booker Prize-winning novel *Moon Tiger*, her aging protagonist Claudia examines her face in a mirror, deciding that it is "an appalling caricature of what it once was." Although the features that once identified her as a handsome young woman are still evident, "the whole thing is crumpled and sagged and folded, like an expensive garment ruined by the laundry." In contrast, in May Sarton's journal *At Seventy*, she considers her now-aged face to be a more accurate reflection of her inner self. Comparing it to her younger face, which had "a surface of sophistication that was not true of the inside," she suggests that she now wears "the inside person outside."[42] And in some sense, this is what it means to kiss the hag: to recognize and to be able to embrace the deep, radical beauty of the person inside, regardless of the nature of the superficial external mask.

Nevertheless, the task is made more difficult because so many depictions of older women — especially those in folklore — present them as hideously ugly. And however fine our intentions might be, I don't think any of us finds it easy or especially desirable to identify with those often-gruesome images. But it's important to bear in mind that in folktales everything is exaggerated, by design — whether it's beauty or ugliness, wealth or poverty, good or evil. Additionally, many folktales were written down at a time when it was really quite impossible to retain your youthful charm. There was little in the way of dentistry, no mascara, and certainly no cosmetic surgery; nutrition wasn't great, either. Back in the day, living to a ripe old age was a rare thing, and those who survived that long probably wouldn't have been especially easy on the eye. But I think it's also true that there was often a deliberate effort to make old women seem to be particularly ghastly, perhaps because solitary older women who weren't under the control of men were the subject of a great deal of suspicion, and often actively feared. Maybe I'm perverse, but I think we can take a little pride in that.

Apart from that shattering moment of horror at the rapid and terrifying disintegration of Ayesha's face and body in the movie version of *She*, I can't remember ever being particularly afraid of or disgusted by old age — but then, my childhood was dominated by old women. For several years my mother was a single parent, after leaving my father when I was three. As well as her usual day job as a legal secretary, she worked some nights in the local bingo hall, and during that time I was looked after by my mother's elderly aunt, Meg. I would spend much of the week sleeping over at Aunt Meg's postwar council house, which happened to be just down the road from my school.

Aunt Meg was born at the turn of the century, and as a young woman she had cut a fine figure on the local sands. I have a framed, grainy black-and-white photograph of her from the *Hartlepool Mail*, which is captioned "A notable cockle gatherer in business." She has a handkerchief tied around her head, is barefoot, and is holding a large basket.

She looks strong. Her skirt is shucked up around her waist, and the white petticoat below is trimmed with broderie anglaise. Unusually, she is smiling. But in her sixties she was borderline obese and, crippled by ingrown toenails which she refused to have treated, was barely able to walk. It didn't help that she had grown agoraphobic with age, and hardly ever hobbled any further than the garden gate. Aunt Meg might not have smiled much, and she wasn't especially kind, but she could be funny when she cared to be; her pièce de résistance was singing "All I Want for Christmas Is My Two Front Teeth." Unfortunately, all Aunt Meg actually had were two front teeth, each of them clinging precariously to its gum; she would stick her finger in her mouth and wobble them around to make me laugh. In spite of her various disabilities, Aunt Meg had a lovely smooth complexion, though her younger sister, Aunt Florrie, had a face which was scored and lined, as wrinkled as a walnut and just as brown.

These women might not have been physically strong or beautiful, and they certainly weren't always admirable in character, but they had a strange strength and power of their own. Aunt Meg, like my utterly terrifying Aunt Lena in the next grove of houses up the road, would stand on her well-scrubbed doorstep with arms folded and make it clear to everyone who passed by that she was watching them, and she was judging. Anyone who was deemed to be out of line in any way — skirts too short, make-up too heavy, pregnant out of wedlock, trousers in need of washing or mending, out of a job for too long, refusal to nod their head to her in respect — would be treated to a shouted mouthful of creative and gloriously obscene vituperation. The entire neighborhood would hold its collective breath, and flinch. You didn't mess with these old women, and for good reason: more often than not, it seemed, they were the ones who held their families together. Each of them played a significant role in a community which, for all its deprivation, had then a real

sense of belonging — to each other, and to the places where
they lived. Their values perfectly reflected the northeastern
working-class ethic of the times, and they were its matriarchs, its tradition-bearers, its moral compasses.

Aunt Meg never mellowed in her extreme old age; my
aunts would receive regular calls from the care home where
she lived for the last few years of her life, threatening to
toss her out if she didn't moderate her foul language.
Apparently, she was shocking the other residents — even
the men. She lived to be ninety-two; "Only the good die
young" was another of her catchphrases. Well, Aunt Meg
might not have been good, but she was always taken
seriously. On the other hand, my maternal grandmother,
Hannah — Aunt Meg's youngest sister — had none of her
strength and presence. Overshadowed and downtrodden by
a brutal husband, my grandmother was an expert in the art
of learning to disappear.

There are so many ways for older women to disappear,
out of choice or out of necessity. But Doris Lessing, in an
interview when she was fifty-three, declared that the invisibility of growing older, and in particular the disappearance
of youthful beauty, was "one of the most valuable experiences that I personally have ever had. A whole dimension
of life slides away, and you realise that what, in fact, you've
been using to get attention, or command attention, has been
what you look like."[43] When beauty fades, we are free to
command attention in new and more authentic ways.

It's not always easy to accept these changes, though. My
old friend Amy, a London-based professional, has always
been blonde and beautiful. Now, on the threshold of her
seventh decade, she has found this to be one of the hardest
things about growing older. "I've had to communicate with
people — men, really — on a different level," she tells me.
"Guess what? No one wants to flirt with me anymore! Now
that *is* liberating. It was shocking at first when I realized
that I'd always operated on a 'let's flirt' basis, but now I

quite like this new space. It feels more comfortable, and personally I feel more grounded. Noticeably, my male friendships have reduced. Those I've been friends with for a long time remain, but the friendships are less close. I don't mind that either. It's less confusing. My female friendships have become much more important, and I love that."

Lessing's novel *The Diary of a Good Neighbour* confronts this discourse of invisibility head-on. The book's protagonist, Janna Somers, is forty-nine, and her image of the aging female body is above all a threatening one, because it reflects her own fears of what she might become. In the past, Janna "had not seen" the old women in the streets, because she "was afraid of being like them." She had also been resistant to the idea of maturity, always a "child-daughter, child-wife." As the subeditor of *Lilith*, an up-market woman's magazine, Janna is one of those responsible for rendering old women invisible and celebrating young women instead — fully embracing the cultural ideal of youthful feminine beauty. After meeting the older, witch-like Maudie, Janna becomes conscious of the cultural discourses which consolidate all old women into a single category of people: "no individuality allowed them, just 'old women.'" Janna gradually comes to recognize this view of aging for what it is: an ideology which justifies keeping the old away from the young, in case the latter should grow distressed when confronted by the reality of their own future.

We might fear disappearing then — but there's a freedom in invisibility. Women might find it challenging at first, but many of them — eventually — come to find it liberating. There's a pleasure in not being the subject of sexual attention, in not even having to care about the prospect. It's a delight not to be constantly self-conscious. This sense of freedom arrives along with the understanding that yes, something old — youth and beauty — might be fading, but something new is emerging in its place. But what is it

exactly that we're going to find is left of us, when all that
we once held dear is stripped away?

~

I should have known, when I saw the shed snakeskin
waiting for me on the doorstep of the casita I was to stay in,
in the New Mexican desert south of Santa Fe, the summer
before we moved to Wales. I should have known that a
profound transformation was on its way. Because in all the
old mythologies, serpent energy is the energy of death and
rebirth. They slough off their old skins and grow one that's
new; they arrive in our lives when it's time for us to do the
same. I should have known, when I had the dream that
same night, that the transformation was coming whether
I accepted it or not. I kept trying to thrust the insistent
giant snake away from me, but it was determined to bite
me anyway. As often as I took hold of its neck and cast
it aside, it kept on coming back: it simply wasn't going to
be denied. And after I'd grown tired and finally bared my
throat to its fangs, it reared up in triumph, performing its
spine-tingling spiral dance for me like a crackling, golden
Catherine wheel.

I should have known, when a team of madly cackling,
whoop-it-up coyotes broke into the ranch and ran back
and forth under my window in the middle of the night.
Singing some crazy, wild, playful, jazz-inspired howl-and-
yap dancing song that made me want to jump out of bed
and run off with them, off into the cool-skied desert, all
cicadas and shooting stars. There was Trickster energy at
play there, for sure.

I should have known; serious time spent in the desert has
always coincided with major transition times in my life. I
haven't planned it that way, but it seems to have been true
nevertheless. It was in the New Mexico desert around Las

Cruces that, at the age of thirty-nine, I completed the last stage in my yearlong journey of learning to fly to overcome a fear of flying. I tested myself against extremes of heat and wind, and in that crosswind-buffeted, afternoon-turbulent, eccentric Wild-Western desert, I received my pilot's license from an equally eccentric, crusty old ex–US Marine who called me "little lady" at least ten times, but laughed heartily and congratulated me for my "gumption" when I refused to follow a navigation suggestion of his that I didn't consider to be wise. That process was translated into my first novel, *The Long Delirious Burning Blue*. So finding the snakeskin this time around made me laugh, because here's an extract from the opening page of that novel:

> I have my own take on skins. It's a simple one: they're there to be shed. Like the desert rattlesnake, which sheds its skin two or three times a year. To enable it to grow; to remove parasites. It's a process of renewal, you see. It rubs its nose along the ground until it pushes the skin up over its head — and then it just crawls right on out of it. Leaves it there: a ghostly, inside-out skin. There are millions of them, all over the desert.
>
> A sea of shed skins.[44]

So *hello, beautiful, shed skin of a Red Racer snake*, I wrote in my journal, that first evening in New Mexico in 2019. *Yes, I'm still shedding skins too. Through menopause and on into elderhood, there are skins left to be shed, journeys still to be undertaken, transformations still to undergo, in this last third of my life. And so I'm here in the desert again, looking for clues. Because place is the greatest teacher of all. Places teach us everything, if we let them.*

After my time at the ranch (where, appropriately, I was

leading a workshop on the "spirit of place"), I spent three days haunting the Plaza Blanca in the Rio Chama hills near Abiquiu — the "white place," which is the subject of one of Georgia O'Keeffe's finest paintings. I went there mostly at dawn to escape the blistering daytime heat, wandering in solitude through a landscape formed by the residue of an ancient supervolcano's ash. It is a surreal, Otherworldly place, all carved cliffs and towering hoodoos. There are fairy-tale castles here, spiraling spires and obelisks, rows of brooding ancestors lined up in an endless vigil along the top of the cliffs. Rock like white bone, and the bones in my pale face becoming more prominent each year; and, wondering how I looked up against that rock, I did something I had never done before: I took a selfie with my iPhone, to see how my face blended in. I saw that I still had a long way to go. I still had a way to travel before I became all hard rock and white bone, but there was a resonance there, nevertheless. Slowly, but surely, I was starting to fade in, as my flesh began to dissolve and the shape of the bones underneath became more apparent. Like the desert I so dearly love, I would soon become unrelenting in my clarity. Everything but the bones of me would one day be stripped away.

I walked on, sat down on a red-hot, ice-colored rock, and the dry heat entered me and there was something oddly erotic about this place, that feeling; I was reminded of a beautiful poem by my favorite New Mexican poet, Pat Mora, in which she declares that the desert "is no lady." On the final day of my stay, I realized why this place was calling me, what the desert was trying to teach me. She was teaching me what she knows best: how to grow old. Not "gracefully" — that kind of grace is overrated. But playing, yapping, howling — dancing with my skirts high. Stripped of pretension; broken open; relentless light penetrating all my darkest places. The desert might be no lady, but she's a fully paid-up Trickster for sure. She made me cackle, that day, and she made me howl. If that's not hagitude, I don't know what is. And that seemed like a really fine way to begin to grow old.

I will never live in that great American Southwestern desert that I love so much, but I carry its energy in my heart — and in my home. Years ago, a woman who came to Ireland to take one of my workshops gave me a small fragment of cholla cactus skeleton from her desert home near Tucson. Cholla skeleton is precisely what the name implies: it's what's left of the arms and main trunk of the cactus after it's died. My piece is cylindrical, like a small log; it's dry, fragile, and airy. It's a meshwork of perfectly placed holes, like a net. It is the quintessence of cactus; the stripped-down, faded, desiccated core of it — and it's beautiful.

Our own physical fadings and desiccations can be hard to take in at first, and it's hard to see them as lovely. After so many decades of strength, I found it hard to accept a future that was more fragile. On the one hand, I badly wanted to be that stripped-down, bright-eyed, super-focused elder; on the other, I didn't want to give up anything in return. I had railed against the fact that my reddish-blonde hair was stubbornly refusing to turn gray, but, in spite of my yearning for gravitas, I had a secret horror of it. And now, like Sophie in *Howl's Moving Castle*, I felt as if a young woman were trapped inside this aging, arthritic body. But Sophie, like the heroines of so many stories, manages to break the witch's spell and regain her original youthful form. There was no way of breaking the aging spell that had now taken hold of me. And I found myself wondering: If there were — would I choose it, after all? Would I really choose to go back to what I once had been? It's a question that is also faced by the rare elder-woman protagonist of an old Croatian folktale, "The Magic Forest":

Once upon a time, an old woman lived on the threshold of a magical forest with her son. One day, the son saw a snake in the forest which was so beautiful that he wanted to take it home with him — but, as soon as he touched it, the snake turned into a beautiful woman. He brought the woman home to his mother, and announced that she was his bride-to-be.

At first, the old woman was happy for her son, but the more time she spent with the young woman, the more she came to believe that something was wrong with her. She tried to warn her son, but he rejected her. He called her a witch, and set about marrying his intended.

The young couple, having no house of their own, lived with the old woman. But the new wife made the old woman do all the housework, and piled other tasks upon her, requiring her to fetch snow from mountaintops and to catch fish from beneath frozen lakes. As the old woman performed these difficult tasks, she thought about praying for help. But she believed that God might then punish her son, and so for his sake she remained silent.

One evening, the old woman picked up one of her son's shirts to mend it, but she was scolded by his new wife. "Don't do that," she shouted. "You'll only ruin it!" When the old woman turned to her son for support, he simply said, "Obey my wife." So the old woman set aside the shirt and went outside to sit on the freezing front porch.

Soon a young woman from the village walked by with a heavy load of kindling. She asked the old woman whether she would like to buy some, but the old woman replied that she had no need of it. "However," she said, "I see that your coat is torn. May I mend it for you?" The young woman was delighted, and thanked the old woman after the repair had been completed.

That night the son and his wife attended a dinner in the village. Before they left the cottage, the snake woman gave her mother-in-law a long list of tasks to complete, and as soon as the young couple had departed, the old woman set to work. While she was starting the fire, she heard laughter — and turned around to see twelve little men, dancing. They were fire elves, and she was delighted to watch them having such a fine time. She laughed and clapped as they danced, remembering the happier days of her youth, and when they stopped she began to cry.

One of them, who was called Wee Tintilinkie, asked, "What's the matter, old mother?"

She told them about her situation, and they suggested that she visit the Forest King to see if he might have a solution to her plight. She agreed, and so they all left the cottage together and traveled deep into the enchanted forest. At the center of the forest was an enormous old oak tree. Wee Tintilinkie led the old woman inside it, and there she saw before her seven golden castles and a village which looked strangely familiar. They went inside the largest castle, which was the home of the Forest King.

When the old woman approached his throne and told him what had happened to her, the king gestured to the village beyond. "Look!" he said. "There is your childhood village, and there is your mother, your father, and your friends. If you wish, you can join them, and live again during this happier time of your life. All you have to do is clap, and then climb the fence that surrounds the village."

The old woman smiled as she thought about entering the village, but then the smile disappeared from her face. She asked the king, "What about my son? What will happen to him?"

The king replied, "You will have no memory of him, because you will be returning to a time before he was born. He will be left to his own fate."

The old woman knew then what she must do. "No," she said to the Forest King. "I can't forget my past and my son.

I can't forget all the things that have happened to me, and all the things I am. I will return home."

As soon as she had spoken, the king sat up straight on his throne and replied, "You have rejected magic and the joy of returning to your youthful past, in favor of your difficult present circumstances. With that choice, you have broken the enchantment which the snake woman cast over your son." The king then clapped his hands, and the castles, the fire elves, the enormous oak tree, and the king himself disappeared. The old woman found herself alone in the forest, and set off eagerly to return to her cottage.

The old woman ran home to find her son crying at the hearth because his young wife had turned back into a snake, and now he understood how he had been enchanted by her. When he saw his mother at the door, he embraced her and begged her forgiveness. He later married the girl from the village who sold kindling; she remembered the old woman's kindness to her, and the three of them lived happily together for the rest of her days.

And so, in accepting the reality of her age, in deciding to retain the gifts of her long life and refusing to go backward, the old woman breaks the enchantment that has spellbound her son. In making that choice, she displays the true wisdom of elderhood; she enters the House of Elders, and takes her place at the table.

THE HOUSE OF ELDERS

There are several aspects of the journey to and through elderhood that almost all women share. Each of us will encounter the Alchemist, as we submit to the fiery transformative forces of menopause and handle its fallout in whatever individual ways suit our needs and imperatives. At this time in our lives, whether we choose to follow her insistent call or not, most of us then will come face to face with some iteration of the Medial Woman archetype: the Mystic, perhaps, or the Witch. As a consequence, we find ourselves haunted by manifestations of the numinous: experiences of mystery, awe, or "otherness" which arise from some new inner necessity which burns brightly at our core. If we're willing to apprentice ourselves to these new teachers, we begin increasingly to be consumed by questions about the ultimate truth and meaning of our existence.

These are questions that have preoccupied me for over twenty years, but the onset of menopause, and my own interactions with the imaginal world and the witches and wise women of my native traditions, brought them firmly to the forefront of my mind. I still wonder about the fortune or fate that brought me to this particular place in my life, in these strangest of all possible times, and I'm focusing on the traces I might leave behind to an ever-greater extent. While all of this is going on, and without exception — beginning in menopause and lasting well beyond — each of us also looks on (likely with some dismay) as the bloom of youth slowly fades away; eventually, we will all begin to experience the deterioration and dysfunction of our physical body. We each have to learn to love our inner Loathly Lady, and dare to kiss our Inner Hag.

What happens in the years following menopause, though, will be fundamentally different for each of us. Unique as we all are in reflecting the infinite variety of the universe, we consequently embody elderhood in unique and infinitely various ways. We each have our own exceptional gifts and singular vision, and now's the time to uncover them, to fulfill a potential that's been developing throughout our many years on this beautiful, animate earth: the ultimate revelation of who we truly are and always were meant to be. The task here reminds me of a line attributed to Michelangelo: "I saw the angel in the marble and carved until I set him free." The essence of a rich and meaningful elderhood is finally to set our inner angel free.

As we stand on the threshold of elderhood, it's natural to wonder how we go about revealing that inner angel — or, more appropriately perhaps, that Inner Hag. Where will we catch a glimpse of her; where do we find the clues? For me, some of the strongest traces of the person I believe I was meant to become were already unveiling themselves in my childhood years, before I was told what to be — or more precisely, in my case, what not to be, and especially what it was not, apparently, *possible* for me, as a working-class girl, to be. If we look back carefully, most of us will find that we can reconnect with some memory of the child we were which seems to reflect the deepest longings and values that define us today. We can find fragments of those longings and values in the things we were profoundly, and perhaps unexpectedly or inexplicably, passionate about as children;

we can find them particularly in the books and stories that had an especially lasting impact on us.

One of the childhood stories that affected me most, when I was around seven years old, came in the form of a popular movie: *Inn of the Sixth Happiness*. It was made in 1958 and tells the story of Gladys Aylward, a British-born Christian missionary, who set off for China in 1932 when she was just thirty years old and stayed there for seventeen years. I didn't — and certainly still don't — relate in any way to the idea of Christian missionaries and their imposition of Western religious dogma and values on other cultures, but that wasn't the aspect of the story which captured my imagination as a child. What I found so stirring about Aylward's narrative was her immense courage, determination, and the enduring reach of her work with Chinese women and children. Aylward was instrumental in ending the ancient and brutal practice of foot-binding, which had for centuries been customary among the Chinese upper and middle classes. Bones in young girls' feet would be broken, and then the feet tightly bound to change their shape and size so that the girls could walk only with slow, tottering steps. "Lotus feet," as they were called, were a status symbol and considered to be a mark of beauty. During the years that she spent in China, Aylward risked her life in many other ways to help those in need — intervening, for example, in a volatile prison riot and consequently becoming an advocate for prison reform. She cared for orphans and adopted several children herself. In 1938, after the region where she lived was invaded by Japanese forces, Aylward led more than a hundred orphans to safety over the mountains, taking care of them despite being wounded.

Aylward was short and dark in life but was rather incongruously played in the movie by the tall, blonde Ingrid Bergman, and the image of her leading the children over the mountains while singing "This Old Man" to keep up their spirits ("with a knick-knack, paddy-whack, give a dog a bone...") has, much to my surprise and with more than a little embarrassment, stayed with me ever since. But for me, at the grand old age of seven, this movie was more than mere entertainment: it was my awakening to feminism, and the first evidence I had seen, growing up in an impoverished working-class household obsessed with male war heroes, that working-class women like Aylward could also do great and necessary things. Women, I realized, could be courageous, and good, and risk their lives for others. They could save people. They could make a difference. The story made me feel brave, and strong; it fed a deep need in me, even at that young age, to help and nurture others; it showed me both the possibility and the beauty of risking yourself for what you believe in.

Apart from books and stories, we can also find clues in the things we loved to do, and in the things we were un-thinkingly and spontaneously — instinctively, perhaps — passionate about. As a young child, I would regularly grab every doll or teddy bear I could scrape up, sit them down in a nice neat line, and set about teaching them whatever I thought it might be good for them to learn that day. When I wasn't playing at being a teacher, I was writing appallingly bad poetry. I still remember my first; I submitted it with some pride to a children's magazine: "A blackbird came to my window / one fine and sunny day / it cheeped a little song at me / then turned and flew away." Well, no prizes for that one, oddly enough — and I soon gave up poetry for the greater pleasure of scribbling my own stories, or con-structing monologues and imagined conversations between characters I'd invented which I spoke out loud — as long as no one was around and likely to hear. Because although I loved my friends, more than anything I loved to be alone. Inside or outside, with an infinitude of real and imaginal worlds just waiting to be explored. And whatever I might have done in the intervening years, I'm still passionate today about exactly those same things. They inform the elder I've always been growing into; they inform the elder I still hope to become.

That Inner Hag whose image we each carry within us reflects our own unique variety of wisdom, the gift that each of us has to offer this breaking and broken world, and our own particular brand of connection to the numinous. In looking for glimpses of her, we're looking to catch glimpses of what poet David Whyte calls the "truth at the centre of the image you were born with."[45] We're looking for hints that might show up in our dreams, or in unexpected interactions with crows or willows. We're looking for the images that haunt us for reasons we don't at first understand — in poems, songs, books, or movies. We're listening for echoes of the numinous, of a deeper, mythopoetic self — for those tropes and traces which come around again and again, because throughout our lives, like so many fairy-tale heroines, we are forced to endlessly repeat the experience of being lost in the dark woods and having to find our way home. This isn't a cyclical process; as I've often argued in my reflections on the "post-heroic," as opposed to the heroic journey;[46] it's very much more like a spiral. We might seem to be circling back around, but we never find ourselves back in exactly the same place in which we began. We pick up consequence as we go through life, spiraling outward — and sometimes back inward again — as we travel on down the years. But whatever place in the spiral of our lives we might find ourselves in at the time, the journey to elderhood hurls us once again into this archetypal realm of lostness that we find so vividly depicted in myth and fairy tales.

For me, exploring the roles of archetypal older women in myths and in folk and fairy tales has helped me more than anything else to find my way out of those lost places, and to home in on the image of that elder I might someday grow into. But these stories also come with a health warning, because if fairy tales and the archetypal characters within them tell us anything, it is that transformation is not only possible — it's inevitable. At this time in our lives, we're going to change, whether we like it or not. It's only the nature of the transformation that is in question, and what we manage to learn from it — and to give.

The archetypal older women in our native stories aren't, like so many of the younger female protagonists, simple and straightforward characters. Usually, there's a complexity about them. They rarely, for example, fit neatly into an unequivocal "goodie versus baddie" typology, even when they appear in the guise of the "Dark Feminine": slightly mad, maybe more than a little bad — but always dangerous to know. When we think of the Dark Feminine we tend to imagine the Terrible Mother, the Death Goddess, the exiled and spiteful Fairy Godmother; we tend to think of the Evil Hag — the "Hansel and Gretel" witch who swallows up the lives of lost children rather than finding a way to meaningfully inhabit her own. The notion of the Dark Feminine certainly incorporates a series of archetypes that Western culture finds profoundly uncomfortable, but the truth is that they're by no means incontrovertibly negative. In a Jungian sense, such images might indeed represent the Shadow of the Hag, but in these often-simplistic classifications encouraged by an overculture which specializes in trivializing and demonizing women, we don't much encounter the other faces of the Dark Feminine: the faces of transformation, healing, and rebirth. This does women a great disservice, because it leaves us estranged from the full range of qualities that belong to the feminine. The Dark Feminine, rather, is the expression of the sometimes ambiguous, but always very necessary, mix of energies that encompass the mysteries and magic of womanhood: the chaos of creation and destruction, the cycle of birth and death, wrath, fierce compassion, eroticism, and spiritual ecstasy.

On the surface, these may seem to be threatening qualities — but they're necessary to feed the forces which keep life going. The Dark Feminine is above all the transformative feminine, teaching us that there can't be genuine growth without pain, challenge, unpredictability, uncertainty — and, especially, awareness of the dark. Wisdom comes from the darker places, not from having always lived in light; and the creative impulse — which can motivate and sustain life only by constantly making way for new life — arises out of the friction which exists between the two. Without which, there is only stasis. Each of the archetypal women we'll encounter in the House of Elders reflects this ambiguity; not a single one of them is all sweetness and light, and each of them is powerful, necessary, and transformative in a different way.

Each of the elder women in the stories I'll be speaking about in the chapters which follow expresses a different aspect of that set of qualities I call hagitude: a comfort with the unique power they embody, a strong sense of who they are and what they have to offer the world, a strong belief in their necessary place in the ever-shifting web of life. Not everyone who reads this book will identify with all of these characters; that would be unusual. We each embody and express our hagitude in different ways. Not all of us are natural creatives, for example; not all of us are natural troublemakers and truth-tellers. But I believe that each of us might find, among the scatterings of stories and archetypes in the pages to come, some key reflection of the essence of our own unique Inner Hag.

4

THE CREATRIX

Old Women Weaving the World

When I look back, it's strange to notice how often, at difficult periods of major change in my life, I've taken to the fiber arts. When I left an increasingly obsessive and controlling first husband in Ireland and ran away to America at the age of thirty-five, I distracted myself with patchwork quilting. The monthslong act of meticulously hand-sewing a complex twelve-inch-square Celtic knotwork pattern thirty times through the three pinned layers of a king-size quilt not only calmed me, but made me feel as if I were stitching the layers of myself back together again after a distressing and sometimes frightening breakup. I created the pattern of the quilt myself: it was a Triple Irish Chain with an eight-pointed star at each of the corners where the crisscrossing chains intersected. I called it "Ladder to the Connemara Stars," and sewing it was an act of faith in the idea that somehow, sometime, I'd stitch my way home again. It took twenty years, but I worked my way back to Connemara in the end; and even though I've now left again, that quilt still has a place on my bed. It's a symbol both of hope and of the power of intention. It's a symbol of all the ways in which women weave themselves — and the world — back together again after they've been broken.

I was inspired to take up quilting in good part through

reading the wonderful *Happenstance* by Carol Shields, a Canadian author whose novels I'd always devoured.[47] *Happenstance* consists of two companion stories: those of long-married couple Jack and Brenda Bowman, during a rare period of time spent apart. In "The Husband's Story," historian Jack is at home attempting to cope with domestic crises while tortured by self-doubt. In "The Wife's Story," Brenda, traveling alone for the first time at forty years old, is at a quilters' convention in Philadelphia, a city which is strange to her. Quilting was once just a hobby for Brenda, but now her quilts, classified as works of art, sell for hundreds of dollars. But the patterns and colors she works with are shifting, just as her life is shifting, along with her sense of self; in Philadelphia, she finds herself "assailed by a sense of opportunities missed," and contemplates a piece of work which she calls "The Unfinished Quilt."

> She was, in fact, uncertain about how to finish it…She wanted a pattern that was severe but lyrical; she would have to be careful or she might rush it toward something finite and explanatory, when all the while she wanted more. Perhaps, she admitted to herself, staring out the window late one afternoon at the weak sunlight striping the garage roof, perhaps she wanted more than mere cloth and stitching could accomplish. Nevertheless, more was suddenly what she wanted. What she spent her time thinking about. More.

In the book, the quilt remains unfinished, just as Brenda's story does. In a scene in the book which I've never forgotten, Brenda takes the quilt she is exhibiting — aptly named "The Second Coming" — and wraps it around herself on a snowy Philadelphia street, "leaving a streak of indelible color on the whitened street and trailing behind her the still more vivid colors of — what? Strength, purpose, certainty. And a piercing apprehension of what she might have been or might still become."

A few years after I'd arrived in America, trapped inside a too-easy, too-safe corporate honeypot and trying to summon up the means and the courage to reimagine my life, I took up knitting. In the evenings after work, and on weekends, I would knit obsessively, as if somehow to straighten and then bind the snarled-up strands of myself together — an actively raveling antidote to the unraveling of a life which somehow had lost all purpose. And another decade on, cast adrift on an island in the Outer Hebrides with everything around me falling apart, I learned to spin. Now I was creating new threads: threads born of the land, fashioned from the hand-carded fleece of the little black Hebridean sheep we tended on our wild and windy west-coast croft. I still have a small, dusty ball of the yarn I spun in those dislocated, dislocating island days. It's special to me, because the wool came from the fleece of a much-loved sheep who broke her leg on the crossbar of a feeding trough the very same day that we brought her home as a small but feisty ewe-lamb. We named her Wonky after watching her hobble around the croft in her homemade splint, loudly expressing her displeasure. Wonky also happened to give birth to our first-ever lamb, plopping it out in the middle of the field and fleeing from it in horror, then stubbornly refusing to acknowledge that she had had anything to do with it for a troublesome forty-eight hours. To retain its water-repellent properties, her fleece wasn't washed before spinning, and so the resulting yarn is raw, heavy with lanolin, and after all these years still smells of earthy, healthy ewe. Its texture is lumpy and uneven; it has clearly been spun by an amateur.

Stitching, knitting, spinning — whenever I undertook

it, this ancient women's work seemed to perfectly express whatever changes I happened to be going through at the time. And indeed all of these crafts, along with weaving, are connected in myth and folklore to women's magic, and especially to the mysteries of transformation. Let's focus, as an example, on the practice of weaving: it's an ideal metaphor for understanding the methods we use to construct a sense of who we are. Imagine that each of us, at birth, is presented with a loom on which to weave the cloth of our lives. First, the foundations of the pattern must be established, and this is achieved by means of the warp threads. The warp represents the structures that we build our lives upon: our values, our beliefs, our sense of purpose. So the basis of the cloth — what ultimately will hold it together — is laid down in the warp, but the pattern itself can't be perceived until the weft threads begin to be woven through it. The weft represents our everyday actions and experiences, and these threads repeatedly cross over and under the formative warp threads, so creating the cloth.

It is this interaction between warp and weft — along with the colors and textures of the threads we choose — which creates our own unique fabric, the unique pattern of our own individual life. In a sense, the warp holds the fundamental truth of the finished cloth, and the weft reveals that truth. Once the warp is set up it can't be changed; this limits the possibilities for the final cloth, while providing a necessary stability. But if mistakes are made in the warp, they'll carry all the way through the woven cloth. The weft, on the other hand, can — to an extent — be unraveled and rewoven to correct any errors.

Sometimes we weave our own threads, but sometimes, the old stories tell us, invisible threads are weaving us, and invisible hands are guiding the creation of this cloth which represents our life. In the Greek mythic tradition, for example, three spinning and weaving goddesses were said to control destiny. They were the Fates: Clotho (the Spinner), Lachesis (the Allotter), and Atropos (the Unturnable — a metaphor for Death; sometimes she was called the Cutter). In literature (though not always in the visual arts) they are usually represented as old and ugly. Gods, as well as humans, had to submit to the Fates; they presided over nothing less than the natural order and balance of the entire cosmos. Their role was to ensure that every being, whether human or divine, lived out their destiny within the fundamental laws of the universe; each of these individual destinies was represented as a thread spun from a spindle. In Plato's *Republic*, the mother of the Fates is said to have been Ananke, whose name means Necessity. Ananke is usually depicted holding a spindle, and in Orphic mythology, together with her mate Cronos (the personification of Time), she was said to have formed the universe and embedded order into it.

In ancient Greece, the Fates were originally called the Moirai, a term deriving from a noun which means a "share" or a "portion." By extension, then, the Moirai are "The Apportioners": the ones who allot to each human being her own permitted portion of life. Obtaining more than your fair portion was certainly possible — whether it be a greater portion of the spoils of war, or of other good things in life — but it really wasn't advisable. Severe consequences would follow, because taking more than you were entitled to was a violation in the natural order of things, and would result in a cosmos that had lost its equilibrium. To prevent this happening, the Fates would step in. And on balance, if they did, you probably wouldn't like it.

We find comparable characters in Nordic myth too: three women called the Norns, who similarly personify Fate. Like the Moirai, the Norns spin, knot, and weave the threads of individual lives into the ordered pattern of the cosmos. "The

Song of Helgi," from the medieval *Poetic Edda*, describes
them in this way:

> Each night they wove the web of Fate...
> They wove the golden threads,
> They made them fast in the moon's hall.
> At East and West they hid the ends...

The Norse idea of Fate as meted out by the Norns, like
that of the Greeks, wasn't purely deterministic. The old texts
suggest that an individual was held to be morally responsible
for their own actions — but without necessarily being in
control of the circumstances that contextualized them.
In other words, we can make choices — and with those
choices come personal responsibility, of course — as well as
being subject to the constricts of Fate. So the notion of Fate
doesn't imply that the individual has no choice — only that
she is predisposed to make certain kinds of choices. Fate, in
this sense, is the unfolding of a preexisting truth which is
inherent in a person: the weft illuminating the foundations
that have been laid down in the warp. In other words: we
don't *create* ourselves through the choices that we make:
like Michelangelo uncovering the angel within the marble,
we *reveal* ourselves.

In the Celtic tradition, a single old Irish text refers to
"the seven daughters of the sea who are forming the thread
of life";[48] unfortunately, though, this is the only written
reference to such beings. In the Germanic tradition, it is an
old creator-woman called Frau Holle, or Mother Hulda (or
Holda), who spins the world into being and foretells Fate.
In early mythology, Holle was an ancient goddess who
also ruled over the weather and protected agriculture and
women's crafts. She was often depicted holding a distaff or
drop spindle, or sometimes sitting at a spinning wheel. Holle
is related to the Germanic goddess Perchta (or Berchta),

who was also known as the Dark Grandmother; children who died in infancy were said to go to her. In Catholic German folklore, Holle — likely many pre-Christian mythic elder women — came to be associated with malevolent witchcraft; in these tales, she rode through the air with witches on her distaff — which in visual depictions of her closely resembled the brooms that witches were said to ride in folktales throughout Europe.

Old women who weave the world into being and mediate the fate of those who inhabit it, then, are ubiquitous in European culture. In his beautiful book *Why the Moon Travels*,[49] Oein DeBhairduin offers a traditional story from the Irish Traveller community. Once upon a time, he tells us, there were old women who would wander through the land gathering roots, bark, and herbs in baskets made of willow. They particularly loved to gather fleece which was caught on brambles. These old women wore black dresses, but the bottoms of their dresses were adorned with red, white, and yellow stripes. Sometimes, they'd have extra stripes made of different colors — one for each of their children. They carried beaded purses which were studded with medals, buttons, and other tokens, and their long gray hair was neatly braided.

At the end of every day, the old women would return to their camp and dye the wool they'd gathered in a large cast-iron pot which they boiled over their fire. The wool would be colored red. They'd spin the dyed wool all night, singing as they worked; and as they spun, they'd weave prayers and charms into the cords they were making from the wool for all the children of the world. Then, during the day, the old women would sleep. But with the passing of the years, the number of children born into the world grew, and the old women struggled to keep up. They worked as hard as they could to make their red cords, but they couldn't find a way to make enough of them for all the new children. So, one day, they decided they'd weave a single red cord which would be long enough to encircle the world, so that no child would be left without access to a blessing.

It was long, hard work, and the old women didn't stop to rest or even to eat. Over time their fingers grew dark from the ashes of their campfire and the coal which fueled it. Still, the old women who gathered continued to work, and their camp grew ever more silent as they focused solely on this one task. They worked so hard and the fire grew so hot that they sweated, and the sweat which ran down their faces washed the red dye from the cords, and the cords began to turn gray. Thinner and more delicate the cords became, and gossamer soft — but at their heart they were as strong as the old women who wove them. And those old women worked on. They worked so hard that they grew thin and bony, and eventually they began to shrink and their fingers started to wear away.

As time went by, the old women who gathered grew smaller and smaller. They began to fade, to become creatures less of this world and more of the Otherworld, until eventually the day came when they looked like little more than a bundle of fingers, always spinning and weaving, with their baskets on their backs, as they went about their gathering and their work. The old women who gathered, you see, had become the very first spiders. And even today, the spiders spin on, spinning the strong, silken cords, weaving the webs that bring blessings and healing to the people of the world.

Spider: her threads seem delicate and fine, but they are strong. She spins and twists, constantly weaving the threads she creates into new patterns. Spider is the ultimate weaver: the weaver who makes the world. Sometimes, to be a weaver means you must mend a broken web; other times it means you must start again, weaving new and more functional stories into being. And it is the grandmothers in our oldest European myths and stories — women as old as time itself — who define and shape the ongoing story of the world. They set the context for right action; they maintain the natural balance and harmony of the cosmos. They wield the ultimate creative power: the power of life, death, and transformation. In order to take on such weighty responsibilities, they must, of course, be old; they need every ounce of the wisdom they've gained through their many long years.

Back in the mortal world, by the time we women reach our elder years, the creative, life-giving power we wield is no longer about birthing children. Those of us who are childless, by choice or otherwise, will likely find this idea easier to embrace; our creative energies have always been directed elsewhere. But all of us are working now on different looms; what is it, then, that we should be weaving into being at this time in our lives? In most mythical traditions, as I've described, what the grandmothers are weaving into being is the world itself. So perhaps it's time for us to move out of the domestic sphere and into the wider reaches of the world; perhaps it's time to shift the focus of our creativity away from individual expression and into the realm of the "cultural creative." It's time for us, with whatever unique skills and gifts we each possess, to become influencers and transformers — because, like those beautiful, mythical old women, we are the ones who now hold the necessary long view. Because, to quote Ursula K. Le Guin again, only an old woman has "experienced, accepted, and acted the entire human condition — the essential quality of which is Change."[50]

In this context, it's important to stress that expressing creativity isn't simply about making things yourself — patchwork quilts or paintings or books. A passion for creativity can also express itself in a passion for reading and promoting the books of others, for supporting the work of artists and craftspeople. It can express itself in supporting the creation of anything that has the possibility to transform the world for the better. To be creative is also to have the ability to make the leap from image to idea to reality; creativity, then, is not just a way of thinking about the world, but a way of being in it. It's a talent for seeing possibility in the most impossible circumstances, and adopting an approach to living that is, above all, imaginative.

Thriving in the heart of the creative fire is often presumed to be largely the province of the young — or, at least, of people "in their prime" — but elderhood, approached consciously, can open the door to a period of late blooming such as that experienced by Carl Jung after his heart attack at the age of sixty-nine. The years that followed were the most creative and visionary years of his life, and during them he wrote some of his most profound and complex works. Such late bloomings aren't uncommon. I remember, in my twenties, reading everything by the English novelist Mary Wesley; she took up writing full time at the age of fifty-eight to try to earn a living after her husband died. Her first novel, *Jumping the Queue*, was published when she was seventy-one, and she wrote another nine bestsellers before she died at ninety. Wesley's unique voice stemmed from an idiosyncratic life fully lived: it was eccentric, funny, ironic — but always compassionate. In the course of her own elderhood, she neatly demolished several societal assumptions about old people, confessing to regular bouts of "bad behavior" and strongly recommending sex as a panacea for a multitude of ills. The stereotype of the narrow-minded, judgmental, "past-it" old woman vanished in a puff of delighted, obscenity-tinted smoke. In a review of a biography of Wesley in the *Observer*, Rebecca Seal tells the story of Wesley's encounter with a plumber who came to unblock her toilet; the blockage was found to have been caused by a collection of used condoms. Seal writes that "the plumber, clearly embarrassed, said: 'Nothing to do with you, Mrs Siepmann' (her married name). When he left, she turned, incensed, to her granddaughter: 'Fucking cheek! How dare he assume that?' (How dare he, indeed, even if her last affair, with writer Robert Bolt, had ended some time before; she had been 69 when it began.)"[51]

At its best, though, the creative work of elder women is about making art that matters, transcending self-expression in an effort to make the world a better place. As I'm writing this book, a retrospective exhibition of the work of artist Paula Rego is taking place at the Tate Gallery in London. Rego was born in Lisbon in 1935 and grew up in the fishing village where her grandparents lived. She was born into a liberal family in a country which was ruled by a Catholic right-wing dictatorship, and growing up in a country riddled with censorship fueled her insistence on freedom of expression in her art. Her work was political from the beginning, and in the course of her seventy-year career, her art has focused on the curse of fascism, on abortion, and on the tragedies of women's lives as well as their sisterly solidarities. Her paintings of women who had backstreet abortions, completed when she was in her sixties, are among the most iconic of all, and it's been suggested that when the Portuguese voted in favor of abortion in a 2007 referendum, Rego's paintings played a major part. One of the things I love about Rego is that she draws deeply on folk and fairy tales for her art: "I've found traditional Portuguese folktales the most useful, because they are me, they are my background. I understand their brutality and perversity. They get to the root of many things."[52]

Judy Chicago, born in Chicago in 1939, is another culturally influential artist who also happened to use needlework and weaving in many of her best-known projects.

In the early seventies, Chicago pioneered feminist art and education in a unique program for women at California State University. Her best-known work, *The Dinner Party*, was an enormous piece of installation art which offered up a symbolic history of neglected women in Western civilization, with elaborate place settings around a triangular table for thirty-nine mythical and historical famous women — including fourth-century Alexandrian philosopher, astronomer, and mathematician Hypatia; Hildegard of Bingen; Sojourner Truth; and Georgia O'Keeffe. The names of another 999 women are inscribed in gold on the white tile floor below the table. In the *Birth Project*, Chicago collaborated with more than 150 needleworkers to create dozens of images that celebrate the birth-giving capacity of women along with their creative spirit. In a series of drawings, paintings, weavings, cast paper, and bronze reliefs called *PowerPlay*, Chicago brought a critical feminist eye to the construct of masculinity, exploring how associated definitions of power have affected the world. *Resolutions: A Stitch in Time* combines painting and needlework in a series of images which rewrite traditional sayings and proverbs in the light of the social and environmental challenges we face today. Her most recent body of work, *The End: A Meditation on Death and Extinction*, was exhibited in Washington, DC, in 2019. For several decades then, and now in her eighties, Chicago has remained steadfast in her commitment to the power of art as a vehicle for social and intellectual transformation.

Our acts of creativity can help us, and show others the way, to transcend and transform our dysfunctional cultural narratives. Art, along with other creative pursuits, is more than just entertainment: it can represent an act of revelation, or of resistance. It harnesses our emotions and captures the imagination, and so helps us to see the world through a different lens, or to reimagine it in a different way. At its best, art transcends borders and barriers and culturally imposed dogma. Whether it's through music, visual imagery, dance, drama, writing, or other modalities, art can open us up to new ways of being. As elder women, the nature of our creative output also often reflects our ability to understand the conditions and dimensions of life that will be faced by the next generation. As Betty Friedan suggests in her marvelous book *The Fountain of Age*, "'late-style' artists and scientists, creators and great thinkers seem to move beyond tumult and discord, distracting details and seemingly irreconcilable differences, to unifying principles that give new meaning to what has gone before and presage the agenda for the next generation."[53]

As I grow older, I realize that my own writing is very much more than just a pleasurable form of self-expression — at its heart, it's a way of trying to change the story, of weaving the possibility of a better world into being through the power of words. The books that I write — whether fiction or nonfiction — are born out of a yearning to help people reimagine themselves and the world around them in more beautiful and functional ways. In particular, they're born out of a deep desire to help women reclaim our unique and necessary power, to step out into a challenged and challenging world and make a difference to it. That word-weaving and story-weaving is how the archetype of the Old Woman Who Weaves the World is reflected in me.

The truth is, I've always believed that the inherent value of writing lies in its capacity to stimulate transformation, because the books I've read throughout my life have contributed more than anything to fashioning the person I am now. Novels especially have always had an enormous influence on me. Opening the pages of a novel is in many ways an act of faith; it's to open myself up to potentially disruptive influences, to challenges to my whole way of being in the world. The best of novels, to me, are alchemical;

you come away from them utterly changed. I love such challenges; I love such changes. My husband, on the other hand, has the same belief in this reconstructive capacity of novels, but his response is quite different; he chooses not to read them, for fear of entering too deeply into their worlds and being affected in ways that he finds disturbing. He's pretty porous.

But by entering into someone else's world through the pages of a novel, I've found it possible to begin to see beyond the limitations of my own. I've found it possible to understand, and to empathize with, people who are radically different from me. Several strands of recent research confirm that reading fiction can increase empathy in this way. At the Princeton Social Neuroscience Lab, for example, psychologist Diana Tamir has shown that people who frequently read fiction have better "social cognition": in other words, they're better at working out what other people are thinking and feeling. Using brain scans, Tamir found that when people who are reading fiction are compared to those who are not, there is more activity in the parts of their brain that are involved in simulating what other people are thinking.[54]

I was lucky to grow up in a family which for most of my childhood and teenage years had no television, but which had a great respect for books. My Saturday treat was a trip to the local library with my mother, taking out as many books as we were allowed, in the hope of getting through a whole week without running out of reading material. Like so many troubled children, I lost myself in books; the world around me simply ceased to exist. And although reading might have been a way of escaping from difficult times, it was also so very much more: quite simply, books lit up my world. Even today, if I don't have a good novel on the go, and one or two more lined up behind it, life seems somehow lacking in sparkle, and I still look to fiction to broaden my understanding of the ever-shifting world around me. Just as I did as a child, when books like *What Katy Did* and *Little Women* made me think about what it meant to be good and kind and strong. And as a teenager, when the books we studied in English literature classes — the Brontës, George Eliot, even Jane Austen — helped me to understand the ways in which women's lives had come to be so confined, and illuminated the passions that they were not permitted to display. Virginia Woolf opened me up to a world of depth and introspective possibility. Marilyn French's seminal and bestselling 1977 novel *The Women's Room* shook me to the core at the age of sixteen, and fueled a fledgling feminist sensibility that accumulated considerable traction through the years. In my early twenties, the poems of Edna St. Vincent Millay and the diaries of Anaïs Nin mirrored my own inner life and emotions and made me feel less alone in the world. A few years later, Margaret Atwood's *The Handmaid's Tale*, along with Doris Lessing's *Shikasta* and *The Golden Notebook*, woke me up to the flaws in our cultural narrative and the danger of its ongoing trajectory.

I could, of course, go on and on. These women writers not only changed my life — they helped me to imagine it. Their books were both formative and transformative. And as a writer, that's the only thing I've ever wanted to do. I think that's why I didn't begin writing my first book till I was forty-two: *The Long Delirious Burning Blue* told the only story I'd ever felt utterly compelled to tell — the first story which came to me that I ever believed really mattered.

The unique gift of those writers who influenced me was their ability, in their different ways, to represent the truth of our experience; and, of course, that's what visual artists like Paula Rego and Judy Chicago do too. But you don't have to be a brilliant artist or Nobel Prize–winning writer to reflect the truth of women's experience; we all have our ways of creating, and so many different creative acts can be revelatory. My Scottish friend Irene, a now-retired teacher, has just begun to create what she calls "spirit dolls," made from felted wool. Her dolls all represent old women, and they're dressed in tweed and linen, adorned with moss, twigs, feathers, and all manner of fragments of the land and the natural world around her. The act of creating these dolls, she tells me, feels like a kind of spell, an enchantment. "When I make a doll," she says, "I feel as if in the act of creating it I'm revealing myself — revealing aspects of myself that I didn't know existed. I don't always have a clear idea of what they'll be before I start to make them. A phrase relating to an imaginal character will pop into my head one day — for example, 'moss witch' — and as I'm felting the doll's body, I'm dreaming about what that means to me, and why 'moss witch,' and what that says about me and my yearnings, and I'm literally making it up as I go along. The felting itself is part of the magic; like any repetitive activity it puts you into a kind of trance state, so that insights and ideas come to you which otherwise wouldn't get through the busyness of your monkey mind. Then once they're made, I stand back and look at the dolls — and I've only made three so far — and it's as if they show me what I want to be as I continue to grow old. There's one, for example, who has a dress made of nettle yarn, and a bag of dried nettle leaves around her neck. She reminds me of the power of plants and the importance of connecting to them, of spending more time in that kind of connection with the land as I get older. There's just something magical about nettles, isn't there? I also feel as if I'm connecting back to a line of earthy old women who once lived in this land, working with wool and natural materials just as they would have done then. My ancestors."

Irene has no background in arts or crafts; felting is something she learned to do in her spare time, and it's been revelatory for her. There's a strange magic in objects we create ourselves, by hand, and an even greater magic when they're made from natural materials — especially those we've gathered from the land. They tie us back to the rhythms of the Earth; they help us to remember where we come from and where we belong. They're a link between human imagination and the imagination of the land itself. And in practicing these skills, and passing them on to others, we do that all-important work of weaving ourselves into being and into greater consciousness of the beautiful, animate world around us.

5

A FORCE OF NATURE

Guardians and Protectors of the Land

In a remote glen in the Scottish Highlands — one of the few which are inaccessible by car — lies a unique and hidden treasure. Glen Cailliche is home to a little-known shrine to a pre-Christian deity and to the remnants of a tradition of honoring it which folklorists believe dates back centuries. Rising up organically out of the peat, as all such temples of the people would once have done, is the house of the Cailleach: the archetypal Old Woman of Scottish and Irish mythology. In neither Celtic literature nor the folk narrative tradition does there exist a myth which specifically explains the creation of the universe, but in the folklore of Ireland and Scotland (and, to a lesser degree, the Isle of Man) there are many references to the Cailleach, who gives shape to the land throughout all its ages. Her stories are strung out across these Gaelic-speaking countries like the necklace of rough granite boulders which one old tale says she wore.

Looking for this unique shrine, I set off, one gloriously crisp, clear autumn morning, to walk the dirt road along Loch Lyon's northern shore, heading west on the five-mile journey to the Cailleach's glen. Even on this rare rain-free day, I felt as if I were walking through a waterworld. The loch glistened and glowered on my left, and waterfalls and tiny streams tumbled down the mountains on my right.

A merlin sped across my path at head height — one of many rare birds, including golden eagles, which are known to breed in the area. In spite of the grazing sheep, there's a wildness to this landscape which is rare in the British Isles. It's a long enough walk to Glen Cailliche, but not especially difficult; the only real challenge presents itself when you come to Allt Meran, a plucky little river which has to be crossed before you can carry on west into the glen. Once I had forded the river, a mile or so later I found the shrine down near the fast-flowing Allt Cailliche, to the left of the narrowing path. It's known as Tigh nam Bodach,* and is a simple, miniature thatched stone hut which is home to a small family of stones shaped by water into sort-of-human forms. The largest stone, with a squat base that narrows into a thin neck and is topped by a roundish head of pink stone, represents the Cailleach; the other two stones represent her husband and their daughter.

The folk tradition here says that the Cailleach and her family were once given shelter in the glen during a period of heavy snow; they liked it, and so stayed a while. So grateful was the Cailleach for this hospitality that she left these stones at the house she'd occupied — with the promise that, as long as they were cared for, the glen would always be peaceful and prosperous. And so this small shrine was constructed by the local people, and every Bealtaine (May 1, an ancient seasonal festival) the three stones which represented the three deities would be taken out of the house and placed facing down the glen. There they'd stay until the house was rethatched for the winter, and they'd be moved inside again at Samhuinn eve (October 31, the old seasonal holiday which today is more often called Halloween).

---

* Although it's often translated as "house of the old man," it's a plural construction — which probably, in premodern Gaelic, actually meant "house of the cotters" or "house of the countryfolk."

The Cailleach's glen is fertile and green; it's also strikingly tranquil. As I sat for a while by the carefully constructed dwelling, my only companions were a few curious sheep and a pair of thuggish ravens clattering around the slopes of Beinn a'Chreachain. I left the offerings I'd brought with me: half a sandwich and the remnants of the coffee from my flask. As I walked, weary now and sore-footed, back along the lochside, I carried in my heart the strength of the ancestral stories which I'd long been researching about that Old Woman; I'd always found in them the perfect role model for the times. An elder woman who stands firm, who holds strong against the plundering of the land and its creatures. If the mythology and history of our culture includes elder women who are strong and fierce guardians and protectors of the land, then it opens up a space for women to grow into and live up to those stories. To be taken seriously, and have our voices heard — not only for our own sakes, but for the sake of the land itself, and the other-than-humans who inhabit it alongside us.

Although the word *cailleach* in modern Scottish and Irish Gaelic simply means "old woman," it is believed to derive from the Latin *pallium*, meaning "veil." The Cailleach, then, is "the veiled one." The veiled old woman — the hidden one, the keeper of mysteries? The truth is, we don't know why the idea of a veil became attached to this particular archetypal Old Woman of the World. What we do know is that stories exist about Otherworldly old women who bear several variants of this name throughout the myth and folklore of Ireland, Scotland, and the Isle of Man, though it's not always apparent whether they relate to just one (very widely traveled) Cailleach, or several different *cailleachean* scattered throughout the Gaelic lands. In Ireland the most commonly occurring Cailleach is called the Cailleach Bhéarra, a name which might (or might not) relate to her close associations to the Beara Peninsula, in the southwest of the country.* In the Isle of Man she is most often called the Cailligh ny Groamach ("Old Woman of the Gloom"), or sometimes Cailligh ny Gueshag ("Old Woman of the Spells"), and in one old poem she is referred to as Berrey Dhone. In Ulster folklore she is known as Cally Berry, and in some of the folktales of the Scottish Lowlands she is named Beira, or known as the gyre-carlin — a terrifying and often malevolent witch-figure.

In 1927, Eleanor Hull described the Cailleach as one of the "ancient goddesses, known both in Ireland and Scotland, but unknown in Wales, and therefore probably purely a Gaelic deity."[55] Nevertheless, gigantic old women reminiscent of the Cailleach are known in Welsh-language folklore, and they are also known in Brittany: Ahès, the old goddess of the Osmises (the Gaulish tribe which once inhabited most of what is now Brittany) and a builder of causeways, has much in common with the Cailleach. The Cailleach has been called "the most tremendous figure in Gaelic myth today," "the most famous old lady in Irish literature," and "the divine hag of the pagan Celts" — although Irish folklorist Máire Mac Neill has suggested that she was actually most likely a pre-Celtic deity who persisted into the Celtic era and beyond.[56]

In Irish folklore, the Cailleach is consistently portrayed as an immensely old and powerful goddess; many of the stories emphasize her great age, and such stories are deeply

---

* Irish folklorist Gearóid Ó Crualaoich has suggested that other forms of her name which occur in Irish sources (Cailleach Bhéarrach and Cailleach Bhiorach) are instead associated with the adjective *biorach*, which means "sharp," "shrill," or "inimical," rather than the place name. Lending weight to this idea, in Scotland she is most commonly referred to as the Cailleach Bheurr, or Bheur, which according to Gaelic scholar Michael Newton almost certainly relates to adjectives in Scottish Gaelic meaning "keen, sharp, pointed, witty."

embedded in the landscape. Their usual setting is wild and rocky places, like the place names which are associated with her and which are usually attached to mountains or locations in which ancient dolmens and cairns are to be found. More often than not, the stories say that the Cailleach is the creator of these places. For example, one of the most significant sites associated with her is Loughcrew, in County Meath. The 904-foot-high hill known as Sliabh-na-Caillighe, a prominent feature in the landscape, is said to have been constructed by the Cailleach, who dropped a stone from her apron to create each of its three peaks. Two of the peaks are covered with tumuli and cairns, and the "Hag's Chair" is a particularly well-known monument: a large stone with a seat hollowed out in the middle of it, on which the Cailleach is said to have sat to look out across a wide expanse of the country. A story from Moycullen, County Galway, tells of the Cailleach throwing rocks at another Cailleach, eventually burying her under a pile of rocks on the hilltop so that she becomes part of the landscape, which is then said to have been created from this Cailleach's body. This and other stories like it show the Cailleach bringing about major and lasting changes to the land and so, mythically, she can be said to represent the ever-shifting forces of a landscape which is still very much in flux.

In Scotland, as in Ireland, the Cailleach is an important deity; some traditions say that she was the mother of the gods, and there are many legends of a giant Cailleach-like woman throughout mainland Scotland and the islands. As in Ireland, place names associated with such characters abound, such as "The Burial Place of the Big Women" on Tiree; stories about giant women are common on the Isle of Eigg, which is also known as Eilean nam Ban Mòra: the Island of the Big Women. Here too the Cailleach is said to be so old that she remembers previous geological ages. In most of the Scottish stories about her she has a fearsome and decidedly seasonal character: she is associated with the harsh and wild winter half of the year. In some folklore, particularly in the west of Scotland, she appears in conjunction with her sister (or alter ego) Bride (or Brighde), who is a reflection of the Irish goddess Brigid, and who, in contrast to the Cailleach, rules over the summer half of the year. The Cailleach's close identification with the natural world is shown in many folktales in which she mimics the cycles of death and rebirth in nature. These stories tell of her ability to renew herself — becoming young again, after she has grown very old. In one story, the Cailleach rejuvenates herself every hundred years by bathing in the waters of Loch Bà on the Isle of Mull at Bealtaine, before the sun has risen and before a bird has sung or a dog barked.

Several old Scottish stories depict the Cailleach as a guardian of the natural world's balance — especially when it comes to the need to protect it against humans. In some of these stories the Cailleach might appear as a Glastaig (a "Green Woman"); one such tale recounts a Glastaig preventing Donald Cameron, a hunter in Lochaber, from killing a herd of hinds which she was driving. Seeing him raise his gun, she called to him: "You are too hard on my hinds, Donald! You must not be so hard on them!" Donald, quick-witted, answered her immediately, saying: "I have never killed a hind where I could find a stag." He allowed the hinds to pass, concentrated ever afterward on taking the occasional stag, and the Glastaig never bothered him again. In another story, a man returning from hunting on Beinn a'Bhric one day heard a sound like the cracking of two rocks against each other. At the base of a large stone by the road, he saw a woman with a green shawl around her shoulders. The woman, clearly a Glastaig, held a deer shank in each hand, and constantly beat them together. He asked her what she was doing, but she would only cry, over and over again, "Since the forest was burned! Since the forest was burned!" She kept repeating this refrain for as long as he could hear her. Here, the Cailleach mourns the cutting of the forest for human profit. But, showing for once a gentler aspect to humanity, she was said to have given a warning about the conversion of shielings (summer grazing lands) into grouse-shooting places during the Clearances: "If the Gaels only knew the value of the top of the heather, or of the hen's egg, fowl would be more valuable than cattle, and the glen more valuable than the strath."[57]

Many other stories tell of the Cailleach's close affinity with the animal world, whether domestic or wild. In one story, she scolds a servant boy for setting out to turn hay on what would be a wet day. He asks how she can be so sure of her weather forecast; she tells him that the scald crow and the deer are her reliable advisers. In Scotland she is said to have had a herd of wild deer that she milked, and she traveled with them through the Highlands. Folklorist J. G. McKay suggested that such stories about the Cailleach might have reflected the remnants of an ancient tradition of deer-goddesses, noting a plethora of stories about "colossal Old Women" who owned, herded, and milked deer.[58] These stories, along with others which have her shapeshifting into the form of a crane, offer us images of this archetypal Old Woman embodying a more-than-human wisdom.

Old women like the Cailleach who are so deeply identified with the Earth and its creatures aren't confined to the Celtic nations; they occur in several countries throughout Europe. To take just one example, there's a strong resemblance between certain characteristics of the Cailleach and giant-esses in Nordic mythology, and it's been suggested that the earliest Norse settlers brought their tales about giant hags to the Shetland Islands, though later Scottish settlers brought their own versions of the Cailleach along with them too, and the two traditions undoubtedly merged together over time. The early Norse giantess, who was variously called the *trollkona*, *gryla*, *gífr*, or *gygr*, haunted the Shetland landscape, and was a terrifying personification of nature: a chthonic figure, a wild, dangerous deity; a female who, above all, was not to be taken lightly.

Stories of the Cailleach and mythic old women like her arise out of a time when the Earth was commonly represented as the body of a woman. Caves were thought of as wombs, rivers as veins or the flow of life-giving milk, and hills were seen as breasts... but then, with time, the Divine became disembodied, transcendent, and the physical became something to overcome or supersede. As we saw in the previous chapter with Frau Holle, in many parts of Europe, these powerful and life-giving elder women were transmogrified in the folklore into stereotypical witches. But what is interesting to me is that, although so many old gods vanished from memory after the adoption of Christianity, the Cailleach did not; her stories, and the stories of gigantic old women like her, are abundant in the landscape, and still very much alive. It's the old women who remain here then; it's the grandmothers who endure. This gives me confidence that, once upon a time in these islands, elder women were revered — and sometimes feared. It's more than time, I think, to make our voices heard again, and to stand up for the land that we too embody.

To me, and to many other women I know in Britain and Ireland and the wider Celtic diaspora, the Cailleach — along with other gigantic old women like her — is the greatest archetypal inspiration of all. Our Old Woman is not to be messed with. She teaches us that to be elder is to be strong — strong and hard as the oldest rocks of this Earth, which she personifies. To be elder is to be powerful and to stay the course — not just to endure, but always to remain fully alive through all the long years until our work here is done. One of the characters in contemporary fiction who wonderfully represents this quality is Marvellous Ways, the protagonist of Sarah Winman's beautiful novel *A Year of*

Marvellous Ways. The book begins on the banks of a Cornish creek in 1947, where eighty-nine-year-old Marvellous lives alone, "good for nothing except hanging on." Marvellous hasn't died yet, because she's waiting — but she doesn't know exactly what it is that she's waiting for, "because the image was incomplete." It soon becomes clear that she's waiting for a person: Francis Drake, a young man recently returned from the battlefields of France, whose current mission is to deliver a letter to the grieving father of a fellow soldier who didn't make it back home. Although in many ways Drake seems lucky to have escaped it, the traumas of the war nevertheless run deep, and it's Marvellous's job to gently coax him back into the land of the living.

Marvellous helps Drake through the power of story-telling, as she slowly spins tales about the three great loves of her life. In places, the narrative feels like a fairy tale, replete with characters with odd names and slightly magical pasts. And so, for example, she tells the story of her mermaid mother, who was shot shortly after her daughter's birth, having been mistaken for a seal. As Marvellous shares these stories, Drake learns how to find wonder in life again. It's a beautiful narrative, but it's the character of Marvellous who made this novel so magical for me. She engages in meaningful conversations with the world around her, and is Cailleach-like in her insistence on valuing the world's simple and natural pleasures over a headlong rush to "progress": "Some things are best left untouched, she said. Tides rise and tides fall. That is perfection enough." At almost ninety years old, knowing that her time is short, she is nevertheless fully alive in all the ways which matter, fully herself — and in spite of her ongoing struggles with memory loss, diminished in no significant way.

To become elder in my native traditions, then, following the Cailleach, is to fight for the integrity and health of the wild places and creatures of this world, and to be the fierce protector of the Earth, guardian of its balance. Her ubiquity throughout the landscape — not just in the grander "sacred sites," but in scattered rocks and hills and lakes across these islands — shows us the necessity of being fully embedded in and belonging to our places. We can only engage in a meaningful way with the overwhelming scale of our current environmental crisis if we start with the place that we call home, so that, in whatever ways are open to us, we can take responsibility for, and help to protect, the land that we occupy — the land which we, like her, can merge into and personify as we age alongside it. The Cailleach also teaches the importance of understanding the language of the natural world, and the other-than-humans which inhabit it alongside us — because she exists in the wider flow of life, fully enmeshed in it. Ultimately, she reminds us that there is a very intimate relationship between old age and the Earth. One way or another — through traditional burial or cremation — in the end, we all go back to the land.

Although we rarely see the Cailleach in "tame" places or domesticated settings — she's very much a creature of the wild — one of the archetypal images I'm especially fond of, and which I associate with her nevertheless, is the Good Gardener. Being in service to the Earth also includes tending it; tending our own little patch of Earth, in whatever ways are possible for us, then becomes, by association, a sacred activity. I've always had a strong desire to tend the land — in the sense of caring for it — and for most of my adult life I've been lucky enough to live in houses with small gardens. Simple acts, like growing beautiful flowers, aren't just for human pleasure; they also attract bees and butterflies and other insects, and provide food for them. Every garden I've ever been responsible for, no matter how tiny, has had a wild patch, and a pile of dead wood and grass clippings in which hedgehogs, toads, and other creatures can shelter and so live alongside me. Struggling to grow my own food and herbs on a peat-ridden croft in the Outer Hebrides taught me so much about the gifts that the Earth gives us, about gratitude and reciprocity. And here in Wales, where I live now, in an old farmhouse with eight acres of fields, my preoccupation is to ensure that grazing happens in a balanced way. We have a small flock of Hebrideans — the little black sheep with horns which are known for conservation grazing; moving them around from field to field at critical times allows disturbed areas to coexist with sections that are rested and ungrazed, which leads to a greater diversity of habitats. And so our fields are filled with grasshoppers, moths, and butterflies, and all through spring and summer there's an abundance of wildflowers — yarrow, harebells, foxgloves, cow parsley, cuckooflowers, vetch, bird's-foot trefoil, speedwell, and many others.

As she's grown older, my friend Faith has also felt an ever-increasing pull to being on the land, and working with it in meaningful ways. She now lives on a farm in the Shropshire hills, and although she earns her living through long hours spent at a computer, is growing her own herbs as part of her herbalism practice. "Ever since I was in my teens, and came to realise that life was a strange, unfathomable and wonderful thing, I've been searching for the meaning in it all and trying to live in a way that feels authentic," she tells me. "Now, at age fifty-eight, when becoming old is beginning to feel very real, the pull towards soulful living is stronger than ever. I've been feeling a powerful need to prepare for returning to the earth from which I came, and for me this has meant coming into a deeper relationship with the land itself — the soil and the rocks, the plants and the trees, the birds and the air.

"I'm strongly aware that I will go alone into death at the end, but if I go out and sit in the field behind our house I can find a kind of peace with that. I sit quietly and stare across the valley in a trance, feeling the earth beneath me, listening to the wind in the trees — just being me, without distraction or expectation, without the people I love and the demands they make on me, without the everyday business of my life. Losing myself in that state, I really feel as if I'm part of the web of life. And out of this has come a deep sense of communion with certain plants. So I can feel the presence of hawthorn in my chest now as I speak, and see the color that sometimes envelops me as I sit and stare at it. I can feel the wisdom of a greater whole presenting itself to me in specific forms — all so different — and I feel humbled and yet safe in that connection.

"On the days when I feel as though time is running out and I still haven't got my life right, the stones and the plants are my guides. I walk back down to the house with a deeper sense of how I want to spend the years I have left — the coming to fullness that is still possible — and I'm slowly, very slowly, learning how to live from that sense, moment by moment. And when the gnarled old hawthorns blossom each year and I see how much beauty and creative genius can come from those who are bent by the wind and fallen to the ground, I feel full of vigor, inspired to make bold new plans and dream the dreams that I couldn't have dreamed until now."

As he grew older, Carl Jung spoke of similar revelations about his own life and personality through simply being in the land. Toward the end of his memoir *Memories, Dreams, Reflections*, he wrote:

> At times I feel as if I am spread out over the landscape and inside things, and am myself living in every tree, in the splashing of the waves, in the clouds and the animals that come and go, in the procession of the seasons. There

is nothing... with which I am not linked....
There is so much that fills me: plants, animals, clouds, day and night, and the eternal
in man. The more uncertain I have felt about
myself, the more there has grown up in me a
feeling of kinship with all things. In fact it
seems to me as if that alienation which so
long separated me from the world has become
transferred into my own inner world, and has
revealed to me an unexpected familiarity with
myself.[59]

And I think it is this sense of merging with the life of the
land — of the land in some way showing me who I am and
might become — how I reflect the land and its creatures and
how they reflect me — which has influenced the gathering of
my "found objects" over the years. One of my very favorite
things is a fragment of hard black bog oak, roughly three
inches square. Bog oak, like other kinds of bogwood, is
created from the trunks of trees that have lain in bogs — or
in peaty, bog-like conditions in lakes, river bottoms, and
swamps — for millennia. Deprived of oxygen, and resting in
these acidic conditions, the wood fossilizes and is prevented
from decaying. Water movement is also important to the
creation of bog oak, as the flow of currents causes minerals
and iron in the water to bind with tannins in the wood,
causing it over the centuries to turn from a golden brown
to a deep, rich black — at the same time radically increasing
its hardness so that it can only be carved with the use of
specialized cutting tools.

Bog oak is strong, old, hard, and enduring, like the
Cailleach, and like my very favorite fictional character — the
one on whom I most definitely plan to model my old age.
Her name is Esmerelda ("Esme") Weatherwax — more

commonly known as Granny Weatherwax — and she appears in several of the Discworld novels written by the late English writer Terry Pratchett. Granny Weatherwax is a witch — but she's rather different from the witches we typically find in other stories, old or new. Granny finds her strength in practical tasks and hard work, and has little time for the bells, whistles, and miscellaneous contraptions associated with what she sniffily refers to as "magick." She has no time for witches who find pendants, crystals, and pentagrams necessary for the practice of their craft, and in spite of her own considerable power she rarely uses magic in any obvious form; instead, she prefers to rely on headology: an idiosyncratic and wonderfully pragmatic brand of folk-psychology.

In *Equal Rites*, the first novel in which she appears, Granny's definition of headology highlights the deep differences between the magic of witches and wizards:

> "It's all down to —" she tapped her head "— headology. How your mind works. Men's minds work different from ours, see. Their magic's all numbers and angles and edges and what the stars are doing, as if that really mattered. It's all power. It's all —" Granny paused, and dredged up her favourite word to describe all she despised in wizardry, "— jommetry." ..."It's the wrong kind of magic for women, is wizard magic...Witches is a different thing altogether...It's magic out of the ground, not out of the sky, and men never could get the hang of it."

She also refers to witches as "the handmaids of nature." And it's this focus on the ground and the natural world that makes Pratchett's witches unique, because each of his witches not only has an intense relationship with the land that she inhabits, but is an expression of its geology. Granny, for example, is a granite witch; she not only derives her power from the mountains where she lives, but she reflects them in her own character and in her practice of magic. And so, in *Wintersmith*, Granny Weatherwax says of the new teenage witch Tiffany Aching: "'She calls to the strength of her hills, all the time. An' they calls to her! Hills that was once alive, Miss Tick! They feels the rhythm of the dance, an' so in her bones does she, if she did but know it…She has the strength of her hills,' said Granny."

In *The Wee Free Men*, and Pratchett's other books involving Tiffany Aching, there is considerable discussion about this power of geology, and the ways in which it determines the kind of witch who comes from the land in question. Miss Tick, who specializes in identifying girls with the potential to become witches, declares that it's just not possible to grow a good witch on chalky ground, because of its softness.

> "You need good hard rock to grow a witch, believe me." [Miss Tick] stopped running, and leaned against a field wall as a wave of dizziness hit her… "It's this wretched chalk! I can feel it already! I can do magic on honest soil, and rock is always fine, and I'm not too bad on clay, even…but chalk's neither one thing or the other! I'm very SENSITIVE to geology, you know…Chalk…is a hungry soil."

The witches of Discworld don't just inhabit wild places, though: in *I Shall Wear Midnight*, an urban witch named Mrs. Proust waxes lyrical over the geology of urban environments.

> "Granite and marble, chert and miscellaneous sedimentary deposits, my dear Tiffany. Rocks that once leaped and flowed when the world was born in fire...And what did we make from the stones? Palaces, and castles and mausoleums and gravestones, and fine houses and city walls, oh my!...Can you imagine how it feels to lie down on an ancient flagstone and feel the power of the rock buoying you up against the tug of the world? And it's mine to use, all of it, every stone of it, and that's where witchcraft begins. The stones have life, and I'M part of it."

As well as drawing power from the bedrock of the land, Pratchett's witches have a deep relationship with the other-than-human creatures with which they coexist, and so Granny Weatherwax is able to sense the underlying mood of plants and animals, as well as the earth itself. She is highly adept at "borrowing," a kind of shapeshifting: the art of entering the mind of another creature so that she can borrow its body, seeing through its eyes and steering its actions.

In these funny but profound books, Pratchett presents us with grounded, pragmatic witches who are wholly entangled with their places, and derive their power from the land itself. Just as in the best old stories, the practice of witchcraft here has nothing at all to do with dressing up to do fabricated rituals in darkened rooms. It's about being out in the land, listening to it, reading it, and learning from it. Pratchett's witches — and Granny Weatherwax in particular — have taught me to inquire very deeply into the

geology of all the places I've lived in since I read the first of
his books, around twenty-five years ago. I'm used to living,
like Granny, on the hardest of old rock — on granite or
Lewisian gneiss; perhaps that's why I identify with her so
deeply. But now, here in the Cambrian mountains of Wales,
I'm living — for the first time since I was a child — on
a foundation of sedimentary rocks like sandstone and
mudstone. If I were a character in one of Pratchett's books,
what would it mean, to be a sandstone witch? What are the
old voices of the stones here whispering to me? How would
I reflect the nature of this rock which holds the memory of
seawater, here on this little farm at the top of a hill in the
middle of a very much greener and pleasanter land than I've
become accustomed to?

Right now, I'm still learning; I'll let you know when I've
figured it out.

When I think of elder women here in the West who are
Cailleach-like in their fierce care for the land and its creatures,
the woman who first comes to mind is Joanna Macy. Macy,
who was born in 1929, has been an environmental activist
for six decades now. She describes herself as a scholar of
Buddhism, systems thinking, and deep ecology, but she is
also a writer; a respected and much-loved voice across many
movements for peace, justice, and ecology; and a passionate
advocate for the cultivation of ecological awareness. As
the founder of The Work That Reconnects, Macy created a
groundbreaking framework for personal and social change,
with the aim of helping people to transform despair and
apathy into constructive, collaborative, positive action.
Her work is rooted in a vision of the world as an extension
of ourselves, as our larger, living body, and she coined the
phrase "The Great Turning" to describe what she calls
"the essential adventure of our time": the shift from an

"industrial growth society" that is rapidly consuming the planet, to the possibility of a civilization that sustains life, rather than killing it. In the afterword, which she wrote as her contribution to an anthology about her work, Macy shares the motivation for her life's work: "Carl Jung once said that at the core of each life's journey is a question that we are born to pursue. For me, that question has been *How can I be fully present to my world — present enough to rejoice and be useful — when we as a species are destroying it?*"[60] It's a question, I believe, that each of us needs to ask as we grow into elder women — and in answering it, each in our own way, we can draw inspiration from the great age, strength, and endurance of the Old Woman in so many native mythic traditions. The Cailleach teaches us always to be present and to mindfully witness what is happening to the world — even as we grieve for it.

Another woman who has inspired me since I first came across her work in the early 1980s, as part of my studies in psychology, is Jane Goodall. Goodall was born in 1934, and although she's known primarily for being an expert on chimpanzees, she is also very much more than that. She's the founder of the Jane Goodall Institute and its Roots & Shoots program, an environmental education project for young people; she has also worked extensively on a miscellany of conservation and animal welfare issues. She's an outspoken environmental activist who has raised awareness about the effects of climate change on endangered species, and *Time* magazine named her as one of the one hundred most influential people in the world in 2019. Goodall, like the Cailleach protecting her pregnant deer against the predations of men, is ensuring to the best of her ability that nothing precious is allowed to disappear from this world without a fight.

Macy, Goodall, and other inspiring elder-woman activists

like them teach us the importance of cultivating a wide circle of elders around the world who will stand up for this increasingly threatened planet on which we entirely depend. Like the mythic Old Women of our native traditions, our affinities lie with waterways, forests, and seashores — with the heart of mountains and the ancient bedrock of our places. We are the Earth, and the Earth is us. That is the nature of the deep, embodied knowledge which we can pass on to our young.

6

FAIRY GODMOTHERS, AND PURVEYORS
OF OLD WIVES' TALES

During my younger years, I would have loved nothing more than to have an elder woman as a wise adviser, friend, and guide. When I was ten, we moved from the far north of England to the Midlands and I was separated from my extended family — but even if that hadn't happened, our older women wouldn't have been obvious candidates for that role. Both of my grandmothers were the victims of domestic violence and had learned the hard way that speaking up for themselves, or trying to take control of their own lives, wasn't ever going to end well. As a teenager and then a young adult profoundly lacking in confidence, unsure about what it meant to be a woman in such a profoundly patriarchal world, I would likely have flourished under the wing of such a mentor — but unfortunately it just didn't happen. No wise and strong grandmother, no kindly old neighbor, or aging family friend. I lived with a mother who didn't really make friends, and in a house where visitors were rarely welcomed.

I missed out, then; I was never on the receiving end of one of the key gifts of elders in indigenous cultures all around the world: to teach and to mentor the young. From a broader psychological perspective, Carl Jung also believed that as the "guardians of mysteries and the heritage of his/her culture," the older person is called to foster wholeness in younger people, and to help them deepen their appreciation of life's meaning.[61] This process doesn't involve telling young people what to do, but rather is about pushing them beyond the perceived limitations which define and confine what they imagine they can be. This is exactly the kind of role which can be fulfilled by a wise grandparent, and a particularly fine example of it can be found in Finnish author Tove Jansson's novel *The Summer Book*. It's about an elderly artist and her six-year-old granddaughter, who spend the summer alone together on a tiny island in the Gulf of Finland. Sophia's mother is dead, and her father is defined more by his self-important absence than by any kind of meaningful presence. She and her grandmother wander around the island, talking, fighting, and having adventures. Their discussions cover a wide range of subjects, from the profound: "'When are you going to die?...will they dig a hole?' the child asked amiably" — to the mundane: "'Don't look so cross,' Grandmother whispered. 'This is socialising, and you have to learn how to do it.'" Sophia can tend to the obstreperous, and the old woman seems always to be on the verge of fatigue and dizziness, but by the end of the book they understand each other beautifully, and a great love has grown between them.

Such mentoring possibilities might well be open to those who have had children and now have grandchildren, but for those of us who do not, and especially if we don't have siblings or close friends with children either, growing older means that we can sometimes struggle to find the best ways of serving younger people — and of defining ourselves in a culture which still seems to value procreation in women above all else. I found myself in conversation about all this with Jody Day, founder of Gateway Women, a global friendship and support network for childless women.[62] We began by talking about the paucity of stories which celebrate childless women in any way at all. "Fairy tales really haven't been kind to childless women," she suggests. "From Snow White's paranoid stepmother and the child-eating witch of Hansel and Gretel, through the evil fairy godmother who curses Sleeping Beauty, we're shown to be not just 'other' to mothers, but downright deviant. So, now that I'm fifty-seven, an idea that I've been mulling over, and which has now started to take more solid form in my ongoing 'Conscious Childless Elderwomen' project, is this: in a culture where the only respected term for an older woman is 'grandmother,' how does the journey to elderhood differ if you've never had children? Because it does seem to matter. And if older women in general have been symbolically annihilated by the culture, older women without children are usually the first to be crossed off the guest list."

We reflect for a while on instances of this happening — in 2021, for example, when the right-wing American TV channel Fox News aired a segment wondering if people without children should be allowed to vote, as they have no "physical commitment to the future."[63] This is a question which echoes a statement made during the UK Conservative Party's 2016 leadership campaign, when Andrea Leadsom (a mother) said that, compared to her childless rival Theresa May, she felt that "being a mum means you have a real stake in the future of our country, a tangible stake."[64]

"Although an understandable concern of those aging without children is 'who's going to take care of me when I'm old,'" Jody continues, "I'm also curious about what it takes to *be* us when we're old. One of the reasons we need role models of conscious elder women without children is to counterbalance the archetypes *other* than grandmother that are often used in its place, all of them drawing from the rich shadowy underbelly of the feminine archetype. So we're the dangerous child-eating witch (not the wish-fulfilling, twinkly fairy godmother); we're the smelly, crazy, hoarding cat lady (not the benign, friendly grandmother in her cottage with cakes and a sweet pet); we're the dangerous, irascible virago, particularly if also unpartnered, and then best left to rot alone ... it seems the only good use the patriarchy has for us is as a cautionary tale for younger women on how not to screw up your life! We're shamed into silence and disconnection so that the inconvenient truth can remain hidden — that a life without children (and perhaps without a partner too) can be just as powerful a way to be a woman, and to be an elder, as grandmotherhood."

It's a good point, and certainly one that I've struggled with at various times in my life. In some sense, it seems to me that those of us who never become mothers run the risk of perpetually remaining daughters. We never quite grow up; we never quite learn to own our authority. It's something I've noted in a couple of close friends who similarly haven't had children: it's hard enough for us to step out of the role of young person and into our own adulthood — let alone our elderhood.

"For myself, and for many of the childless women I've worked with over the years, accepting that you are 'the end of the line' — an acceptance that only really becomes real after menopause — can be a fierce truth to make peace with," Jody tells me. "But what I've noticed as I've settled into that truth is that, rather than it making me care *less* about the future, it's gifted me a deep concern for the future of *all* the children of the world, both human and more-than-human. And instead of feeling that I've let my ancestors down in some way by failing to procreate, I have a sense that they *chose* me and shaped me precisely so that I could be their representative during these epoch-shaping, liminal decades of human life on this planet. I may not have children, but, hell yes, I *do* have skin in the game — ancient skin, the skin of the thousand generations that led me to this moment, who prepared me to do my small part in standing up for the voiceless. I may be childless, but I can still be a good ancestor. Never before in recorded human history have so many educated, liberated women without children or grandchildren been alive at the same time; what if this was no accident? Could it be that our edge-walking wisdom and the outsider sensibility gifted to us by patriarchy is just what is needed? New solutions never arise from the mainstream and so we are the natural allies of youthful radicals, if we allow ourselves to be: they have everything to lose; we have nothing to lose; to me, that sounds like a powerful relationship between mentor and student; a cauldron in which both can be transformed."

In so many mythic tales, elder women — whether they're grandmothers or not — are there to help young people find their way in the world. They emerge suddenly out of the dark heart of the frightening forest with precisely the gift which the protagonist needs to stay alive and allow their story to progress. Sometimes, they make apprentices of them, teaching them to engage in the hard but necessary work of discernment and order, and allowing them to acquire the necessary qualities (usually involving kindness, and cooperation with the other-than-human world) which will enable them to go back home and lead a fulfilled, useful, and meaningful life. This occurs in the classic German folktale of Frau Holle (who we also encountered in chapter 4 as one of the Otherworldly spinning and weaving creator women in the European mythic tradition). At the beginning of this story, we meet a widow who lives with her daughter and her stepdaughter. As is usually the way of it, the widow favors her biological daughter, who grows spoiled and remains idle while her older stepdaughter is required to do all the work. Every day, the stepdaughter sits outside their cottage and spins beside the well. One day, she pricks her finger on the sharp point of the spindle. She leans over the wall of the well to wash the blood away, but drops the spindle so that it falls into the well, soon sinking out of sight. The stepdaughter is afraid that she will be punished for losing the spindle, and so she jumps down into the well after it.

The girl finds herself in a meadow and happens upon an oven full of bread. The bread cries out to her, asking to be taken out of the oven before it burns; she carefully removes all the loaves and then walks on. Next, she comes to an apple tree, which asks that its heavy burden of apples should be harvested. The girl picks them and gathers them into a neat pile before continuing on her way. Finally, she comes to a small house of an old woman, who offers to let the girl stay with her if she will help with the housework. The old woman says that her name is Frau Holle, and she tells the girl that she will need to shake the featherbed pillows and coverlet well when she makes the beds, because that will make it snow in the girl's world.

The girl agrees to stay with Frau Holle, and she serves her well. But after a while she becomes homesick, and asks Frau Holle if it might be time for her to return home. The old woman has been impressed by the girl's kindness and hard work, and so when she escorts her to the gate of her property, a shower of gold falls upon her. Frau Holle also presents her with the spindle that had fallen into the well. The girl then suddenly finds herself back home, not far from her stepmother's house.

The stepmother greatly desires that her biological daughter should have the same good fortune as her stepdaughter, and so she sets her to sit by the well and spin; the daughter then deliberately throws the spindle into the well before jumping in herself. She too comes to the oven, but she refuses to assist the bread; nor will she later help the apple tree. When she arrives at Frau Holle's house, she too takes service there, but before long falls into her usual lazy, careless ways. The old woman soon dismisses her, and as the girl stands at the gate, instead of a shower of gold, a kettle of pitch spills over her. "That is what you have earned," says Frau Holle, as she closes the gate behind her.

The blackthorn (*Prunus spinosa*) is a shrub or small tree which is common in hedgerows in this part of the world; for those of you who might be unfamiliar with it, it has long, thin thorns which can cause unpleasant wounds if you're not careful. It produces bittersweet sloe berries, which ripen after the first frost of the year, and which are commonly used to make that most delicious of winter tipples, sloe gin. The tree is said to be beloved of the Cailleach, the feisty Old Woman of Gaelic myth who we met in the last chapter. Her staff, so the stories tell us, was made from the wood of the blackthorn, and in other folklore witches were said to carry blackthorn wands. I too have a beautiful, smooth-sanded, polished blackthorn wand which began life in the native woodland planted by my friend Moya in County Leitrim, in Ireland. But I don't really think of it as a witch's wand, because for some reason I don't usually think of witches using wands at all. Wands, to me, are the province of the archetypical Fairy Godmother. In Disney movies and their ilk, those wands would probably have a twinkly little star on top — but I'd much prefer to be the kind of Fairy Godmother who would wield a wand of blackthorn. I do admit to being especially enamored of this particular archetype, though — perhaps because those of us who can't become grandmothers nevertheless always retain the possibility of becoming a Fairy Godmother.

In fairy tales, the Fairy Godmother is a supernatural being with magical powers who acts as a mentor or surrogate parent to the protagonist — usually, they appear in stories in which the protagonist is female — and who plays the role that an actual godparent would have been expected to play in those cultures which had them. Fairy tales which include Fairy Godmothers are actually quite rare, but these delightful women have become so familiar to us because of the popularity of the French literary fairy tales in which they originally appeared: those of Madame d'Aulnoy, for example, and Charles Perrault. The Fairy Godmother is usually an elder woman, and so embodies a wisdom and knowledge of the world which she's able to utilize for the benefit of those around her. She can see the potential which others possess and foster it, encouraging them not only to believe in themselves but also to help themselves, and so to become the best and most authentic person they can possibly be. Without her Fairy Godmother to help her and show her the way, the girl under her care will never be able to leave home and grow into a unique and confident woman.

She might be associated with glitter and glamour, but more often than not the fairy-tale Fairy Godmother is actually a profoundly practical soul. In the story of "Cinderella," for example, the Fairy Godmother takes considerable pleasure in using whatever happens to be at hand to help her protégée, transforming a pumpkin into a coach, and a rat and mice into servants who'll escort Cinderella to the ball. A fine example of this kind of Fairy Godmother in the movie world is Mary Poppins, who, as well as having many serious qualities, is possessed of a profound sense of fun — and an ability to make even the most mundane tasks enjoyable. Mary is the kind of Fairy Godmother who teaches those under her care that nonconformity can be a virtue, and she demonstrates to them the value of making decisions which reflect who they truly are.

The character of the Fairy Godmother might have her roots in stories of the mythical Fates; this is especially clear in Perrault's "Sleeping Beauty," in which the princess's multiple Fairy Godmothers declare what her destiny will be, and in which they also, like the Fates, are linked with the craft of spinning. In this fairy tale, there is a naming ceremony shortly after the birth of a princess, and seven fairies are invited to be her godmothers. One notable old fairy, however, has been overlooked because she has been holed up inside a tower for many years and everyone has imagined her to be dead. Furious at being forgotten, she turns up anyway, but instead of bestowing a gift on the princess like the other fairies, she curses her: on her sixteenth birthday, she declares, the princess will prick her finger on a spindle and die. But, happily, there's one last fairy at the ceremony who hasn't yet given her blessing — and although she can't remove the curse, the seventh good fairy has the power to change it. So, instead of dying as the wicked old fairy had intended, the princess — and all those in the castle with her — falls into a deep sleep after pricking her finger on the spindle; the sleep lasts for a hundred years, until a prince comes along and kisses her, so bringing her and all those around her back to life again.

As with all fairy tales, there's a power in this story, and a profound relevance for older women today. Sometimes, looking at the state of the world around us, it's hard to imagine that we're not all Sleeping Beauties — sleeping as the large swaths of the planet variously burn or drown. Sleeping as the world that we grew up with crumbles, and so many precious species of flora and fauna disappear. It's hard to imagine that we're not under some kind of curse. A curse of our own making, for sure — but a curse, nevertheless. Do we have it in us, as elder women, to take up the mantle of that seventh good fairy — the one who redeemed what seemed like an irreparable situation, who diverted the curse and transformed it into something more hopeful? If the

Fairy Godmother archetype teaches us anything, it's that we always have the power to transform the lives of even the most unlikely children and to subvert even the most impossible curses. The Fairy Godmother teaches us never to give up on anyone or anything — and that, if we only cultivate the will and the imagination, we will always be alive to the possibility of changing things for the better.

When I was living in Kentucky and Georgia in the late 1990s and going through what seemed like an endless procession of midlife crises, I read a book which reawakened that old longing for an elderly mentor: Fannie Flagg's *Fried Green Tomatoes at the Whistle Stop Café*. Flagg's novel was made into a movie in 1991, starring the glorious Kathy Bates as Evelyn Couch, a timid, unhappy housewife in her forties who meets elderly Ninny Threadgoode (Jessica Tandy) in the Alabama nursing home where her aunt is now living. Evelyn is excessively fond of doughnuts and candy bars, and so struggles with her weight; she is utterly lacking in self-esteem and is incapable of asserting herself. She's taking classes in an effort to rejuvenate her loveless marriage to the utterly insensitive, beer-guzzling, baseball-watching Ed. And, as if all that weren't enough, she's depressed.

During the course of several conversations with Evelyn, Ninny tells her the story of a now-abandoned town called Whistle Stop, and the people who lived there. But Ninny, disguised as the fiercely independent and unconventional Idgie Threadgoode, is actually telling Evelyn her own story: a story of strength and determination, which ultimately inspires Evelyn to take charge of her own life and to change it. On several occasions, when Idgie did something she'd been forbidden to do, or something that a well-brought-up girl wasn't ever supposed to do, she would shout the word "Towanda" — the name of an Amazon-like warrior woman she'd created in her imagination — as a kind of personal battle cry. This profoundly affects Evelyn, who gives up junk food, starts working out, quits her women's meetings, stops cooking her husband dinner every night, takes up a new career selling cosmetics, and tears down a wall in her house to let in more air and light. In what is probably the best-known and most iconic scene in the movie, after Evelyn complains to two young girls who have stolen the parking space she'd been waiting for, they laugh and tell her, "Face it, lady: we're younger and faster." Evelyn, furious, rams their car six times. When they run out of the grocery store screaming, "What are you doing? Are you crazy?" Evelyn calmly replies, "Face it, girls: I'm older and I have more insurance." As she drives away, she realizes that she has finally taken on the qualities of the great Towanda.

At the end of *Fried Green Tomatoes*, in recognition of their now-deep friendship, Evelyn invites Ninny to come and live with her. Ninny, we can imagine, will continue to tell Evelyn stories of female empowerment, and Evelyn will continue to learn from her. That process of passing wisdom down through the generations is as old as humanity itself. Women have always spun and woven together, cooked together, sung and danced together. We've always passed down our stories to the young ones, grounding them all the while in the land and the cycles of the seasons. We've always shared our life experiences, our knowledge of what it is to be a woman. This is the knowledge that we still need to pass on today; there's a thirst for it. I experienced that myself recently, when in my online community The Mythic Imagination Network, a virtual sharing circle was instigated by members approaching menopause who wanted to ask the advice of those elder women who'd already gone through it.

In the book *Red Moon Passage*, Seneca and Cherokee author Jamie Sams speaks about the Grandmother Lodge in her native traditions.[65] It's also called the Wisdom Lodge, and it's a place for older women to counsel younger women who are going through puberty, or for young mothers to leave their children. It's a place, she writes, where "women would learn how to think, how to be industrious, how to be problem solvers and peace keepers and good mothers." For the elder women themselves, "The Grandmother Lodge was a place for women elders to go if they were beyond their bleeding years and needed to come together for a time of quiet. They would go to the Grandmother Lodge and discuss how they could help tribal members who were off balance. Anything they chose to do was honored as wisdom." The "grandmothers" in such cultures also act as bridges, connecting the more meaningful traditions of the past with viable visions of the future.

In the West today, the wisdom of elder women is rarely acknowledged, let alone valued. Think of the phrase "old wives' tales" — in common parlance, it's used to refer to a story which is told and presented as a truth, but which ought to be discounted as foolish or superstitious, and as containing exaggerated or inaccurate details and facts. This, the phrase suggests, is the kind of conversation that older women specialize in; it's really all they're good for. But old wives' tales actually originate in the ancient tradition of oral storytelling, and many fairy tales, such as those collected and written down by the likes of the Grimms, Hans Christian Andersen, and Charles Perrault, have their roots in the traditions kept alive by older women. In many indigenous traditions, older women are repositories of the memory of the culture; the memories are passed down in stories. I'm a huge fan of Laguna Pueblo writer Leslie Marmon Silko; in her book *Storyteller* (in which Grandmother Spider acts as narrator), the elderly Aunt Susie belongs to the "last generation here at Laguna, / that passed down an entire culture / by word of mouth / an entire history / an entire vision of the world / which depended upon memory and retelling / by subsequent generations."[66] A major theme of novels like Silko's *Ceremony* and Paula Gunn Allen's *The Woman Who Owned the Shadows* is the healing of cultural amnesia by elder women who keep the old stories alive.

Elder women's stories have historically been important in my culture too, but it's interesting that the stories women told in these islands tended to be different from the stories offered up by men. In "The Gaelic Story-Teller," a lecture by folklorist J. H. Delargy which was delivered to the British Academy in 1945, he notes that:

> The recital of Ossianic hero-tales was almost without exception restricted to men...There are exceptions to this rule, but still the evidence is unmistakable that the telling by women of Finn-tales was frowned upon by the men. Seanchas, genealogical lore, music, folk prayers, were, as a rule associated with women; at any rate they excelled the men in these branches of the tradition. While women do not take part in the storytelling [of men], not a word of the tale escapes them, and...it is no uncommon experience of mine to hear the listening woman interrupt and correct the speaker.[67]

The most important venue for traditional storytelling in Ireland was the "ceilidh": nightly visiting among neighbors which was common until relatively recently during the winter months when nights were long and cold, and the demands of the agricultural cycle were fewer. Storytelling was a key component of a ceilidh, along with music, dancing, and singing, and it was sometimes the case that men and women would each hold their own gatherings. At women's ceilidhs, fairy tales — rather than sagas and hero tales — would be the usual fare, and during the summer months when they would take their cattle to summer pastures and stay there for a while, women would share these stories together then too.[68]

It seems to have been different in Classical times, when women also told the mythic narratives which, in the Irish tradition, seem to be confined to men. They specialized in tales of gods and metamorphoses, in the form of songs and stories which usually happened while they were working together — especially when spinning and weaving. Ovid in particular makes much of female storytelling; in his *Metamorphoses*, the Minyeides — wool-working women — are the first human narrators of the text, and, as they weave, they tell stories of love and transformation.[69]

In this age in which computers, TV screens, and so many other gadgets have taken the place not just of storytelling but often of conversation, we run the risk of losing that hard-won old wisdom for good. We run the risk of losing the stories — and that matters. In 1962, in his book *Symbols of Sacred Science*, the French philosopher and esotericist René Guénon argued that we now live in "degenerate times," at the end of a long era during which important spiritual truths have been forgotten, the ancient centers of wisdom have been destroyed, and the guardians of that wisdom are long gone. However, he suggested, the safest repository for such old truths has always been folklore. He believed that knowledge which is in danger of being lost can be translated into the symbolic code of a folktale and then passed on through the storytelling tradition. For a while, people who hear them will perhaps only be concerned with the stories," surface meanings — but they will at least preserve them and pass them down to their children. Then, in better times, people might once again appear who understand the code, and who will penetrate the symbolic disguise and uncover the wider meaning behind.[70] I believe that elder women today can fulfill that role. We are tradition-bearers, wisdom-keepers, tellers of tales. It's incumbent on us to tell the old stories — and to use those stories, when necessary, to hold the culture to account.

7

TRICKSTERS AND TRUTH-TELLERS

Holding the Culture to Account

Once, when I was in practice as a psychologist in the early 2000s, I had a client who I'll call Ursula. Ursula lived in a rural cottage in the Highlands of Scotland; she'd moved away from southern England after her husband suddenly died, and she was struggling to come to terms with her grief. Extracting herself from the location they'd shared and embarking on a life in a new place had helped, but not surprisingly, she was still distraught. Nothing could shake her out of her listlessness, and her first winter in her new home was sad and lonely. Then, in early spring, Ursula's small cottage garden was overrun with magpies. They chattered and cackled; they swooped down suddenly from treetops as if to tease her. They stalked around the lawn like kings, poking their beaks inquisitively into all corners of the garden. All at once, magpies were everywhere. They made her laugh, and it was that simple gift of laughter, in the end, which loosened her tight body and dissolved Ursula's depression once and for all.

I am a great lover of magpies, and of corvids of all shapes and sizes. They are my favorite familiars; I talk to them all the time. On the windowsill by my desk sits a jugful of their feathers, which I've collected from many different places over the past couple of decades. The largest and most dominant of them is the tail feather of a raven, left behind in some strange exchange as it took off with one of our just-born goslings, one late-spring day in 2013 on the Isle of Lewis. There are magpie feathers from our Connemara garden and jackdaw feathers from our beautiful townland in Donegal — but most of the feathers in my little yellow jug come from crows. There are black crow feathers, of course — but also gray, because in the many years I lived in the north and west of Scotland, it wasn't the all-black carrion crow which was the most common of these creatures, but the "hoodie," or hooded crow, with its slate-gray back and belly. The dominant grayness of the hooded crow always makes me think of her as an old woman, and I've grown so used to talking to her in that way over the years that it's strange not to find her particular brand of tricksy hagitude here in this part of Wales.

Ursula's stories about her magpies remind me of a rare comedic moment in Greek myth, which arises in the tale of Persephone (sometimes called Kore). Persephone's mother, the goddess Demeter, is lost in inconsolable grief at the disappearance of her daughter, who has been abducted by Hades and taken to the Underworld, and is wandering the earth in search of her. After many travels, she comes finally to the town of Eleusis, where she refuses all food and drink and rejects all efforts to help her — until she encounters an old woman called Baubo. Baubo approaches Demeter, lifts up her skirts and displays her genitals. Demeter bursts into sudden laughter — and earthenware figurines identified with Baubo, which were found in the ruins of the fourth-century BCE temple of Demeter and Kore in Ionia, offer some insight into the reason for this amusement. In each of the statues, the head and female genitals are merged together, with the vulva on display immediately below the figurine's mouth, blending into her chin. So back in our story, after she has recovered from her bout of hilarity, Demeter accepts the drink that Baubo offers her, and becomes herself again.

Like Ursula's magpies, my much-loved crows, and other corvids in cultures all around the world, Baubo isn't just a joker; she's a Trickster. She shocks Demeter out of her grief, and so restores her to her natural state; Demeter is then able to summon the strength and confidence to petition Zeus, the father of the gods, for the return of Persephone. Such acts of disruption are characteristic of that archetypal figure we refer to as the Trickster: the one who, in myths and folktales across the world, shifts his or her shape or identity in order to shine a light on deeply rooted human follies.

The particular way in which this aspect of the Trickster archetype is expressed varies from culture to culture. In some parts of the world, Trickster characters are strongly related to the Clown, Joker, or Fool, and achieve their ends through buffoonery or other comedic means; like Baubo, the Native American Coyote and Black American and Caribbean Brer Rabbit are examples of such Tricksters. In British folklore and early literature, mischief-making sprites and fairies — such as Puck in Shakespeare's *A Midsummer Night's Dream* — represent this kind of Trickster too. Prometheus, Titan and Trickster in Greek myth, stole fire from the gods and gave it to humans — so disrupting the order of the cosmos in the most profound of ways. In other traditions, though, the archetype is much darker; the Norse Trickster-god Loki, for example, is more often malicious than he is helpful, and plays a part in bringing about Ragnarök, the end of the world.

In other places, Trickster is ambiguous, neither good nor bad, neither moral nor immoral — but whatever specific methods are used, Trickster is above all a disruptor of the established order, upsetting it so that necessary change might come about. Trickster happens along when something urgently needs to shift, sweeping out the old, arid, and useless to make way for the new. Sometimes, the methods used are more extreme than we might like: Trickster is rarely a comfortable, warm, and cozy character. But in times of need this archetype can be the greatest of teachers — because Trickster holds up a mirror to all that is dysfunctional, hypocritical, and perverse in us or in the culture, and challenges our deepest assumptions about our own nature, or the nature of the world around us.

One of the more interesting features of Tricksters around the world is that they frequently have a penchant for subverting cultural expectations around gender. In Western Trickster traditions, it's usually a male Trickster who disguises himself as a female, rather than the other way around; Loki, for example, switches gender from time to time — in one case even becoming pregnant. A real-life Trickster who disrupted gender in this way was French surrealist photographer, sculptor, and writer Claude Cahun.* In her book *Disavowals*, Cahun writes: "Masculine? Feminine? It depends on the situation. Neuter is the only gender that always suits me."[71] During the early 1920s, she settled in Paris with her lifelong personal and artistic partner Suzanne Malherbe, who subsequently adopted the pseudonym Marcel Moore. In 1937, Cahun and Moore moved to Jersey, and after the fall of France and the German occupation of the Channel Islands, they turned their energies to resistance efforts against the invaders. They produced anti-German fliers, many of which were German translations of fragments of BBC reports about Nazi crimes; they created many of these messages under the name "Der Soldat Ohne Namen," or "The Soldier With No Name," to deceive German soldiers into thinking that there was a conspiracy among their own troops. They would

---

*   Cahun was born as Lucy Renee Mathilde Schwob. Moore was also Cahun's stepsister; her divorced father and Moore's widowed mother married eight years after their relationship began.

attend German military events, strategically slipping their pamphlets ("paper bullets") into pockets and placing them on chairs for soldiers to find. In 1944, Cahun and Moore were arrested and sentenced to death; the sentence was never carried out, though, as Jersey was liberated in 1945.

In his biography of Cahun,[72] Jeffrey H. Jackson associates the two women's involvement in resistance work with their personal experiences as artists — and as lesbians. Cahun had always transgressed against convention, and their life together consistently departed from what was expected of them as the daughters of wealthy families. Among the cultural values they so effectively disrupted was that classic Tricksterish flouting of mores around gender identity and expression, which they explored both in their personal lives and in their art.

Trickster, then, in all her diverse forms, is the character who breezes in and breaks something in an attempt to wake us up, revealing to us the shakier truth which underlies a seemingly stable situation. And so Trickster can also be thought of as an archetype of the apocalypse — in the original sense of that ancient Greek word, which means *revelation*: "an unveiling or unfolding of things not previously known and which could not be known apart from the unveiling."[73] When civilizations start to become moribund; when social, economic, and political systems stagnate, and empires become degenerate and unresponsive to the needs of the people, in walks Trickster to shake it all up — embodying that disruptive intelligence which all cultures need if they are to remain lively, flexible, and open to change.

What follows after Trickster's intervention, of course, depends on many things — among them, the specific qualities of the Trickster who happens along in the story we are living through. And although we don't always get the Trickster we imagine we might want, we mostly get the Trickster we deserve — because Trickster is often, in Jungian terms, the one who also reveals the cultural Shadow. In the same way that the personal Shadow is the dark, unacknowledged complement of an individual's persona, a culture will cast its own collective Shadow, which includes all the things we imagine that other cultures are, but categorically believe that ours is not — racist, sexist, xenophobic, or undemocratic, for example. Whenever a society believes strongly in its own moral righteousness, superiority, or entitlement, the collective Shadow is likely to be present in spades — and it's then that we most need Trickster. Trickster holds up a mirror to us and helps us to see what we have become. The good news is that, although the Shadow is the hidden place where we can hardly bear to look, if we manage to look it in the face anyway, it may carry the promise of a better life that hasn't yet been lived. The Shadow doesn't just represent the dark side of our collective unconscious: it represents opportunity as well. But we can only begin to acknowledge, heal, and integrate our Shadow behaviors by becoming aware of them — and more often than not, that happens because someone stands up and tells us the truth.

The Shadow side of Western culture, it seems to me, is clearly visible in contemporary debates about gender identity. There are few issues that are quite so polarizing. From a personal perspective, as a psychologist and mythologist whose focus is on story, I'd love to work with more trans and nonbinary people to delve into the narratives and archetypes which reflect their unique ways of being in the world, and their unique experiences of womanhood. Many years ago, on a blog of mine which no longer exists, I wrote an article about powerful women's stories in the native mythology of the British Isles; it was during the years when I was preparing the ground for *If Women Rose Rooted*. A trans woman commented on the post at the time, wondering where she might find such powerful mythical stories that reflected her own rather different experience of the feminine. Unfortunately, I didn't know of any back then, but I replied that from my perspective this was an exciting opportunity: if the old stories don't reflect who we are today, then let's get radical and imagine some new ones.

With this exchange in mind, when I set up my online Mythic Imagination Network[74] at the beginning of 2021, I wrote, "If there's demand, we would be more than happy to set up spaces for men, for transgender men and women who'd like to explore and reimagine their own unique stories and mythic and archetypal patterns, and for those who identify as queer/nonbinary." So far, there have been no takers, but I wish there were. There might be elements of the experience of those born as women that trans women can't participate in but, equally, there are elements of the experience of trans women that those of us who were born as women can't participate in — and they are valuable too. Gender identity is an important and genuinely intriguing issue — but today, we are increasingly robbing it of its wonder and mystery through dogma and didacticism, through our seeming inability to engage in reasoned and reasonable discussions, and our growing inability as a culture to differentiate truth from "fake news." The truth of such a complex matter, of course, isn't always quite so easy to identify. Truth can be Tricksterish too, in its way: slippery, shapeshifting, chimerical.

There's no question that transgender men and women are routinely marginalized and discriminated against in a culture that is designed around binary conceptions of gender; Shon Faye details this history of oppression and disadvantage in her book *The Transgender Issue*.[75] Trans people can face overwhelming political and media hostility, and vital healthcare is often impossible to access. The UK charity Mermaids, in a 2021 report,[76] quotes research

indicating that an astonishing 92 percent of trans young
people have thought about taking their own life; 84 percent
of trans young people have self-harmed, and 45 percent of
trans young people have actually tried to take their own
life. Raising awareness of gender fluidity in Western culture
is in good part about bringing into the open what was
always there, but was once hidden, or forbidden. This has
to be a good thing. But it would be a pity if, as many women
increasingly fear, the very necessary changes to this unacceptable situation came about at the expense of those
who were born as women — who have also been oppressed
and marginalized for centuries, and in most parts of the
world still are. If you'll forgive the repetition of an old but
apposite cliché, throwing the baby out with the bathwater
rarely ends well.

I've always admired women who are courageous enough
to speak out in the face of societal disapproval — because
truth-telling can be dangerous, and often requires courage;
lives and careers can be ruined by challenging the prevailing
cultural orthodoxy. In the United Kingdom today, for example, women have been fired from university positions and
from editorial boards, excluded from lecture theatres, and
regularly face a barrage of abuse and death threats on social
media — for exercising their right to believe and to speak
about what all of us, until quite recently, had been taught
was a straightforward scientific fact: that biological sex in
humans is not a "social construct" — unlike gender, which
clearly is. In a notable recent case in the UK, philosophy
professor Kathleen Stock was effectively hounded out of her
job at the University of Sussex for expressing her belief that
biological sex matters and cannot be changed. Stock happens
to be lesbian; she has written movingly about the experience
of coming out and finally being able to tell the truth about
her own sexuality:

For lesbians in particular, the shame-inducing narrative of one's attraction to women is likely to meet other shame-inducing cultural scripts for women, exponentially increasing self-loathing. The combined effects of such scripts — predicting deviancy, failed femininity, and strangeness — are still alive and kicking. They are especially pertinent for some younger lesbians, or so they tell me.[77]

She repeatedly declared her support for trans people's right to legal recognition of their identities and protection from discrimination, violence, and harassment, but didn't accept that this should require her to accept that people can quite literally change sex.[78] After angry student protests and denunciation by several colleagues on social media, Stock resigned. Similarly, in spring 2022, a student at a private girls' school in England who suffered sustained and "enforced public shaming" because she asked questions of a visiting politician about her definitions of sex and gender, subsequently self-harmed on school premises and was forced by the school to leave and study at home.[79]

It's important to recognize that abuse — whether in person or online — clearly affects people on all sides of this issue; Shon Faye, along with many other trans activists, was forced to permanently delete her Twitter account in 2021 because of incessant trolling. Seemingly uncrossable battle lines between two diametrically opposed sides have now been drawn. In some quarters, as Kathleen Stock experienced, to suggest that the deeply embodied experiences of those human beings who are born with two X chromosomes (the profoundly transformative, life-changing potential for menstruation, pregnancy, giving birth, menopause) might make them different (not better — just different) from people who have an X and a Y chromosome and so can't experience these

things,* is now taken to be evidence of transphobia. Even
to refer to people with two X chromosomes as "women"
these days can be problematic; we're increasingly now
described by governments, companies, charities, and media
outlets, as "people who menstruate," "pregnant people," and
"chestfeeders."

All of this is particularly upsetting to women who fully
support the rights of trans people, or any people, to live in
a way which reflects their authentic self, whichever gender
that may be — and yet who feel that we too should retain
the right to refer to ourselves, and be referred to by others,
by an ancient word which similarly reflects our sense of who
we are. But the state of the profoundly polarized cultural
discourse around these issues right now, whipped up into
frenzy after frenzy on social media, is such that nuance gets
lost. And so too, after long, painful centuries of fighting for
them, can the notion of women's rights as something that
must be preserved while we're going through the profound
and necessary cultural changes which will allow people with
more fluid, or different, gender identities to live in safety
and peace.

The main concern of most of the women who are asking
that biological men who self-identify as women should be
prevented from accessing women-only safe spaces isn't — as
far as I've been able to determine — to prevent anyone from
living in a way that seems to them to be most authentic,
but simply to insist that the reality of women's experience,
and their reasonable fears, must also be acknowledged.
It's easy, perhaps — especially for those who haven't lived

---

* It's often stated, during discussions about sex and gender, that
biological sex is assigned at birth by the appearance of a baby's
genitals. But biological sex is actually determined by the particular
combination of chromosomes that we possess; that combination of
chromosomes, which occurs in every cell in the human body except
for gametes, happens also to determine the appearance of our genitals.

through long decades of fighting for things which we now take for granted — to forget how difficult the many battles for women's rights have been, and to understand that in so many areas of life we still haven't achieved anything remotely resembling equality with men. We seem to have made little progress on sexual and domestic violence. It's important that we consider these reasonable concerns in the context of equally reasonable concerns expressed by transgender people for their own safety, in a world in which they're also subjected to violence and abuse: trans people must have safe spaces too. Nevertheless, the concerns which older women have expressed about an ideology which they perceive as stripping away women's rights and protections have been ridiculed on Twitter as evidence of "old lady feminism." Susan Dalgety, in the *Scotsman* newspaper, recently sought to remind younger activists of the decades-long feminist legacy that they take for granted:

> Along the way, you will have benefited from the changes in society secured by those old lady feminists. Because it was those women, the very people you now scoff at, who fought for — and won — domestic abuse shelters, rape crisis centres, equal pay legislation, the right to choose... They marched with their brothers to secure gay rights. They protested wars, nuclear weapons, climate change. And they have lived experience of the intersectionality of class, race, disability, sexual orientation and yes, age, that affects all women. These old lady feminists changed your world for the better, and they are still doing it.[80]

In July 2020, referring to discussions around gender ideology and similar issues, 150 leading authors, academics, and thinkers from around the world — including elder-women writers Margaret Atwood and Gloria Steinem — signed a letter published in *Harper's Magazine* in which they condemned growing challenges to freedom of expression in higher education, journalism, philanthropy, and the arts.[81] They warned that a "stifling atmosphere" was restricting the exchange of information and ideas and public debate.

> The free exchange of information and ideas, the lifeblood of a liberal society, is daily becoming more constricted. While we have come to expect this on the radical right, censoriousness is also spreading more widely in our culture: an intolerance of opposing views, a vogue for public shaming and ostracism, and the tendency to dissolve complex policy issues in a blinding moral certainty.

It doesn't, of course, have to be this way. In order to be a truth-teller, you don't have to anchor yourself firmly to one side of an impossibly divisive debate, and you don't have to join in the shouting competitions on increasingly shrill and polarized social media platforms. You don't actually have to shout at all. You can express the truth that you believe in with dignity and empathy, and by living it in a way that, to paraphrase the Hippocratic Oath, above all does no harm.

A particularly apposite example of this can be found in the person of Jan Morris, who I first came to love when, a couple of years after my mother had moved to Wales and married a Welsh sheep farmer, she presented me with a copy of Morris's *The Matter of Wales: Epic Views of a Small Country*. It is still one of my favorite books about the notion of a sense of place: poetic, insightful, incredibly enriching. I was a good long way into the book before I happened across the information, somewhere, that Jan Morris had spent the first half of her life as James Morris, a soldier in the British military who subsequently found international acclaim for his chronicles of Sir Edmund Hillary's historic ascent of Mount Everest. The second half of her life was spent as one of the most famous transgender women in the world, and a celebrated writer of nonfiction. At twenty-two, while living in Cairo and working for the local Arab News Agency, Morris met and married Elizabeth Tuckniss, the daughter of a British tea planter. The couple had four children and stayed together, first as husband and wife, then as ex-spouses, and finally as domestic partners, for the rest of Morris's life — around seventy years. Morris, much loved and deeply respected by so many, died in Wales in 2020, at the age of ninety-four.

Jan Morris's remarkable, slim memoir of transitioning, *Conundrum*, epitomizes this altogether different way of truth-telling, emerging naturally out of the gentle and intensely lucid way of being in the world that she embraced during her long and rich life. Morris helps us to understand and empathize with the phenomenon that we now call gender dysphoria by fully interrogating her own experience of it — with compassion, honesty, and profound understanding of the complexities of the human condition. *Conundrum* is an exquisitely beautiful read; it offers up insights into an experience which most of us will never have, and at the same time, illuminates new aspects of a struggle that all of us will face in one form or another during our lives: the struggle for belonging, meaning, and authenticity. Morris's epiphany came early: she describes, at just three years old, sitting under a piano that her mother was playing, very distinctly feeling as if she had been born into the wrong body. The conviction, she writes, was unfaltering from the start — and indeed, it never faded, in spite of the challenges

of repeated surgery and hormone treatment during her
transition.

> Trans-sexualism...is not a sexual mode or
> preference. It is not an act of sex at all. It is a
> passionate, lifelong, ineradicable conviction,
> and no true trans-sexual has ever been disabused
> of it...I equate it with the idea of soul, or self,
> and I think of it not just as a sexual enigma,
> but as a quest for unity. For me every aspect of
> my life is relevant to that quest — not only the
> sexual impulses, but all the sights, sounds, and
> smells of memory, the influences of buildings,
> landscapes, comradeships, the power of love
> and of sorrow, the satisfactions of the senses as
> of the body. In my mind it is a subject far wider
> than sex: I recognize no pruriency to it, and I
> see it above all as a dilemma neither of the body
> nor of the brain, but of the spirit.

Morris published *Conundrum* in 1974, when most
people's understanding of gender dysphoria was limited,
and when, for all her own visibility — she wrote more than
forty books, which stretch across her life as a man and then
as a woman almost equally — the subject was rarely spoken
about in public. By writing *Conundrum*, Morris bravely
brought her perspective on gender identity into the open.[82]
And that perspective is one that we might still do well to be
informed by today:

> Gender...is a more nebulous entity, however
> you conceive it. It lives in cavities. It cannot
> be computerised or tabulated. It transcends
> the body as it defies the test tube, yet the

consciousness of it can be so powerful that it
can drive someone like me relentlessly and
unerringly through every stage of life.

Morris was forty-eight at the time of writing, and a
particularly fine exemplar of what so many older women
discover: that understanding and articulating our inner
truth becomes something of an imperative as we age. And
so, for me, the most beautiful passage in *Conundrum* is
Morris's celebration of elder women:

> Distilled from those sacramental fancies of my
> childhood has come the conviction that the
> nearest humanity approaches to perfection is in
> the persons of good women — and especially
> perhaps in the persons of kind, intelligent and
> healthy women past their menopause, no longer
> shackled by the mechanisms of sex but creative
> still in other kinds, aware still in their love and
> sensuality, graceful in experience, past ambition
> but never beyond aspiration. In all countries,
> among all races, on the whole these are the
> people I most admire: and it is into their ranks,
> I flatter myself, if only in the rear file, if only on
> the flank, that I have now admitted myself.[83]

It would be difficult to find a more perfect expression of
hagitude.

In all such discussions, it's important to remember that there
is rarely just one single truth operating in any particular
situation; indeed, there are quite different kinds of truths at
work in the wider world. "The truth" can sometimes refer
to undeniable scientific or objective facts, and sometimes

we use the word to refer to our own personal, subjective sense of what is true for us. Philosophers disagree about what truth is; different theories abound, and many of them challenge the notion that truth and falsehood are simple binaries. Many writers and artists believe that art can be a way of expressing, and even acquiring, truth:[84] William Wordsworth, for example, argued for a "poet's truth" which sees deep into the heart of things, and by expressing its discoveries, enables others to see in the same way. Poetic truth in this sense, he believed, binds humans together with love and a sense of oneness.

Wordsworth's contemporary, John Keats, ended his poem "Ode on a Grecian Urn" with these lines: "Beauty is truth, truth beauty — that is all ye know on earth, and all ye need to know." Here, Keats is representing the philosophy of Plato who — in the simplest terms — believed that Beauty and Truth are virtues which descend from Goodness (a facet of the Divine); all things can be judged in terms of these virtues. Knowledge, for example, which comes from the Good, is only worthwhile when it can be judged as both truthful and beautiful. And I believe that there is a complex, poetic kind of truth and beauty in Jan Morris's deeply personal perspective on sex and gender, just as there is an equally necessary recognition of the value of objective truth in the work of Kathleen Stock and other "gender-critical feminists."

The truth is that truth is complicated these days. It's become something of a cliché recently to declare that we're living in a "post-truth" age; according to the Oxford Dictionaries online, "post-truth" — their "word of the year" in 2016 — means "relating to or denoting circumstances in which objective facts are less influential in shaping public opinion than appeals to emotion and personal belief."[85] And when large numbers of scientists and journalists seem to be afraid to speak what they believe to be true for fear of losing their jobs or being tried in the kangaroo court of social media, we certainly find ourselves living in very dangerous times. I believe that a growing contempt for truth — especially in the political arena — along with a growing inability of people to evaluate complex or multiple truths, is (with the current environmental crisis excepted) one of the greatest threats to freedom and democracy that we've faced here in the West for a very long time.

Whatever the genuine complexities of the situation, it nevertheless seems to me that we've been in this same place — where women are threatened and denounced for simply insisting on the reality of their own embodied experience — many times before. Not least, during the long, dangerous centuries of the witch trials. The disregard we're increasingly seeing for women's fears and realities — not just in debates about gender, but in issues around safety — seems to represent nothing less than a new era of witch hunts. And so women have once again grown afraid of expressing their beliefs for fear of being "canceled," or publicly excoriated, or mostly both. As older women, I think we can sometimes fear truth-telling more than most; over the centuries, we've been burned at too many stakes not to. It's always been too easy to silence us, and we've had few champions other than ourselves. This deeply ingrained and often very visceral fear of the consequences of holding unpopular beliefs, or challenging the cultural orthodoxy, is one of a cluster of characteristics that has been called the "witch wound." Centuries down the line, it still holds us back. Centuries down the line, society seems to have learned nothing.

As we grow older, we have to be able to leave the world that we know behind, and allow it to change — perhaps in ways that we dislike, or find hard to understand. We have to let go of it. But that doesn't mean that we also have to wash our hands of it. Sometimes, we need to tell uncomfortable truths, and to warn about problems that maybe only we, with our many decades of lived experience, can see coming. But all we can do is pass our wisdom on; the world might not listen to our warnings, and we need to be able to accept that too. People — even people who we might expect to understand us better — will purse their lips and roll their eyes; will dismiss us completely or mutter that we're overreacting, or out of touch with the zeitgeist. People would often prefer the women who challenge the cultural mythology and insist on engaging with "forbidden" issues to just keep quiet and stop rocking the boat. Sometimes that can be difficult, and often the reactions of others can be hurtful. But nevertheless, in a world which is still, and in ever-more-inventive ways, dangerous for us, and especially in a world which is still dominated by patriarchal values and structures, we need our elder-woman truth-tellers today more than ever. We need women who will challenge the worst excesses of the patriarchy, and who won't pull their punches while they're doing it.

One of my earliest heroines, who did precisely that, is Australian feminist icon Germaine Greer. Greer rocked the West, and especially the worlds of its women, with her book *The Female Eunuch*, which she wrote in 1970 when she was thirty-one. Now, in her early eighties, she still refuses to play nice and pander to cultural orthodoxies. Whatever you think of her outspokenness and her occasional glaring insensitivities, Greer is nothing if not fiercely interesting. She might sometimes be outrageous, but she is incontrovertibly astute. It was clear from the start that Greer has never been motivated by a desire to be loved. "Hopefully this book is subversive. Hopefully it will draw fire from all the articulate sections of the community," she wrote at the beginning of *The Female Eunuch*. The book was certainly subversive, and it did indeed draw fire — just as her opinions do to this day. Greer is cast as a "scold" by many because she speaks uncomfortable truths, and speaks them with wit and force. But she's one of a band of brave women who have fought this hardest of battles not only on behalf of their own generation, but for the future of generations to come.

Germaine Greer is a fine — if sometimes exhausting — example of the archetypal elder woman as truth-teller: the woman who speaks out against moral failings and other great wrongs in the world. The woman who speaks what no one else dares, and what no one else can — because she has both the lived authority and (relatively) little to lose; the one who knows when it's time to say "Enough" or "No More." The truth-teller reminds us that, if we will only open ourselves up to the possibility, the journey to elderhood can return our silenced voice to us.

My favorite mythical truth-telling hag is the fierce and wondrous Cundrie,* from Wolfram von Eschenbach's thirteenth-century Grail romance, *Parzival*. Cundrie is the classic Loathly Lady: "A plait of her hair fell down over her hat and dangled on her mule — it was long, black, tough, not altogether lovely, about as soft as boar's bristles. Her nose was like a dog's, and to the length of several spans a pair of tusks jutted from her jaws. Both eyebrows pushed past her hair-band and drooped down in tresses... Cundrie's ears resembled a boar's." In a particularly fine example of the art of understatement, von Eschenbach concludes that Cundrie "did not look like a lady." In addition, he says, "Her mouth suffered from no impediment, for what it said was

---

* The original Cundrie is quite different from the vision of Kundry offered in Richard Wagner's opera *Parsifal*, where she is portrayed as an enchantress who tempted Amfortas, the Fisher King, into the sin that caused his wound.

quite enough. With it she flattened much joy upstanding."
Cundrie, then, clearly didn't mince her words, and men
didn't much like it. But Cundrie was so much more than an
ugly face and an outspoken disposition: her nickname, we
are told, was The Sorceress; she spoke all known languages,
and had mastered dialectics, geometry, and astronomy, and
the healing arts.

In chapter 3, we met one of the most famous "Loathly
Ladies" in Irish mythology: the hag by the well, encountered
by Niall and the other sons of Eochaid Mugmedón, who
represented the quality of Sovereignty. In the Grail literature,
the Loathly Lady serves a different (but not entirely
unrelated) purpose. She is the "Grail messenger," a keeper
of the Grail mysteries, and the bearer of the Grail itself; she
determines the fitness of heroes to become the protector
of the Grail, and chastises them when they lose their way.
And so Cundrie, wild, terrible but educated hag that she is,
must above all be a truth-teller. With the piercing vision of
a bird of prey, she sees right to the heart of people and the
situations they find themselves in. And she doesn't hesitate
to let them know how she feels about all that — whether it
"flattens much joy upstanding," or not.

Parzival is a long and complex story, but here is a brief
summary. The young and rather foolish Parzival, who is
eager to become a knight, leaves his mother and the forest
home in which he has led a secluded and sheltered life. He
finds his way to the court of King Arthur, but is judged
there to be too young and unready to become a knight
of the Round Table. Later, after many adventures and
misadventures, he is deemed to have proven himself and is
finally granted knighthood. But when one day he stumbles
across the Grail Castle and visits the invalided Grail King,
he stays spectacularly silent in the face of many wonders,
and then fails to ask the one obvious question — a question

that would also happen to release the old man from his suffering — "What ails thee?" And so, as he sits chatting with the other knights after finding his way back to Arthur's court, the hideous Cundrie rides in from the forest and curses him for his failure to ask that all-important question. Cundrie sees, in Arthur's court, a world which is full of finery — but also full of falsity, and one which is lacking in heart. She sees, in Parzival, a young man who might be part of that seemingly great and sophisticated society — but to her he too is false, and lacking in "manly virtues." Cundrie is the perfect contrast to Parzival: she is outwardly ugly, but filled with inner beauty; he is outwardly handsome, but lacking in inner beauty. Cundrie tells him:

> A curse on your beautiful visage
> And your manly limbs.
> Had I conciliation or peace to give
> You would find them both hard to come by.
> I seem an unnatural monster to you,
> And yet I am more natural than you are — [86]

— more natural, because she follows her inner convictions, rather than meaningless rules dictated by a rigid and narcissistic culture. She curses Parzival because he is lacking in compassion and other genuine emotions — and, as if to show him what such a thing might look like, she allows her own emotions to freely flow. Eventually, though, her compassion gets the better of her anger, and she weeps. Upon which, having made Parzival brutally aware of the aridity of his own soul, she turns and simply rides away.

Her harsh words create a moral imperative for the shattered Parzival: his challenge now is to reimagine himself, so that his handsome body will also contain a beautiful heart. But Parzival's first reaction is to curse God, whom he believes has turned against him. When finally he encounters an old hermit who helps him understand the true nature of divinity, Parzival reaches a turning point in his personal and spiritual development. We then see Cundrie for a second time, as she comes to tell Parzival that he has now been elected to the Grail Company as the new King of the Grail, and she acts as his guide on the journey to take up its guardianship. This time, Cundrie comes to him veiled, clearly bearing the insignia of the Grail, and on a fine horse. She apologizes to Parzival for having doubted him, and so adds dignity to her long list of virtues. He returns with her to the ailing Grail King, and this time, having gained much wisdom as well as compassion, he understands the question that must be asked.

One of the reasons why I find Cundrie so interesting is that, in her first appearance, she epitomizes righteous wrath. Not mere rage, or anger, but wrath. Cundrie is the voice and guardian of the Grail, the voice and guardian of the Earth, and she demands that people take its tasks seriously, and perform them well. She demands that they examine themselves honestly, and face up to the truth. She refuses to allow Parzival to rest on his (frankly, modest) laurels, and to sit around at feasts feeling pleased with himself. She wants him out in the world again, doing what he is called to do. Cundrie, that gloriously loathly, truth-telling hag, is the gnarly old tree root which trips us up when we fall into complacency or otherwise lose our way. She's the truth which can't be ignored. She might be frightening, but all she wants is for each of us to get up and set about doing what we were called to do. When we do that, she'll be the first to cheer us along, as Parzival finds out when he meets her for a second time. And in the end, she'll treat us with compassion.

The Loathly Lady character epitomized by Cundrie is reflected in most other Grail stories. In the medieval Welsh tale of *Peredur*, in which the main character is also re-proached by a Loathly Lady for not having asked the Lame King about the Spear and the Dish at this story's equivalent of the Grail Castle, she reappears in the story to berate Peredur whenever he falls short of her expectations. In Chrétien de Troyes's *Perceval*, the Loathly Lady is a hideous old woman with rat-like eyes, long ears, and a beard, riding a mule; she tells Perceval that if he had had the wit to ask the "Grail question" then the Fisher King would have been healed and the Wasteland restored. In the Didot *Perceval*, the Loathly Lady is called Rosete li Bloie, "the Blonde Red One," who sometimes is old and ugly and sometimes beautiful. Another romance, *Perlesvaus*, offers up the bald Maiden of the Cart, who travels around the land carrying messages about the Grail, and offers advice to the Grail-seekers. She is also the Grail-bearer, and keeps her right hand tied up in a sling so that it might never hold anything less sacred than the Grail itself.

As an example of the archetypical truth-teller in con-temporary art, Frances McDormand is gloriously fierce in her performance in the 2017 Oscar-winning movie *Three Billboards Outside Ebbing, Missouri*. She plays grieving small-town mother Mildred, who takes justice into her own hands after the brutal rape and murder of her teenage daughter on a deserted road near the town. Angry over the lack of progress in the investigation after seven long months, Mildred rents three abandoned billboards near her home and posts on them: "Raped While Dying," "And Still No Arrests?," and "How Come, Chief Willoughby?" The billboards upset many of the townspeople, including chief of police Bill Willoughby and the racist, violent, alcoholic officer Jason Dixon. Despite being harassed and receiving threats, and disregarding the objections of her son Robbie, Mildred is determined that the billboards should remain.

Mildred is warrior-like in her quest for justice, striding through her days with jaw clenched, fists tightened, and a bandana around her head, as she absolutely refuses to accept inaction. It's her refusal to back down in the face of disapproval that defines her and makes her admirable, in spite of her clearly depicted flaws.

The movie also had real-life consequences: Mildred's actions inspired a series of copycat responses. In February 2018, Justice4Grenfell, an advocacy group created in response to the Grenfell Tower fire in London, hired three vans with electronic screens in a protest against state inaction in response to the fire. The vans were driven around London, and displayed messages in the style of the billboards in the film: "71 Dead," "And Still No Arrests?," and "How Come?" Similarly, in response to the Stoneman Douglas High School shooting that took place in February 2018 in Parkland, Florida, activist group Avaaz had three vans circle Republican senator Marco Rubio's offices displaying signs declaring: "Slaughtered in School," "And Still No Gun Control?," "How Come, Marco Rubio?" Several other examples followed, across the world.[87]

Although I grew up in a world of outspoken older women, and in a northeastern culture in which bluntness of speech was valued — and the enormity of the insult hurled at you reflected the amount of affection the speaker had for you — as a child I was taught nevertheless that being "nice" was the finest of all feminine virtues. My mother firmly subscribed to the old adage that, when they were asking uncomfortable questions, or challenging "truths" that seemed to make no sense, children should be seen and not heard. It was important, I was told, not to rock the boat. As a child and then a teenager, I took that lesson to heart, and it wasn't until I was well into my thirties that I very slowly began to learn how to challenge others in a way that didn't feel threatening — either to me or to them. But I never really felt comfortable doing so; I always felt as if I were treading on very shaky ground.

In menopause, as I've already described, I lost much of that sense of caution, swept away on a tidal surge of rage at all the iniquities visited on women by the overculture through the millennia. I'd had enough of silenced female voices; I wanted to speak out again, to challenge the perpetrators of abuse and indignity. I wanted to express my perspective on the things that I believed were wrong with the world, and I wanted that perspective to be heard — whether it needed to be heard or not. But the most important thing that I learned during my own personal burning times was that *balance* is a critical part of that sweaty, exhausting journey through menopausal rage: acquiring and finely honing the skill of understanding how much is too much and how much is just enough. It takes a while to learn how to manage the fire which burns in us. We don't want to turn that fierce fire off, and we don't want to let it burn itself out in a conflagration. We need, rather, to learn how to add just enough fuel to keep it burning steadily and surely, and to preserve its beautiful, glowing flames through the rest of our lives.

The wisdom which allows us to carefully tend our inner fires as we grow older also helps us to understand just when it is that truth really needs to be told: when it has the capacity to result in healing and transformation, rather than just destruction. Today's "call-out culture" can mask bullying, and the act of truth-telling can mask rudeness and aggression. What we gain with age is the wisdom to know when and how the truth should be told: when the culture is properly ripe for disruption, and when that disruption will do the most good.

You don't have to look far to find stories of elder women in contemporary life who hold the culture to account. Some of my favorite activists are the "Raging Grannies," members of a group who rely on satire and humor to spread their message.[88] The Grannies, originally mostly comprising white, educated women in their fifties and sixties, began their work in 1987 in Victoria, British Columbia, and quickly spread across Canada. The group was founded in reaction to the health and environmental threats posed by the operations of nuclear-powered or nuclear weapons-carrying US Navy warships and submarines in the waters surrounding Victoria. The Grannies began by experimenting with street theater to make their points, dressing in lab coats and, armed with makeshift Geiger counters and turkey basters, testing water puddles for radiation at popular malls. They then joined a protest at the British Columbia legislature during hearings on uranium mining, and brought with them a laundry basket full of women's underwear, which they said contained the "briefs" they wished to present at the hearings. Their actions, incisive but always good-humored, proved to be hugely popular, and from then on the Grannies adopted increasingly colorful clothing to play on cultural stereotypes of older women, wrote witty and satirical songs, and succeeded in challenging authority through the simple power of irreverence.

According to their website, the delights of grannying include: "dressing like innocent little old ladies so we can get close to our 'target,' writing songs from old favorites that skewer modern wrongs, satirizing evil-doing in public and getting everyone singing about it, watching a wrong back down and turn tail and run, sharing a history with other women who know who they are and what they're about." Their actions are archetypically Tricksterish, employing apparently simple buffoonery to highlight the futility of contemporary power structures — and the frequent foolishness of those who hold that power. And in doing so, they have managed to empower themselves in a world which disparages the experience of older women and consistently discounts their point of view, so turning their identity, which ought to be a liability, into an asset. "Grannies are best equipped to make public, corrupt things that have been hidden (often for profit)," their website declares. "Grannying is the least understood yet most powerful weapon we have. Sometimes, looking back, we can see grannying was the only thing that could have met the need. ... From the most ancient times, the strong, wise, older women were the ones who advised, mediated and fought for what was right."

If that isn't hagitude, I don't know what is — and the Grannies' willingness to engage with a challenged and challenging culture in these ways certainly reflects a much-needed optimism about the value of elder women today.

8

THE WISE WOMAN

Deep Vision

Not all of my found objects are "natural," although all of them have been found in nature. On the windowsill next to my desk is a small pale-blue bottle — well, perhaps closer to aqua than pure blue — which I came across when I lived in Connemara. There, on the shorcline of the village lake, with its roots firmly embedded in a cluster of gigantic granite rocks, was a solitary hawthorn tree. Right beside it, hidden in a deep hollow created by the rocks, one day I discovered a pile of bottles. Most of them were of fairly recent vintage — a good stack of Guinness bottles, for sure — but there was a handful of anomalies, and among them was this flat, battered, and rather older bottle. I called the tree the Bottle Tree — a name which I hope wasn't too disrespectful to a hawthorn tree which, especially when it stands alone, is known in the Irish folk tradition to be home to the Good People: the fairies.

It amused me to find a blue bottle there among the roots of a fairy tree, because it reminded me of the famous blue bottle which belonged to legendary County Clare wise woman Biddy Early, and through which it was said she could see into the Otherworld. It was the denizens of that Otherworld — the fairies — who gave the bottle to her, or so the story goes. The fairies were responsible for Biddy's deep knowledge, and her ability as a consequence to foresee the future, spy on her neighbors, and determine the location of lost objects and animals. Biddy's knowledge and healing skills, then, were attributed to her personal interactions with the Otherworld, and because it was believed that she consorted with the fairies at night to obtain useful knowledge which she brought back into the community, folklorist Nancy Schmitz has suggested that she, and wise women like her, would have fulfilled a similar function to that of the village shaman in indigenous cultures through the ages.[89]

I have to admit that I've never seen into the future or the Otherworld when looking into my own little blue bottle, but I'm fond of the connection to Biddy nevertheless. She is perhaps the most famous wise woman in Ireland, and her reputation was such that people traveled from great distances to see her. Biddy is believed to have been born around 1798, and was said to be a benevolent but forthright and strong-willed woman; she took her mother's surname rather than her father's; she drank, smoked, played cards, refused to attend Mass, ignored the priests, and had a liking (especially when she was old) for husbands far younger than herself.

Biddy wasn't interested in normal healing methods; although she would offer the occasional herbal remedy in connection with her other skills, she would step in only if an individual couldn't be cured by traditional means. In that case, the problem at hand would be presumed to result from a supernatural cause, and Biddy would begin to ask whether the person in question might have disturbed the fairies on their particular ground — by plowing across a fairy ring, for example, or blocking a fairy path — or whether certain necessary prescriptions and rituals — such as saying "God bless" in the right places and at the right times — might not have been observed.

This particular approach to healing, employed by Biddy Early, is typical of the archetypal Wise Woman who's known in the Irish language as the *bean feasa* — which literally means the "woman of knowledge." The *bean feasa* is different from the *bean leighis*, the "woman of healing," who (like the bonesetter and herbalist) used traditional physical healing methods. What specifically characterizes the *bean feasa*, and differentiates her from other healers, is that her methods are predominantly symbolic. In her primary role as a mediator between the community and the Otherworld, the native Irish wise woman was part spiritual guide and part folk psychologist. As a psychologist, she was called upon to heal emotional and psychosomatic disorders for which, in those earlier times, there was no other treatment. Her spiritual role involved establishing a kind of equilibrium between the two worlds, which would in turn foster spiritual equilibrium within the community. So, for example, certain psychological disturbances were thought to be a consequence of "fairy abductions," the practice of which resulted in a disturbance of the balance between worlds; restoring the abducted individual to something approximating normal function also restored that balance. These ideas, of course, were perfectly natural in a society which believed that both individual and community well-being could only be achieved by maintaining harmonious relationships with Otherworld forces, as well as with the spirit of the land itself.[90]

It's interesting to note that the *bean feasa* was never considered to be a witch. The typical European witch, of the kind that we encountered in chapter 2, was largely unknown in Celtic tradition, and in Ireland only really existed in those areas that were under Norman influence. According to Irish folk belief, access to supernatural power in the form of spells and charms, and admittance to the Otherworld, was available to anyone who wished to make

use of it; no contract with a particular figure of evil, like
the Christian Devil, was necessary to achieve this. It's been
suggested that the character of the *bean feasa*, and the
practice of her particular kinds of powers, might originally
have derived from the female druids — *bandraoi* — who in
more ancient times would similarly have acted as conduits
to the gods and the Otherworld.

Wise Woman characters reminiscent of the *bean feasa*
also existed in Scotland, though they were usually viewed
with much greater suspicion. There, if they were perceived
to be entirely benign, they were often called "cunning folk";
if not, the conventional and more negative label of "witch"
would be attached to them. The bar was quite high; for
example, Edinburgh wise woman Bessie Dunlop delivered
babies, healed the sick, consoled the bereaved, identified
criminals, and recovered lost and stolen goods — and yet
was tried for witchcraft in 1576. Like many others killed as
"witches," she attributed her powers to a spirit — a ghost,
perhaps — whom she called Tom Reid. In line with Nancy
Schmitz's suggestion, folklorist Emma Wilby in her book
Cunning Folk and Familiar Spirits draws parallels between
cunning folk and the shamans of Siberia and the Americas,
arguing that they entered into similarly "visionary" altered
states of mind to access the Otherworld.[91] Both the cunning
woman and the *bean feasa*, then, acted as a kind of
oracle — an individual who could see into the true meaning
and nature of events and situations, and discover the course
of action which should be pursued to restore cosmic, social,
and psychological harmony. Or, in other words, to transmit
to the community the wishes and insights of the gods.

Wise or cunning women like Biddy Early aren't the only
oracles in the history and folklore of these islands; in the
Orkney tradition, a character known as the spaewife
acted as a prophetess, seer, and diviner. The name has

been used as the title of several literary works, including Robert Louis Stevenson's poem "The Spaewife"; John Galt's 1823 historical romance, *The Spaewife: A Tale of the Scottish Chronicles*, and Paul Peppergrass's 1871 novel *The Spaewife, or, The Queen's Secret: A Story of the Reign of Elizabeth*. According to the nineteenth-century Orkney folklorist Walter Traill Dennison, the Orcadian spaewife was said to possess "all the supernatural wisdom, some of the supernatural power, without any of the malevolent spirit of witches... The women of this class were skilled in medicinal and surgery, in dreams, in foresight and second-sight, and in forestalling the evil influence of witchcraft."[92]

The character of the spaewife originally derives from Norse folklore, in which she was called a *spákona* or *spækona* — a seeress — and stories of such women are found throughout Norse mythology. But they're not just mythical beings: archaeologists have identified several graves that may contain the remains of Scandinavian seeresses. These graves contain objects that are believed to be wands, seeds with hallucinogenic and aphrodisiac properties, and a variety of objects associated with high status, such as jewelry.

Mentions of Germanic seeresses occur throughout the Roman era, during which period they're known to have played a role in leading rebellions against Roman rule, as well as occasionally acting as envoys to Rome. According to Tacitus in his book *Germania*, the Germanic tribes "believe that there is something holy and an element of the prophetic in women, hence they neither scorn their advice nor ignore their predictions."[93] Greek historian and geographer Strabo wrote of the Germanic Cimbri tribe that:

> Their wives, who would accompany them to their expeditions, were attended by priestesses who were seers; these were grey-haired, clad in white, with flaxen cloaks fastened on with

clasps, girt with girdles of bronze, and bare-
footed; now sword in hand these priestesses
would meet with prisoners of war throughout
the camp, and would lead them to a brazen
vessel of about twenty amphorae; and they had
raised a platform which the priestess would
mount, and then, bending over the kettle, would
cut the throat of each prisoner after he had been
lifted up; and from the blood that poured forth
into the vessel, some of the priestesses would
draw a prophecy, while still others would split
open the body and from an inspection of the
entrails would utter a prophecy of victory for
their own people; and during the battles they
would beat on the hides that were stretched
over the wicker-bodies of the wagons and in
this way would produce an unearthly noise.[94]

Elder-woman seeresses were clearly common throughout
Europe, then, but the best known of them is probably the
oracle at Apollo's temple in Delphi, who was called the
Pythia. For many centuries, women acted as the priestesses
and mouthpieces of the god, but we know very little about
them, or why and how they were chosen. Plutarch, though,
tells us that when the Pythia fulfilled her prophetic role, "she
does so quite artlessly and without any special knowledge
or talent."[95] One of the more interesting things that we do
know is that it came to be necessary for the Pythia to be a
woman over fifty, to avoid a focus on her sexuality and to
reduce the risk of her being violated.

The Pythia wasn't a fortune-teller, and she wasn't
consulted for anything so unsubtle as what might be going
to happen in the future. Rather, she would be approached
for advice about a particular situation: for example, on how
a specific goal might be achieved. Her role, then, seemed

to be focused on offering guidance rather than simple revelation, and her responses, as far as we can tell, seemed to be purposefully ambiguous. Apollo himself was known as Apollo Loxias, "the ambiguous one," but according to Plutarch, this ambiguity would also have been adopted in part to protect the Pythia from the powerful people who came to consult her. Historian Michael Scott notes that the Pythia was particularly useful at moments of community indecision. After the oracle had offered her advice, it was often sent back to the community for continued deliberation; the initial visit to the oracle, then, paved the way for the community to make its own decisions. The oracle, he suggests, didn't so much offer a fortune-telling service as provide a sense-making mechanism.[96]

Although there's inevitably been a good deal of skepticism about it in these more rational times — particularly given the known ambiguity of the Pythia's "prophecies" — the oracle as an institution was nevertheless considered to be useful in Greece for over a thousand years. In his last novel, *The Double Tongue*, William Golding addressed this question of belief and skepticism head-on. The manuscript was left in draft form at the author's death in 1993, but it was published anyway; it is the fictional memoir of a prophetess at Delphi who is, at the time of recounting her story, now in her eighties. As a young girl, Arieka is ugly, unconventional, and a source of great shame to her parents, who fear they will never find a husband for her. However, she makes some chance remarks which give her a reputation for prophecy; as a consequence, she comes to the attention of Ionides, the High Priest of the Delphic temple, who manages the shrine and selects the candidates who train to become oracles. Ionides takes her off to Delphi to become one of them. But Arieka is shocked when Ionides casually expresses disbelief in the gods, and fears divine wrath when she learns about the politicking which goes on behind the scenes at the Delphi shrine. Nevertheless, she respects Ionides's desire to bolster the declining importance of the oracle. "In the old days, when Hellas was great," he tells her, "the replies to questions came in hexameters, poetry, elevated speech, because the questions were elevated ones." And so he encourages Arieka to read books to educate herself, and eventually she serves as the Pythia — the earthly voice of Apollo. Interestingly, Golding writes of Apollo metaphorically raping Arieka by forcibly impregnating her with the seed of oracular truth: "The god would have me there in the holy seat whether I would or no, oh yes, it was a rape, this was Apollo who fitted me in the seat, twisted me anyway he would, then left me" — but it is the conflict between belief and skepticism that lies at the heart of the novel. Does a god really speak through the Pythia, or is she simply imagining it? As Arieka grows older, this question remains at the center of her life.

For the first forty years of my life, I was caught up in a similar conflict between belief and skepticism. My childhood belief in "magic," which lingered on during my teenage years as a sense of wonder and possibility in the world, was pretty much wiped out after three years of a profoundly scientistic psychology degree in which we were taught not only to question everything, but to disbelieve everything. The part of me that still dreamed, and insisted there was more to life than this, was locked away neatly in a shadowy corner of my psyche, and it wasn't until I was in my late thirties that a series of "big dreams" and remarkable synchronicities reawakened that old sense of mystery. The rekindled sense of possibility which I experienced as a consequence amounted to a belief in something more than a dead, purposeless universe in which the only reasonable "religion" was centered around the doctrine of rationalism, but I couldn't have defined my beliefs any more clearly at the time. I wasn't brought up in a religious household, though I spent about a year, when I was fifteen, embedded in an evangelical Christian church, playing the guitar and earnestly belting out "Lord of the Dance" along with everyone else. It was one of those odd, and later profoundly embarrassing, teenage blips — the ones that happen when you're trying desperately to find something, anything, to belong to. But I just couldn't retain a belief — and frankly, didn't want to retain a belief — in the rather misogynistic and largely unforgiving God of the Old Testament, and by the time I'd educated myself about atrocities committed in the name of the New Testament God by the Christian Church over the centuries, I didn't much want to believe in him, either.

In my late thirties, a series of happenings — which I described in more detail in *If Women Rose Rooted* — led me to discover the hitherto completely unknown (to me) world of the Divine Feminine. I'd really never imagined that such a concept existed. In my Western Protestant upbringing, divinity was a purely masculine attribute. The goddesses I'd encountered in Greek myth or Celtic myth were simply fictional characters — or at least, that's how they had always been presented to me. But now, I began to broaden my concept of what spirituality could be, traveling a very long way beyond the "authorized" monotheistic religions that lay at the heart of my formal education about such matters. This kind of spirituality wasn't just about some dictatorial, grumpy, and often misogynistic old man in the sky anymore, and it didn't require men to mediate between humans and the Divine — all this was something that was relevant to actual women, and today. Nevertheless, fine as I found the ideas of the "goddess movement" to be, it didn't make much sense to me to simply replace a male god with a female god, or even several. I was looking for something else; something I couldn't possibly have put words around.

All I knew was that I believed in *something* — something beyond the purely human world; something beyond the purely physical world. Some overarching meaning, or design, or purpose...

My discovery that, in the Celtic tradition, divine women were seen to be immanent in the land, meant that my focus turned to finding a sense of the sacred in the places I lived, and an interest in the spirits of place; my long years of research into the beliefs of our ancestors opened up a whole world of fascinating animistic and panpsychist ideas. Those belief systems grounded me, and connected me to the land and the other-than-humans who occupied it along with me in a way that I'd never begun to imagine before. But it wasn't until I combined these old ideas with the writing of contemporary depth psychologists that I finally found a way of seeing the world that made sense to me. I found it in the work of post-Jungian psychologist James Hillman, and in the work of Henry Corbin, a twentieth-century French theologian and philosopher who wrote extensively about ancient Sufi beliefs and who profoundly influenced Hillman's thought. But, most transformative of all, I found it in reading the ancient Greek philosopher Plato.

Philosophers in Plato's tradition believed that the cosmos was brought into being by a divine "creator" being who infused soul throughout the cosmos. That soul — the *anima mundi*, or "soul of the world" — joins all phenomena together, Plato suggested, forming a living ensouled universe of which we are a part. Soul, then, is the underlying principle of reality; the entire universe is a living organism and all levels of being are linked together in it, in an unbreakable chain. As well as being transcendent (at a level of reality beyond or "above" our physical world) the *anima mundi* was also thought to be immanent in the physical world, just as traditional animistic cultures have always imagined it; soul, then, is present in all matter. Following Plato, Aristotle went on to suggest that the cosmos is itself in a flow of becoming, and that we (along with all other-than-human beings in the world) are a critical and necessary part of that ongoing growth and transformation of the cosmos.

These ideas don't just appear in ancient Greek philosophy, but in other traditions too. Henry Corbin used the term *mundus imaginalis* (the "imaginal world") to describe a particular order of reality which is referred to in ancient Sufi texts, and which has many similarities to the Greek concept of the world soul. These texts tell us that, between the physical world of our senses and the world of abstraction, of intellect, lies another world: the world of the image — and a world that is just as real as either of these other two. The *mundus imaginalis* is the stomping ground of the *anima mundi*. It's the place that all spiritual and transcendent experience comes from. It's the source of synchronicities, of "psychic" experiences and creative insights; it penetrates into our dreams and other visionary experiences, including the places we visit during deep meditation or imaginal journeying. This imaginal world can be perceived by what Corbin called the "psycho-spiritual senses," and it communicates itself to human beings through images, so that the act of imagining then becomes an act of connection to it. Corbin was quick to differentiate between the simple everyday acts of daydreaming and fantasizing (which are what we often mean today when we speak about "imagining") and the reality of this world of archetypes and visions.

The imaginal world is one of the many layers of reality which all ancient spiritual traditions, in one way or another, tell us are layered around this world that we perceive with our physical senses (the physical world which, our "enlightened" Western culture insists, is the only one that is "real"). As I mentioned in chapter 2, the idea of an Otherworld (or several) which penetrates and is entangled with this one has always been a defining feature of Celtic culture and literature. And so the Otherworld, or imaginal world, is the place where the Others dwell: the archetypal energies and beings which, when clothed in the garments of a particular culture, we sometimes call gods and goddesses. And the psychopomps, or soul guides, who James Hillman called the "necessary angels." To fully engage with psyche — with our own soul, with the soul of this beautiful planet, and with the cosmos itself — we need to engage with these images and archetypes. Because the imaginal realm is not an unreal fantasy or an abstraction or a metaphor: it's the very basis of reality. If you're cut off from it, then, as our super-rationalistic culture has caused most of us to become, you're not really fully alive. You're walking through the world as if you were wearing a veil. You're out of touch with your own soul and with the soul of the world. You have no anchors, no guides. You're adrift and lost in a world which has no meaning.

In reacquainting myself with these old ideas, I began (without abandoning my practice of building relationship with the land) to think about the ways in which the imagination-based techniques I'd once used in therapeutic practice, and in the practice of mythic imagination which I now teach, could help me delve more deeply into the imaginal world. Because it's my belief in an imaginal world, my daily engagement with my dreams, with myth and story, and other acts of imagination, which allows me to develop my own deep vision: to understand the deeper nature of the world around me, and to discern my own path within it.

We might not have direct equivalents of the Delphic Oracles today — women who are part of an established religious or spiritual order, who pass on the wisdom of the gods to all, and have it accepted — and given the damage done by centuries of religious dogma and hierarchy here in the West, that's probably a good thing. But we do have women with

deep vision, whose various personal spiritual practices lead
them to insights and so to projects which directly address the
problems we're facing in this ever-more-challenging world.
I'm very glad to know one of those women and to count
her — along with her partner, Faith, who we met in chapter
5 — as a friend. Manda Scott is best known as a writer, and
I first came across her through her wonderful series of books
about Boudica. Manda also describes herself as a veterinary
surgeon, a podcaster, a sustainable economist, regenerative
farmer, conscious revolutionary — and shamanic teacher.

Unlike many contemporary spiritual systems that describe themselves as shamanic, Manda's teaching is based
on her conceptualization of what our ancestral traditions
might have been, right here in these lands we inhabit. In
her Boudica novels,[97] she conceived of a practice which she
calls "shamanic dreaming," in which the characters connect
with the gods of the land through waking and sleeping
dreams, becoming channels for healing, wisdom — and a
degree of foretelling. "Nothing is perfect," Manda stresses
when we talk about it: "this is not a Disney reality where
every foretelling is precise and every healing staves off dead
and suffering forever. Rather, it's a melding with the weave
of the world, which enables the dreamer and her tribe to
walk more lightly on the earth, to exist as companions of
the gods rather than servants, to have agency and a sense of
a life lived in partnership with the living world."

These practices aren't just fictional constructs to Manda;
she believes these practices are just as important today, and
so she runs courses and workshops in which she teaches
them. "A life built around these practices is focused on a
constant search for the authentic self, and the connections
we can build from it to the world around us: the rocks and
the rivers, the mountains and the moorland, the squirrel in
the city park, the pattern of water on a pond," she explains.
But although she acknowledges the connection with other

shamanic traditions around the world, she is nevertheless hesitant to use the label "shaman" for those who do this work. "We're not being shamans when we do these practices," she insists. "We're using the tools of shamanic practice to help our lives and, ultimately, those around us. That doesn't make us shamans. We don't live the way our forager-hunter forebears did — or those in shamanic cultures still existing — whose entire lives were and are an integral part of the world around them. We can't return to that, and there's no point in pretending that we can. We live in the twenty-first century, in the Anthropocene age, a time when our presence here has pushed us to the brink of, if not yet actually into, ecosystem collapse.

"But what this kind of shamanic practice offers us is the ability to find our place in the world and on the earth. With discipline, practice, and commitment, we can learn to walk with clear intent and full awareness, and to offer ourselves as the connection between those spirits that guide us, whatever we might call them — the gods, the guides, ultimately, the heart-mind of the Universe — and the Earth. We can do it moment by moment: sitting, walking, running. We can do it as we eat, as we take a shower, as we wait for a train. We can do it waking and sleeping. In the end, this is what it all comes down to — that we're fully present on this Earth, listening, observing, watching. We become, in a sense, the eyes and limbs of the heart mind of the Universe at this moment, in this place, and the boundaries of the world dissolve and we become part of the matrix of life. We bring a commitment to listen with integrity and clarity, to have done the inner work so that we don't cloud our perception with our own projections, fears, hopes, or ego. This isn't trivial — it feels to me like a constantly unfolding exploration.

"I think this is the end point of all spiritual practice, whatever the creed. But what this kind of shamanic work offers is a living practice without dogma, based on our own moment-by-moment experience. Our teachers aren't long-dead figures from history, but the rain and the wind, the hawthorn and the red kite, the earth beneath our feet, the patterns of a cloud on the shoulders of the mountain."

I'm curious about Manda's own practice, and the process she follows which guides her, often in very specific ways, to follow her own unique path of teaching and writing. "At the moment," she tells me, "we live on the side of a hill in Shropshire, and my daily practice has been to go up to one of two particular places on the land where I feel most still, and to stand or sit and ask, 'What do you want of me?' and let the answer guide my day. I used to go every morning. Quite recently this changed, and I've been invited to go at sunset, to sit for half an hour in one particular place, to be open then, and there, as the sun sinks below the horizon, to experience the daytime world going to sleep and the life of the night coming to wakefulness. The sense of opening that comes with this feels as close to a living embodiment of the fictional dreaming in the Boudica books as I've ever come. But by the time *Hagitude* is published and these words are read, I'm fairly sure things will have shifted and something new will have arisen — that's the nature of things even in ordinary times, and these are no longer ordinary times. In this time of total transformation, we need a flexibility and a willingness to let go of all the old certainties — even about our own practice — as we continue along the path."

It's this dreaming practice which led Manda to begin her latest project, which she calls Accidental Gods. "It all began at the winter solstice of 2018," she tells me. "As we do every year, my partner and I sat with the fire and reflected on the year just gone, then sat with an open mind looking for insight into the year yet to come." I ask her to describe what happens during that period of dreaming with the fire. "Well, my gaze folds into the flames until they fade, and I am out in the void, looking down on the wondrous blue pearl that is our home, soaring through the black-drop of space. This image isn't new: it arose in my childhood when humans first walked on the moon. But in my vision now, it's changing. With the wisdom of hindsight, I would say it's evolving. My ears whine as I watch a fantastically complex web of light spring up, encircling — en-webbing — the Earth. It's night when we sit with the fire, and so the web-light is the frost-silver of the moon. What's most striking is the complexity of this web: the uncountable array of filaments that counter-cross in a weave of impossible intricacy. Each node is connected to every other node — that's the nature of webs, of course — but what becomes apparent is that each is a node of consciousness. Some of these nodes are human, but most are not. Exploring along the lines, I meet trees and rocks, dormice and red kites, mycelial networks, oceans and toads. This is the web of life, and I can *feel* it. I'm a living part of it. I am empty and open, and I am here, fully conscious, fully aware and fully alive in ways that make my heart explode. This is what I am here for. This. To take my part in the web, so open, so clear, so connected that I can ask, 'What do you want of me?' and respond in real time."

I ask Manda how that particular period of dreaming led her to the idea for Accidental Gods. "At that time," she reflects, "the world felt…momentous. As if many things were opening, many things falling way — and through all of it, the horror of the climate and ecological emergency. We didn't grow up believing that we'd be part of the generation that gave itself the capacity to wipe out life on our planet. But here we are — accidental gods — poised on the brink of climate chaos and mass extinction. And yet, it seems to me that we're also poised on the brink of vast potential transformation. I believe that we have the capacity — here, now, in the third decade of the third millennium — to make humanity's next evolutionary step one of consciousness, consciously chosen. No more slow tweaks to DNA — I'm talking about a radical change in the nature of what it is to be human. This is about all of us becoming the best that we can be and then, together, becoming something so much greater than the sum of our individual parts.

"And so, out of that dreaming by the fire, came Accidental Gods — a website, a podcast, a blog, and a membership program.[98] Accidental Gods is about finding ways to facilitate this evolution of consciousness that I'm talking about, because we believe it's possible, necessary — and urgent. It's our job to be open to connection with the more-than-human world and to free ourselves from ego, projection, judgment, and fear so that when each of us asks, 'What do you want of me?' we can hear clear, coherent, constructive answers. Which is to say, we need to ditch the bullshit and self-delusion that can often cloud our capacity to connect. We have the tools to do this. Connection is our heritage and our birthright. It's not that long ago that our ancestors lived fully in connection with the Earth, and there are indigenous peoples across the world who still live this way. We can relearn it."

When we talk about the tools that Manda offers participants in her Accidental Gods program, I find that they're an eclectic mix. "We can use all the ancient and modern tools of meditation and contemplation and harness them to the latest neuroscience — specifically, our understanding of neuroplasticity — to reshape the way we feel/think/act/BE in the world. And if enough of us can do this, then together the whole that we make can be so very much greater than the sum of our parts. So ultimately, the aim with Accidental Gods is to build a worldwide community of people who get this, who want it badly enough to give up the time in each day to connect, to practice coherence, to walk towards the edge of letting go. None of this is trivial, but it's not impossible, either. We can do it. The more we work together, the easier it will be. And then another world becomes possible."

The elder woman who has come to understand the nature of her own journey through life isn't easily disheartened or daunted by the challenges of the world around her. She's been around for long enough, and survived enough troubles and traumas, that she's unlikely to be shocked or overwhelmed by the crises and conflicts that exist in the world around her. She's seen how easy it is for things to fall apart, but she has also experienced renewal, and she knows how to engage in that necessary work of reimagining better ways of being and living in a troubled world. That's why it's so important that, as elder women, we find our own unique way of expressing our own unique gift, our own unique brand of hagitude — because one of the more important of our roles is to encourage the kind of imagination which serves all life on this planet. The elder woman — not only because of her age, but her experience and deep vision — can see ahead; she can predict what might happen and what might go wrong. But, more importantly, her visionary skills can help her to work out how to help put things right again, and how to restore the balance, because in almost all old wisdom traditions around the world, elders act as a living bridge between the visible world and the "unseen" realms — the Otherworld, in whatever ways they might conceive of it.

This role of the elder woman as visionary isn't always an active, "out there" role; sometimes it's associated with a quieter, more inward-looking aspect of elderhood — perhaps a later life stage, in which she has withdrawn to the solitude and darkness of her symbolic cave, in preparation for her impending death. I think of such elders — the ones we generally don't know, or have forgotten, precisely because they no longer choose to be seen by the wider culture (though they are often very visible to their family and their community) — as sages. These old women have left their strivings behind, and in the clarity of all that not-doing, they've made room for the space in which to cultivate deep vision, insight, and wisdom.

This is an image, I admit, that I find very seductive. For the past several years, there's been a tension in my own life between my natural inclination to be a hermit — which goes wonderfully well with the craft of writing — and my other role as teacher and lecturer, which requires me to be much more visible, much more out in the world. Although I love that work and the connection it brings to real live people, I find it increasingly tiring to be so constantly on display. But I'm not quite ready yet to take up full-time residence in that solitary cave. For me, the trick is to discern what my heart and my body are telling me at any given time, so that I can always find the necessary balance between these two polarities of internal and external work. Now, I try to teach less when I'm in the full flow of creating a book, and then I allow myself to swing back to teaching again once I'm free of writing for a while. This ever-adjusting balance also changes for me according to the season, and these days I allow that, rather than fighting against it: during the winter months I need to spend more time dreaming and writing by the fire; in the lighter half of the year, I open to the world along with the spring flowers.

As the years go by, though, the overall balance is altering. The endless urge to "do" which has been such a defining feature of my life is now beginning to seriously wane. I've a longing to spend more time reflecting on my own vision, on the ways in which it contributes to the world — and allowing my contribution to the world to shift down-gear a little, to reflect those needs for more vision time. This late-elder archetype of which I'm so enamored — that of the quiet, more solitary Sage with deep vision — requires a little detachment from the world. Not in the sense of not caring about it — but because as we grow older and begin to contemplate our personal passage into death, I think we become less focused on accomplishment, or inspiring people with all the things we achieve and more focused on inspiring people with our ways of being in the world.

When I look ahead to my own deep cave years, how would I like to imagine myself? I'm taken by my memory of an old woman I encountered in a guided imagination journey that I undertook around ten years ago. She exuded peace and clarity — but joy too, and the glint in her eyes was evidence of an active sense of humor. She was dressed in black, her hair was white, her face lightly wrinkled, and those gleaming eyes were a clear, bright blue — the same clear, bright blue that they'd always been. That was when I realized that this old woman, comfortable in her solitary cave, calmly seated between a fire and a deep, cool well, was a future version of me. And I wanted to become her, more than I can say. I'd like to be the kind of elder woman who inspires others to understand that, toward the end of a life that will for sure have been full of challenges and sorrows, joy and peace is nevertheless possible. And I've become increasingly obsessed with how it might be possible to embody *grace*. It's a word that I'm drawn to, though I'm not entirely certain what it is supposed to mean. But for me, it has elements of all these things: understanding that my life has formed a meaningful pattern; somehow making visible the mystery which underpins it; and a full acceptance of life as it is, with all its light and dark, its sorrows and its joys.

When I imagine myself as that wise old woman with deep vision, I imagine myself not in a cave — but in a solitary little cottage in the middle of an enchanted forest, guarded by wolves and surrounded by a fence made of bones and skulls. I imagine myself in the kind of cottage that might be comfortably occupied by that most dangerous of Wise Old Women — the fearsome and magnificent Baba Yaga.

9

THE DANGEROUS OLD WOMAN

Carriers of the Fire

When we moved to Donegal in 2014 and lived in a tiny little cottage which (as I described in chapter 1) had neither space nor privacy, I soon began to long for what I came to call a "Baba Yaga hut." I daydreamed about it regularly. The construction of my fantasy retreat would begin with a simple wooden building — more a summerhouse, perhaps, than a shed — which I'd situate under the trees down at the bottom of our garden, by the stepping-stones which crossed our fast-flowing little river. I'd paint it in vivid colors, and I'd dangle my collection of bones from the overhang of the steeply angled roof. Inside, I'd store all my found objects, and other strange bits of this and that I'd collected over the years. There'd be sheepskins and goatskins, drums and rattles, baskets and brooms. There'd be a small table for working at, and a wooden bench with a small mattress for sleeping and dreaming. There'd need to be a tiny potbellied stove, of course, and there'd be candles and maybe an oil lamp or two for when the nights began to draw in early. I imagined myself inhabiting this hut which so beautifully reflected my own longings for the wild and the earthy layers of life, and I liked what I saw.

It remained a dream; the reality of our particular Donegal microclimate made such a thing impractical. During the warmer months the riverbank was swarming with horse-flies and flesh-eating midges, and the west coast murk and dampness meant that anything placed outside a house and in an unheated, uninsulated shed would soon grow moldy and smelly. So reluctantly, I let go of that particular dream. But I've often wondered since whether a good part of that yearning for a Baba Yaga hut wasn't actually the reflection of a yearning to be Baba Yaga. I wanted to become that Wise Old Woman in the woods who doesn't ever think of advertising her wares, but who is there to be found by those who need to find her. I wanted to be alarming enough to live safely there on my own, and also to be a little bit dis-concerting — because the Baba Yaga in her original Slavic tradition is the perfect personification of the archetypical Dangerous Old Woman.

In the Slavic mythic tradition, Baba Yaga is a super-natural being who is depicted as a ferocious-looking old woman. In most folktales, she flies through the skies of the world in a mortar, steers it by means of a pestle, and comes home each night to a cottage deep in the forest which is usually described as standing on chicken legs. This means that her house can walk around, and so you're not always guaranteed to find it in the same place. The house, the stories say, often seems to have no door — but if you repeat the following refrain, it will turn itself around and the door will show itself to you: *Little House, little House / Stand the way thy mother placed thee / Turn thy back to the forest and thy face to me!* On the occasions when it decides to return to its roost and stay still, you'll find Baba Yaga's house surrounded by a fence of human skulls and bones.

Although I never did have my little house on chicken legs, among the stranger objects in my collection of found objects is a dried-up chicken foot. It might sound like a weird thing to have around, but I love it because it is hard and scaly and has something of the dragon about it. It dangles from a black ceramic plaque on my wall which bears the relief of a wild-haired Baba Yaga in her mortar, pestle held aloft, clasped in the long, bony fingers of one hand.

Baba Yaga. Perilous, wild, and wise old woman of the woods — and so many of the elder women I know seem to long to be her. Just as stories about her are found throughout Slavic folklore, variations of her name occur in most Slavic languages. In Old Russian, the first element, *Baba*, may mean "midwife," "sorceress," or "fortune-teller," and in modern Russian, the word *babushka* (meaning "grandmother") derives from it. *Baba* also means "grandmother" in Croatian, Bosnian, and Serbian. Unfortunately, there's no consensus among scholars about the meaning of the second element, *Yaga*. In the nineteenth century, Alexander Afanasyev proposed that it derived from the Proto-Slavic and Sanskrit words for serpent, or snake. Similar words appear in various Slavic languages, such as the Bosnian/Croatian/Serbian *jeza* (meaning "horror, shudder, chill"), the Slovene *jeza* (meaning "anger"), the Old Czech *jězě* (meaning "witch, legendary evil female being"), the modern Czech *jezinka* ("wicked wood nymph, dryad"), and the Polish *jędza* ("witch, evil woman, fury").

Whatever qualities her name might intend to convey, we can be certain that the character of Baba Yaga is almost certainly based on an old mother goddess. The first clear reference to her occurs in a 1755 list of Slavic gods and supernatural beings, next to their equivalents in Roman mythology; Baba Yaga, however, appears without an equivalent, since she wouldn't have had one in those more patriarchal mythic traditions. Suggestions that Baba Yaga was probably once a major deity also derive from the names of her three faithful servants, who appear in many of the folktales about her: the White Horseman, the Red Horseman, and the Black Horseman. She calls them "my Bright Dawn, my Red Sun, and my Dark Midnight," because they control daybreak, sunrise, and nightfall — and so, through them, she is associated with the cosmic order, ensuring that dawn, day, and night happen when they are supposed to. The fact that Baba Yaga travels through the air in a mortar also links her with the sky, and so, mythically, to the cosmos in general. But her natural domain is the forest, which is widely acknowledged as a traditional symbol of transformation, as well as a place of peril. But Baba Yaga's enchanted forest is also the Otherworld: the "land of the living dead," known in Russian tradition as the "thrice-nine kingdom."

The mythic nature of Baba Yaga is also reflected in the fact that she's rather an ambiguous character. This is a feature of many of the older mother goddesses, and reflects Jungian psychologist Erich Neumann's division of the Great Mother archetype into two aspects which often occur together: the Good Mother and Terrible Mother. Baba Yaga isn't entirely good, and she isn't entirely evil; she is a wild and primal force in the hard-as-steel, seen-it-all body of an old woman. If you're the protagonist of a story in which she appears, she might help you, or she might hinder you. You never quite know which face she's going to show to you; it depends how you approach her, and on your response to the tasks that she will certainly set for you. She might appear as a maternal "Mother Nature" figure, or an unpredictable villain who enjoys eating those who fail to complete her tasks; she might also take on both roles within the same tale. But in all of these stories, Baba Yaga's primary role is as initiator: she is the one who tests the boys and girls who find their way to her, the agent of their inevitable transformation. Interestingly, she's usually much harder on the female characters who come looking for her help.

In some tales, a trio of Baba Yagas appear as sisters, all sharing the same name. In some stories, she guards the fountains of the water of life; in others, she accompanies

Death on his travels, devouring newly released souls. In some accounts she's associated with winter and storms, just like the Cailleach in the Scottish tradition, who is an equally dangerous and ambiguous character. According to some traditional tales, Baba Yaga ages a year every time someone asks her a question; this is why she is often portrayed as a cranky old hag — because she is frustrated and angry about constantly being asked so many questions. The only way for her to regain her youth in these stories is to drink a special tea which she brews from blue roses; heroes who bring her a gift of these rare flowers are looked upon most favorably, and are often granted wishes as a reward for their aid.

The best-known story in which Baba Yaga appears is the tale of "Vasilisa the Beautiful." In the most common version, a merchant has just one daughter, the lovely Vasilisa. When the child is eight years old her mother dies, but on her deathbed she gives Vasilisa a tiny wooden doll. She also tells Vasilisa that, if ever she should be in need, she must give the doll a little something to eat and a little to drink, and then it will help her. After her mother dies, Vasilisa does just that, and the doll comforts her. After a time, as commonly happens in such folktales, her father marries again; his new wife has two daughters. Her stepmother is very cruel to Vasilisa and sets her many hard tasks, but with the help of the doll, she is able to perform them all.

One day, Vasilisa's father sets off on a long journey relating to his occupation. In his absence, his wife sells the house and moves the family to a gloomy place near the forest. One day, after all the candles in the house burn out, Vasilisa is sent to fetch light from Baba Yaga's hut deep in the forest. She consults the doll, who advises her to go. While she is walking through the forest in the hours before dawn, a mysterious man rides past her, dressed in white and astride a white horse with red tack; soon after, along comes a similar rider in red. Eventually, Vasilisa comes to a house

that stands on chicken legs and is walled in by a fence made
of human bones. A black rider, just like the white and red
riders she's previously seen, rides past her, and night falls;
the eye sockets of the skulls begin to glow red with a fiery
light. Vasilisa is too frightened to run away, and so Baba
Yaga finds her there when she lands in her mortar later in
the evening.

Baba Yaga announces that Vasilisa must perform certain tasks to earn the fire she has come for, and if she
doesn't perform them to the Baba's specifications she will
be killed. She is to clean the house and yard, wash Baba
Yaga's laundry, and cook her a meal. She is also required
to separate grains of rotten corn from sound corn, and to
separate poppy seeds from grains of soil. Baba Yaga then
leaves on her daily rounds, and Vasilisa despairs as she
works herself into a state of exhaustion. When all hope of
completing the tasks seems lost, the doll whispers that she
will complete the tasks for Vasilisa, and that the girl should
sleep.

At dawn, the white rider passes; just before noon, the red.
As the black rider rides past at sunset, Baba Yaga returns.
Much to her irritation, she can find nothing to complain
about. She summons three pairs of disembodied hands to
squeeze the oil from the corn that Vasilisa has sorted, and
then asks her if she has any questions. Vasilisa asks who the
riders are, and Baba Yaga tells her that the white one is Day,
the red one the Sun, and the black one is Night. But when
Vasilisa thinks of asking about the disembodied hands, the
doll shakes in her pocket and she realizes that she shouldn't;
instead, she tells Baba Yaga she has no further questions.
In return, Baba Yaga asks Vasilisa how she managed to
accomplish the tasks that were set for her. Vasilisa replies,
"By my mother's blessing," and Baba Yaga, who wants
nobody with any kind of blessing in her presence, throws
Vasilisa out of her house. But she sends her away with a

skull lantern full of burning coals to provide the requested light for her stepfamily.

Upon her return, Vasilisa finds that, since sending her out to Baba Yaga's house, her stepfamily has been unable to light any candles or fire in their home. Even lamps and candles that might be brought in from outside are useless, because all of them are snuffed out as soon as they're carried over the threshold. The coals that Vasilisa has carried home in the skull lantern then burn Vasilisa's stepmother and stepsisters to ashes, and Vasilisa buries the skull according to its instructions, so that no other person should ever be harmed by it. Later, Vasilisa becomes an assistant to a maker of cloth in Russia's capital city, where she grows so skilled at her work that the czar himself notices her skill; he later marries Vasilisa.

In the Vasilisa story, Baba Yaga acts as a trickster, a villain — and ultimately a savior, when she helps Vasilisa to rid herself of her stepfamily. In many other stories, Baba's help comes in similarly menacing or shockingly violent forms, but in the end she always seems to be just — she is never simply arbitrary. It's notable that the tasks she gives Vasilisa are about sorting, sweeping, and cooking. They're fitting, because Baba is the mediator of natural law, and these tasks require both patience and a devotion to order. Sorting, in particular, requires very fine discrimination — and it can only ever be achieved with help. Often that help comes from animals, but here it comes from the doll which represents the spirit of Vasilisa's lost mother; in many cultures, dolls are believed, like bones, to be infused with the spirit of their maker.

By doing Baba's housework, Vasilisa in a sense is apprenticing herself to her; she's learning how to do the Baba's work. She questions Baba about some of her mysteries, but she also discerns when she should stop questioning, recognizing that some things must remain hidden — that the answers to some questions are not for us to know, in this life, at this time. But Vasilisa leaves carrying Baba Yaga's fire, and that fire is the ultimate alchemical agent of her transformation. In giving her the fire, Baba Yaga gives Vasilisa some of her power; the girl almost throws it away but in the end she holds strong, and it literally burns away what was holding her back — the mother and sisters — allowing her to pass into a new stage of life. Finally, she weaves herself a new beginning while weaving the beautiful rich cloth which earns her the love of the czar.

Baba Yaga, then, epitomizes the Dangerous Old Woman — because when you encounter her, you don't know whether you're going to live or to be eaten. The Baba can see behind the mask and beyond the veil: you can't hide your true self from her. When we seek her out, we should absolutely be afraid, because she requires us to go beyond what we perceive to be our limitations, to ask dangerous questions, to step outside the world of logic and reason. If we fail her tests, we die. And perhaps that's why we don't usually encounter Baba Yaga–type characters in everyday life; I've only ever met her in my dreams. I'm not entirely sure that Baba Yaga is an archetype we can become. But under the gaze of her discerning eye, we're inspired to discover and to value the truth about ourselves. The powerful tests which she sets for us at critical choice points in our life inspire us to be brave, and to learn how best to fulfill our potential in a world that wants to render us innocuous and overly careful. The Dangerous Old Woman, in whatever guise she appears, is the guardian of thresholds — the thresholds we must each cross to fulfill that potential, to discover our own unique gift, and to act out our calling. She's the elder who tests our mettle, pushes us out of our comfort zone, and challenges us to become the best we can possibly be.

Although I love them all, I think my favorite among the beautiful images that Australian artist Natalie Eslick created for this book is the character of Baba Yaga who appears at the beginning of this chapter. When she emailed it to me, Natalie told me that this was the old woman she wanted to grow into someday — and so, of course, I couldn't resist asking her why. "Baba Yaga, that archetypical hag in the woods that children are taught to be afraid of, has always fascinated me," she wrote to me. "Before I learned about Baba Yaga, it was the witch in 'Hansel and Gretel' and other Grimm tales that captured my attention. Were they really that wicked? Who decided that? What happened to make them want to live in the woods alone and away from everyone and everything we're supposed to want out of civilization? They felt wrongly maligned to me. And as I've grown older, as I've lived longer among the chaos and beauty and horrors of human society, Baba Yaga has pulled ever more strongly at my imagination, and at my heart. If I had to put into one succinct sentence why I love this character so dearly, it would be: because she is wild and free, and she is connected, deeply. She's free to be who she genuinely is — helper to those who deserve it, but refusing to put up with any nonsense. She knows the heart of the forest, she understands the circle of life, the cruelty and curiosity, wonder and wisdom, and everything in between. She lives a life of reciprocity with the world around her, preferring the simple and intricate (and feminine) complexity of nature to the contrived and unnecessarily complicated human communities."

I also asked Natalie about the inspiration for this particular image of the Baba. "She feels so real to me," she wrote, "and so I chose to represent her not as a wild-eyed, iron-toothed cartoon character, but a strong older woman who is deeply intertwined with the forest around her, who has so many tales to tell, and so much wisdom behind those eyes. That's who she chose to represent herself to me as, as she 'fell out' of my pencils — and I do try hard to listen, to be open to the voice of my subject, and let them guide me as I work. She feels deeply feminine, protective (of herself and of her forest), a skilled harnesser of earth magic, and all of this with a good dose of mischief thrown in. The cannibalism? The skulls on her fence? Well, no one begrudges a bear or a lion when they react to unwanted visitors — that's the chance you take if you approach the forest without sincerity and an open heart, if your agenda is selfish and unkind, if you're not prepared to listen and take heed. She represents the complexity of nature, rejecting societal norms, powerful and empowered. Oh, yes, I want to be Baba Yaga. Come and visit me someday, deep in the heart of the forest. I dare you!"

The fascination that Baba Yaga has for so many of us is reflected in the fact that she is a common and compelling character in popular literature inspired by folklore. My favorite version of her comes in two volumes from Taisia Kitaiskaia: *Ask Baba Yaga: Otherworldly Advice for Everyday Troubles* and *Poetic Remedies for Troubled Times: From Ask Baba Yaga.*[99] In these wonderful books, which seem to have taken up permanent residence on my bedside table, Kitaiskaia reinvents Baba Yaga as an agony aunt — but one who, in true Baba style, refuses even remotely to beat about the bush. Her responses to the questions asked by those who turn to her for advice are littered with crazy punctuation marks and delightful misspellings; she also has her own distinctly Slavic grammar. "Agony aunts have reputations to uphold," the author says in an interview on Bustle, "but witches offer a loophole out of what constrains us: social norms, drudgery, morality. Baba Yaga doesn't give a f*ck. She just tells it like it is, with the careless omniscience of a supernatural being."[100]

In an article that she wrote for Lithub online, Kitaiskaia offers one of the examples from her 2020 book:

DEAR BABA YAGA: I'm a thirty-eight-year-old woman who wants to date men, but I've always been terrified of them and have never been in a relationship. My fear has only grown with #MeToo, and sometimes I feel it's truly impossible to find a good-hearted male feminist — someone who would see me as an equal, pure and simple. I've already kind of given up and have found happiness in my work and social life. Is this single-for-life existence the future for women?

BABA YAGA: All my living I have been an old woman, in the woods; alone. I do what I like: I muddy & sweep my hut, carry myself into the sky & listen to what it says, I gather mushrooms, terrorize foxes & men with my fiendly claws & gait, laugh a long time into a bucket until it laughs back with a spit, breathe as a stone at the bottom of a creek — & many other things I do not say. But none of it is done from fearing. Poke at the fear as into the dying fire in yr hearth: which way do the sparks go, how does the fire hiss? If you choose my life — know you are choosing it, not hiding in the woods.[101]

I cannot tell you how much I love this particular iteration of Baba Yaga. But when it comes to fiction, and in spite of a heroine that I sometimes failed to warm to, one of my favorite Baba characters inhabits the pages of a children's book: *The House with Chicken Legs* by British author Sophie Anderson. It's about twelve-year-old Marinka, who lives with her grandmother, Baba Yaga, and dreams of a normal life — one in which her house might possibly stay in one place long enough for her to make normal human friends. But her house has chicken legs and a tendency to move on without warning in the middle of the night — always to "a lonely, bleak place at the edge of civilization." The only people Marinka usually meets are dead, and they vanish when her grandmother guides them through the Gate between this world and the next. Marinka wants to change what seems to be her inevitable destiny — to become the next Yaga — but the house, of course, has other ideas. In this book, Baba Yaga is a cheerful soul who cooks delicious suppers for the dead before they pass through the Gate.

"I've heard them call Baba ugly, hideous, a witch, or a monster," Marinka says. "I've heard them say she eats people. But they've never seen her like this. She's beautiful, dancing among the dead, bringing comfort and joy." And in this, she's the perfect reflection of what all old women come to be in the end: the place where life and death meet.

LEAVING THROUGH THE HOLE IN THE SIDE OF THE HOUSE

10

THE VALLEY OF THE SHADOW
OF DEATH

In 2018, an article on the Dark Mountain website profoundly captured my imagination.[102] In it, James Nowak
wrote about the phenomenon of the *liklúke*, or "corpse-
door," in countries that are culturally Scandinavian: "not
doors in the ordinary sense, with hinges and the like, but
small, window-sized passages in an outer wall. When someone dies in the house, the blocked-up passage is broken open
and the dead person is passed outside; afterwards, it's closed
up again." But why go to the trouble, Nowak asks: Why not
just use the front door? The answer, scholars suggest, is that
corpse-doors are a protective measure meant to confuse and
disorient the dead — a *draugr*, for example (a kind of "walking dead") — who might think of retracing their steps and
finding their way back into the world of the living. If they
tried to do so, they'd be faced with an inaccessible, resealed
wall instead of a front door through which they'd be able to
go back inside the house and haunt it.

But that's not the only reason why corpse-doors exist;
Nowak argues that their major function isn't to prevent the
dead from returning, but to open a passage through which
the dead can leave this world for the next. "The small hole
in the side of the house," he declares, "is a hole in the side
of the world." The *Poetic Edda*, that unique and intriguing

collection of Old Norse poems, states that Hel (the Old
Norse realm of the dead: a cold place, but one that lacks
the punitive associations of the Christian Hell) lies beyond
several layers of fences. These fences have gates, some of
which are named: Helgrind, Valgrind, Nágrind — Gate of
Hell, The Fallen, and The Dead, respectively. The corpse-
door, then, and the funerary rituals associated with it, are
intended to open these gates so the dead can find their way
to the afterlife.

I love the idea that our houses might incorporate a
threshold to the Otherworld; that the liminal hole in the
side of an old Scandinavian house might actually be a
portal to another world: the world, whatever we conceive
it to be, that we go to when we die. That, in the place
where we do most of our living, there might be not just an
acknowledgment of the inevitability of our future dying, but
a method of helping us — quite literally — to navigate it.
The fact of death in the midst of life, you see, is something
that has been preoccupying me for some time.

Earlier, I wrote about our relocation from the wild, bleak
peat bogs of western Ireland to the lusher, green mountains
of Mid Wales. In making this transition, we hadn't just
accomplished a change in culture and landscape: we'd left
behind several kinds of flora and fauna that we'd grown
accustomed to living alongside, and we'd acquired some new
neighbors in the process. Thankfully, the foxes, badgers,
and hares whose shadowy comings and goings have always
been so dominant in my imagination (as well as in my
Irish gardens) are very much present here in Wales. As are
many birds, and especially corvids of all kinds — including
my much-loved familiar, the crow. But the bird which
now commands our skies is one that I've never lived with
before: the red kite. Scavenging species have only ever
been occasional visitors in the places I've inhabited — the

odd buzzard in Scotland and Ireland, but nothing like the persistent presence of the red kites who constantly circle the mountains among which we live.

It's an inevitable consequence of my training and practice as a psychologist and mythologist that I can't help but see the world in archetypal terms. Of course, it's important to know the birds and animals I'm surrounded by as living, physical entities. It's important to understand their behavior, their habitat, their eating habits; whether this is a prey animal or a hunting animal, how it reproduces, what sounds it makes...But entangled with that grounded and necessary knowledge is another layer: the imaginal. And it's activating the imaginal, as much as knowing the physical reality, which helps me to really connect with the world around me and the other-than-humans which inhabit it. So a heron might be a large, long-legged bird which haunts the water's edge, lays large blue eggs at the top of trees, and has a loud, shrieking call — but she is also a hag in disguise, and a guardian of the gates of the Otherworld, because that is how the old stories of Ireland and Wales present her. In *The Enchanted Life*,[103] I wrote about how a gray heron who haunted the banks of the river at the bottom of our Donegal garden came to embody an archetype which I called Old Crane Woman — shapeshifter extraordinaire; part bird, part woman; haunter of the threshold places. The imaginal Old Crane Woman was as "real" a being to me as the physical gray heron I nodded to each morning as I walked the dogs along the old bog roads.

As a species, we've always lived in close physical contact with animals, so it's inevitable that they should play such important roles in our imaginal worlds. It's quite clear from the old myths and stories of Britain and Ireland that our ancestors saw the boundaries between humans and other animals as very much less clearly defined than we imagine them to be today — and more easily crossed. Back then, animals were very much more than simply creatures to be eaten, or to be used as beasts of burden or in battle: they were teachers and allies, and sometimes they were gods. Many stories in our native traditions include powerful animals who embody a kind of wisdom which is different from the ways of knowing that humans have, and in these old tales they embodied an insight and intelligence which humans long ago repudiated. We respected them, but more than that — we needed them.

Identifying the archetypal nature and the unique wisdom of the creatures around me, then, has always been important to me. It's the jumping-off point for relationship; it's the beginning of a sense of what I might learn from them. But I didn't understand the red kite at all. It didn't occupy any particular slot in my imagination, because I could find no old stories in which it appeared. I didn't know where to place it, and that bothered me. If a landscape or a tree or an animal doesn't show up clearly in my imaginal world, then at some curious but very real level I feel separate from it. I don't know how to approach it, or to honor it properly; I don't know what stories it might have to tell me. All I knew was — red kite: *Milvus milvus*. In the family Accipitridae, which includes many other raptors such as eagles, buzzards, and harriers. Reddish-brown body, long angled wings, and deeply forked tail; 23 to 27 inches long, with a 69-to-70-inch wingspan. Consumer of small mammals, supplemented by carrion and worms. Historically, viewed largely as vermin, it was saved from national extinction by one of the world's longest-running protection programs, and especially thrives in this part of the Cambrian mountains.

I understood the red kite at the physical level, then, but I had no clues about its archetypal nature. I didn't know who it was. I asked my friend Manda, who also lives surrounded by kites. "They feel as if the wisdom they share is ancient and wild and utterly uncompromising," she reflected, "in the way the stone at the top of the hill is ancient and wild and utterly uncompromising. There's a ruthless compassion that feels very clear." And that made sense to me — especially the idea of ruthless compassion — but I also wanted something more. Something more personal. I wanted to find something in the nature of the red kite that would reflect something in my own nature, or my own life.

This perplexing state of affairs persisted for a while — until, one morning, I happened upon a kite in the field above our house. The enormous bird was dismantling the carcass of a wood pigeon: plucking the feathers, stripping away the dead meat, cleaning the bones. And then it came to me, in the way that such things have often come to me before — if I've been paying attention and put the work in beforehand; if I've courted the creature, and genuinely reached out for insight and meaning. "Old Bone Mother," I delightedly announced to the red kite, and she stopped what she was doing and stared at me for a moment before dismissing me as neither relevant nor especially frightening, and then carried on with her work as if I wasn't there.

Old Bone Mother. Creator of skeletons, companion of Death. Who cleans away decaying flesh, and picks our bones clean. Mistress of the avian Nigredo; alchemist of the skies.

~

Among all the natural objects that have found their way into my house, I am fondest of my collection of bones and skulls. Perhaps I'm more mirrored by the scavenging red kite than I'd imagined; perhaps I'm Old Bone Mother incarnate, wandering the hills and fields, gathering up any bones that are lying in wait for me. My favorite skull is that of a fox, whose skeleton we found in a peaty ditch on the back border of our Connemara garden when first we moved in;

she sits on a shelf by my bed in the hope that she'll visit me sometimes in dreams. On the wooden bookcase to the right of my desk is a seal skull; I found it washed up on a beach in the islands, in the days when I sang to my seal friend during early morning walks. The old pine corner dresser in my study houses the bulk of my collection: a rabbit skull; a motley collection of bird skulls found mostly on beaches; the skull of a ram, found dead on common grazing land in the Outer Hebrides.

It's been suggested by many scholars that the Insular Celts — the pre-Roman inhabitants of these islands — revered the human head. Archaeological and textual evidence supports this notion, and the veneration of the head as the seat of the soul, and bones as the source of spiritual potency, is widespread throughout Europe; it seems to date back to the Mesolithic period. The idea was handed down and persists in European folklore, and some of my favorite fairy tales celebrate the power of bones. In "The Juniper Tree," a story collected by the Brothers Grimm, the bones of a murdered and cannibalized child are buried beneath a juniper tree. The spirit of the dead child, presumably lingering in the bones, rises up and flies out from the branches of the tree in the form of a bird; it sings a song which tells the story of what happened to him. In "The Singing Bone," another Grimm tale, a man kills his younger brother and buries his body beneath a bridge. One day, a shepherd finds an uncovered bone under the bridge, and uses it to make the mouthpiece for a horn — which also then sings the truth about the younger brother's fate. An Irish fairy tale entitled "Yellow Lily" tells of a princess who asks a prince to kill her and use her bones as steps, so that he might scale a nine-hundred-foot-high tree and save himself, or her, or the world — I can't now remember which — and then she is brought back to life.

But my favorite bone story of all appears within a

strange saga belonging to the Samoyed people of Siberia.[104]
It begins with seven brothers, who are the leaders of a
community of people who live in seven hundred tents. Only
one of the brothers has a son, and that son dreams that all
the people of the village are killed, and only he is left alive.
Well, his dream comes true; he wakes up one morning to
find them all dead. So he sets off by himself, wandering,
and he wanders for many months. As such wanderers do,
he has a handful of adventures, and after one of them he
ends up with a wife and settles down. Everything seems to
be going very well, until one day someone kills him with a
spear. All of a sudden, up pops a one-legged, one-handed,
and one-eyed old man. He wields an iron staff, and he hits
the dead man with it and says: "Why are you lying there?
It's time to get up! Get up and go back to your village; your
father is alive and all your brothers are alive again too."
The dead man wakes up then, but he doesn't believe what
the old man says, and so he stays where he is. Bad choice:
the man who had originally killed him with the spear has
another try, and manages to kill him again.

Along comes the one-legged, one-handed, and one-eyed
old man and hits him again with his iron staff. He says:
"Yesterday I told you to go back to your old village; what
are you doing there in the tent? Turn back if you want to
keep your head. Your father is alive, and he has been alive
for a long time." The dead man wakes up again, looks
around him, and says: "Who could that man be who keeps
asking me to turn back, who talks about my father and
claims that he is alive? My father has been dead for a long
while!" He convinces himself that he's been dreaming, goes
back to his tent, and falls asleep next to his wife.

Yes, you've got the idea: exactly the same thing happens
for a third time. But this time, the old man is rather cross.
"For the third time I tell you," he shouts, "turn back! You
have been killed twice. Both times I woke you up to life,

but I won't do it anymore." Well, the young man isn't having any of it. He returns to his new village, and for no reason that is apparent in the story, calmly slaughters everyone there except for his wife. Unfortunately, the man who'd killed him twice with the spear wasn't among the dead — and so he sets off in pursuit of him. When finally he finds him, they fight together, and both die.

They lie next to each other all through the summer, and their bodies start to rot. Foxes come, and wolves; they eat the corpses, pick them clean — everything, except for the bones. Autumn arrives, and the one-legged, one-handed, one-eyed old man arrives as well. He says to the young man's corpse: "How often have I told you that you have to turn back? Now I say it to you for the very last time; later my power won't be able to help you." He gathers up the young man's bones — collects them all, the tiniest pieces too; he puts them all into a bag, hauls the bag onto his back, and goes on his way.

After walking for a while, he comes to a big stone. He strikes the stone with his iron staff, and it rolls to one side. Under the stone there is a hole, and the old man crawls down into the hole. He arrives in a dark, gloomy place, redolent with strange sounds: shrieking, whistling, and singing. Someone — or something — tries to snatch the bag of bones from the old man, but he resists. And then in front of him he sees a bright light, like a window with the sun shining through it. In the midst of this brightness he sees a group of people — but these people are naked, without coverings of any kind, without skin, without flesh — just bare, naked bones. Their teeth grin widely in their fleshless mouths.

The old man walks toward the light, sees a tent, enters the tent; there is no one there except for an old woman, sitting at a hearth. On the other side of the hearth are two monsters with enormous eyes; they don't move or talk. The old man throws the bag of bones onto the ground and says to the old woman: "Here is some firewood; throw it into the fire." "Good that you brought some," answers the old woman, "I had none left." So the old woman lights a fire and throws the bones into it; they all burn down to ashes. The old woman takes the ashes of the bones, scatters them onto her bed, lies down on the ashes, and goes to sleep. She sleeps for three days, and at the end of the three days a human being — yes, our friend the young man — is born from the ashes.

Well, the strange story goes on for a while longer, and ends even more strangely, with the reborn hero returning to his original village and killing the one-legged, one-handed, and one-eyed old man — as a consequence of which all the people now in his village die, and he ends up alone once again. But what lends the story such a significant place in my imagination is this scene in which the old woman in her underground cave, her tent surrounded by skeletons and with monsters who share her hearth, sleeps on the bones of a dead hero to bring him back to life. If ever there was an Old Bone Mother, she is it, for sure. Old Bone Mother, who calls back the dead and dismembered parts of us, and from them conjures new life.

I've never been particularly preoccupied by death. Not until now. Not until that lockdown-coinciding inflammation bomb I wrote of in a previous chapter — the gift that kept on giving — added lymphoma to its list of life-changing offerings.

It began with the sudden appearance of a small lump on the side of my neck; the lump continued to grow. It turned out not to be a simple swollen lymph node, as my doctor first suggested, but the first sign of diffuse large B-cell non-Hodgkin's lymphoma — one of the most aggressive hematological cancers, centered on lymphocytes: infection-fighting cells in the immune system. By the time it was properly diagnosed within an NHS which was still reeling from the effects of the pandemic, the lump had grown to the size of a very large, dense golf ball. After the various scans and biopsies finally revealed what was going on, I was rushed in to see a consultant, and chemotherapy began just two weeks later. It was, I was warned, a particularly intensive and brutal chemotherapy regime, since surgery in systemic cancers like this one clearly isn't an option. The treatment would last (assuming that my body held up, and no reasons to postpone emerged) for almost six months, during which time all my hair — body hair as well as head hair — would fall out. I would be facing a smorgasbord of delightfully debilitating side effects, ranging from peripheral neuropathy to the possibility of heart or kidney failure and severe gastrointestinal complications, and almost certainly including painful mouth sores which would make eating ex-cruciating. If I were lucky, the consultant calmly announced, I *might* just get through the six months without having to be admitted to hospital with some potentially lethal infection or other, due to the systematic demolition of my immune system by the potent cytotoxic drugs they'd be pouring into my bloodstream. But most people weren't so lucky. Not to worry — just get yourself to the emergency ward as quickly as you can if you don't feel well.

At this early stage, it wasn't the life-threatening nature of the illness itself which frightened me, but rather the necessity of flooding my body with toxic chemicals for six full months. The idea of intentionally and systematically harming my body in this way was the only thing that made me, finally, cry. I tried to embrace the irony of a situation in which it's a poison that provides the cure, but mostly I failed. Up until then, I'd been someone who would need to be crippled by a headache before taking so much as a couple of acetaminophen, and the pharmacology and physiology training I'd undergone during my early years as a research neuroscientist meant that unfortunately I was in a position to understand all too well what those chemicals would be doing to me. And yet, if I wanted to stay alive — and of course, there was no guarantee of that, either — there was absolutely no choice. If I didn't follow this regime, then, at the rate the lump was growing, I'd be dead within months.

Lymphomaniacs. That was the name that David immediately coined for our much-loved old sheepdog, Nell, and me. Four years earlier, Nell had been diagnosed with lymphoma: exactly the same type of non-Hodgkin's lymphoma as I now had, and discovered as a result of the swelling of a lymph node in the same place, and on exactly the same side of her neck, as I now had. She had almost exactly the same chemotherapy drugs as I was due to have — albeit given according to a different, more dog-friendly regime. I'd heard of people growing to look like their dogs, but this was taking the underlying notion just a little bit too far. The good news was that now, at almost twelve years old — and although she had been predicted to live for probably no more than a year, even after chemotherapy — she was fully recovered and running around like a pup, full of wags and well-being, lording it over another fine flock of sheep. I was counting on that being a favorable sign; I had been told that the cure rate these days was high, and that my prognosis was good. So Nell, a dog who I love as much as any human I've ever known, inevitably became my talisman. When she'd begun to lose her undercoat because of her treatment, I'd found her a fleece coat to keep her warm. The only one I could find in her size was a rather louche leopard skin; all she needed was a set of four stiletto-heeled doggy shoes and she'd have looked as if she were all set for a fine night out on the town. She looked decidedly embarrassed to be wearing it. Now, Nell's leopard-skin coat took up residence under my pillow as a good-luck charm.

Once I'd absorbed what was happening, I began to feel a strange tenderness toward my lump. This wasn't some evil alien invader which was trying to take over my body; it was part of me. It was a consequence of a dysfunction in my immune system, and there were no obvious external risk factors for this particular cancer. And at this stage of my life, I felt very strongly that this illness — all of these sudden-onset immune-related illnesses — were trying to tell me something. Something about how to be, and how not to be. Something about letting go of the old — undergoing a little death — to make way for the new. Above all, and regardless of my opinions about it and attitudes to it, this treatment was going to be an enormous rite of passage, and one whose end would coincide with turning sixty — the age I've always thought of as the threshold to elderhood. I promised myself I'd pay attention. So I never felt "betrayed" by my body, which up until that time had always been so wonderfully resilient; I never felt anger. My attitude to this life-threatening illness wasn't to hate it, or to fight it, or to consider myself a victim of it — it was to give myself over to it. I most certainly wanted it gone — but I also wanted to immerse myself in the lessons that it had to teach me. I wanted to know it, to understand it. Survival seemed contingent on not making the same old mistakes again. All I needed to do was to figure out exactly what those same old mistakes actually were.

In the early days, while I was still assimilating what was happening to me, Coleman Barks's interpretation of an old poem by the Sufi mystic Rumi came to haunt me, and to stay with me:

> This being human is a guest house.
> Every morning a new arrival.
>
> A joy, a depression, a meanness,
> some momentary awareness comes
> as an unexpected visitor.

Welcome and entertain them all!
Even if they're a crowd of sorrows,
who violently sweep your house
empty of its furniture,
still, treat each guest honorably.
He may be clearing you out
for some new delight.

The dark thought, the shame, the malice,
meet them at the door laughing,
and invite them in.

Be grateful for whoever comes,
because each has been sent
as a guide from beyond.[105]

This particular guest, I believed, was precisely the teacher I needed, and had arrived at my door at the necessary time. *If you're going to write a book about elderhood*, it seemed to be whispering into my ear, *then you're going to need to know what being older can mean. If you want to live, you're going to have to learn to walk hand in hand with Death. If you're going to write about elderhood as a big initiation — here's an initiation for you. Don't waste it, now. It's time to slough off another tough old skin.*

All such major initiations — the ones with real, tangible consequences, like whether you get to live or die — are containers for meaning. They're invitations not just to learn, but to finally grow into ourselves, to let the dead wood fall and more fully reveal the thriving, living heart of who we are. If you can brace yourself for the rocky ride and surrender to the journey, nothing will ever be the same again. Chemotherapy is strong medicine, both physically and psychologically — and so is the fact of a life-threatening illness. Staring Death in the face in this way is a more powerful rite of passage than any other we might face in our lives. This one is challenging, dangerous — but it also acts as a key. It unlocks the doorway through which, if we're resourceful and lucky, and survive our walk through the valley of the shadow of Death — and if we learn the lessons of the journey well — we'll glimpse the soft, subtle dawn of a new and more meaningful life.

The lessons I was offered during my monthslong walk through that dreaded valley were profound; their unexpected gifts were utterly transformative. The first and most immediate of this new guest's gifts was kindness. And truly, I never expected that: kindness, in what so often ·seems like an impossibly unkind world. After I took the difficult decision to go public with news of my lymphoma and chemotherapy, the outpouring of kindness I received in return was overwhelming. Hundreds of supportive emails; thousands of warm comments on my social media posts. My husband, always something of a cynic, rolled his eyes at first and muttered that it's easy to be nice to someone who has cancer. But there was more than just "niceness" behind the heartfelt generosity of these offerings; much of what was shared reflected me back to myself in a way I hadn't much experienced before. I felt valued, and loved. And it's hard to express how much that mattered.

The world I inhabit — writing, teaching, the "public eye" — isn't always generous. Certainly, there is support and community, but there's also a surprising amount of envy (for what, I've often wondered; who can ever imagine they know the reality of another's life?) and competitiveness. There are cliques and exclusions; there is subtle (and not-so-subtle) belittling; there are people who really do seem to believe they "own" entire fields of thought, endeavor, and imagination. There are, for sure and always, egos the size of a planet which slash their way through a room and leave only ruin in their wake. It's the same everywhere, I know, but it has always — naively perhaps — seemed to me to be all the more shocking when it happens among people who pitch themselves as being in service to the Earth and its wider community. Such behavior, especially when it comes from people who really are not "walking their talk," makes you cautious; it makes you hold back. It hardens your heart, and sometimes it can break it, and over the past several years, resilient as I always imagine myself to be, I'd been damaged in a multiplicity of ways by people whose work I'd once tried to support, and who had once presented themselves as friends. The immediate anger had mostly faded, and now the hurt passed too — eradicated once and for all by the kindness of others. A few unkindnesses don't mean that the world is unkind. You know, that's not nearly as obvious a thought as it sounds: I'd run the risk of believing the opposite to be true.

I didn't believe that anymore. So welcome, kindness. Welcome, lesson-wielding guest. "Every morning a new arrival." For what "new delight" were you clearing me out now? I had inhabited the Exile archetype all my life; now, I was learning to let go of my attachment to it, to shed the illusory cloak of protection it seemed to offer. Because this life breaks us open. It's supposed to. We're not here to be safe; we're here to risk everything. And every breaking open strips away a protective shell, reveals another tender layer beneath — until, one day, there's nothing left to dismantle and we reach the core of who we are. On that day, Old Bone Mother will have completed her work. But, for now, I was grateful that there were still layers of me to strip away, grateful for the ongoing revelations and opportunities to grow and to learn. I was grateful above all that I hadn't yet come to the bottom of my basket of chances to transform myself. And so, beautifully entangled with and utterly intrinsic to my dread of this disease and its possible consequences, I uncovered the strangest and deepest of joys.

The second gift was the revelation of what it means to actually, finally, properly learn to slow down. The inability to achieve this is an ongoing flaw that I've singularly, and often spectacularly, failed to permanently resolve at other critical stages in my life. Welcome again, lovely guest. As soon as I understood what was going to be happening to me, I cleared my calendar for several months ahead. I canceled public events; I began to refuse the constant stream of requests for advice and assistance. My sole focus was on recovery and, if time and energy permitted, on finishing this book. For the past fifteen or more years, I'd hardly stopped. I hardly knew how to relax anymore; I hardly remembered what it was to take a day off. But now, when I was tired, I resolved to stop working and sit down in a comfortable chair to read a book. Aside from the radical impact on my once-infinite to-be-read pile, I thrived on learning again to be still. And in the midst of that stillness, I came to understand what really mattered to me. Instead of just pushing on through, doing everything that came my way — or everything that I thought I ought to do — I learned to recognize the things that I quietly dreaded, and the things I actually loved to do. If you only can learn to stop, I discovered, it all becomes very clear. If you make the space to listen to it, your body will show you what it is that you really love — what it is that you actually need. You'll notice the tension in your throat after you've said yes to something that you know is going to exhaust you. You'll feel your chest swell with joy after you've written a paragraph that you imagine to be particularly fine, or dreamed up another idea for a book. You'll find yourself softly weeping from the simple sensory pleasure of the wind gently caressing the stubby remainder of your once-beautiful mane of hair, and all your sorrow at its passing will fade. The wind loves me anyway, you'll think, and it will be true.

The third and most profound gift was the opportunity to know and to befriend Death. Chemotherapy, as many of you who are reading this book will unfortunately know all too well, is itself a little death; certainly, it's a dissolution. The chemicals we're given cause rapidly dividing cells to die at an accelerated rate — "good" cells as well as "bad." Among them are blood cells, gut cells, skin cells, mouth cells, nail cells — and hair follicles. With the particular regime that I was given, hair slips away little by little — head hair first, then body hair, and eventually (usually) eyebrows and eyelashes right at the end, just when you think you're going to escape this final loss.

After the first cycle of treatment, as my hair gathered its wits about it, stood on end, and ran screaming for the hills, I asked my husband to shave my head. Perhaps it will sound foolish and excessive to say that this was the most traumatic of all my experiences during this illness. I wept all the way through, and sobbed for hours through the night. This wasn't at all what I'd planned. I had been intent on seeing it as a ritual — like the cutting of nuns' hair when they took the veil, or the shaving of heads when Buddhist monks are ordained. I had imagined I would be able to view it as a ceremonial crossing from death to new life, and as a commitment to whatever the difficult journey that lay ahead might bring. It was a pretty idea, but the truth is I was simply devastated. And for all my fine imaginings, I discovered that I wasn't nearly brave enough, either, to bare quite so much of my nakedness to the world. A nice wig — the closest I could find to my original style — was acquired for more public emergences, and I wore it throughout. I'd always been used to having hair to hide behind, and this would have been one exposure too many. When you've had long hair all your life, the loss of it is more than just vanity — it's like losing a sense organ, and it leaves you oddly vulnerable in ways you didn't quite expect.

But in private, when I looked in the mirror, there was no hiding from what I'd become: a strange, featureless thing, almost like a newborn baby. I didn't recognize the curious creature staring back at me; I had no idea who or what I was anymore — no sense of self. How could it be that so much of my sense of who I was, was tied up in my physical appearance? All the usual cues had vanished along with my hair, eyelashes, and brows. My face seemed to have shifted in structure; my eyes seemed to have grown smaller. The loss of energy from an exhausting treatment regime was mirrored in loss of muscle tone throughout my body and an increase in weight. I felt as if I'd slipped backward in time, as if I'd somehow reverted to an earlier stage of development. I felt frighteningly close to disappearing, as if all that I once had been was now dead. Frighteningly close, that is, until I remembered the cyclicity of life which is intrinsic to old European spiritual traditions — and so recognized my new self at last: the aging woman merging into the just-born child. Coming full circle. Circling back, circling around, not just to death but to the potential for rebirth. My hair had fallen like desiccated autumn leaves, leaving me naked and shivering in my barren winter wood. Now, I could begin to imagine what I might become when spring came round again. Like my beautiful, full-of-heart Entwife tree, I'd sprout my new green shoots from what seemed, on the surface, to be little more than wreckage.

Death is a midwife, birthing us into a new stage of being. This is true for the small deaths we encounter throughout our lives, as well as the "great death" that represents our final departure from this world. It's hardly an original idea; Death has always been a midwife in the old traditions of my land. In Britain and Ireland, scattered among medieval religious buildings, castles, holy wells, bridges, and town walls, there exist a surprising number of stone carvings of women exposing their genitals, their cavernous vulvas pointed at or held open by long-fingered hands. These figures are known as Sheela-na-gigs; they are shown standing, squatting, kneeling, or sitting. The upper half of the carvings presents an impression of death: the Sheela-na-gig's breasts are old and withered, she has skeletal ribs, a skull-like head, hollow eyes, and she is often bald. And yet the lower half is redolent of sexuality, of fertility, of the act of giving birth squatting, or standing.[106] There has been a great deal of discussion about the origin of these figures, and the most favored theory is that they represent folk deities associated with fertility and childbirth — but also that they form a link with the realms of the dead. In the oldest European traditions, the two attributes almost always go together. There are two sides of the ubiquitous Great Mother archetype: death and birth. Every life bears within it the seed of its own death — but no end is ever less than a new beginning.

In Britain and in other parts of Europe, there are many folktales in which old women preside over birth and fertility rituals, and which lend weight to this idea. In Scotland, for example, a gamekeeper intent on curing a disease in his grouse once set out for the holy well of Melshach, but found that a group of women were already there, dancing around the well. "An aged crone sat in their midst, and dipping a small vessel in the water, kept sprinkling them. They were married women who had proved childless and had come to the well to experience its fertilising virtues."[107] When we think of fertility in mythological terms, we usually associate it with the Mother archetype and the physical birthing of babies — but the life-giving aspect of the Old Woman is different. The new life that she brings comes not from the physical womb, but the tomb; she brings death to old ways of being, and keeps all things in balance. As archaeologist Marija Gimbutas suggested, the Old Woman "acts on a cosmic plane: she balances the life energy of humans, animals, plants, and even of the moon." She reminds us that "there is no life without death. Thus, she is essentially concerned with regeneration."[108] The Hag in our native traditions, then, embodies the essence of uncertainty: she upholds the seeming paradox that life can only be known in the context of death, and the death she brings is always in the service of life.

~

During this period of intense rapprochement to Death, it seemed somehow appropriate that I should now be living in a house that, in the eighteenth century, had begun its life as a tiny nonconformist chapel. Its community soon outgrew it, and so it was extended a little and converted into a farmhouse which remained in the same family for generations. Traces of its origins still remain: the painted paneling on the stairs and in the dining room was constructed from original pews; the old oak hymnal cupboard is now our pantry. But the most obvious clue to the origin of the building is found in the multiplicity of yew trees which cluster around it like a tribe of ancient guardians, for this is a tree which is traditionally found in churchyards throughout Britain and Ireland.

The largest of our yews stands thick-trunked and stately, firmly entrenched in the grassy ground just outside the front window of my study. It is tall enough that its ferny branches rustle at my bedroom window in the slightest of breezes, and it reaches beyond to the roofline above. From a distance, its glossy, dark green shadow strikes a somber note; but on approach the beautiful scaly, flaking bark comes into view, with its multiple shades of brown, beige, and pink. Judging from the founding date of the original chapel, this yew is likely to be close to three hundred years old. Yews can easily reach six hundred years of age, and some trees live longer; ten yews in Britain are believed to predate the tenth century. With increasing age, they develop a tendency to hollowness. In Brittany, I once visited an ancient yew inside which I could comfortably stand; it was like slipping into the skin of a tree. I closed my eyes, and I could swear that for a moment I heard her breathing.

Most parts of *Taxus baccata* are poisonous; ingestion causes cardiac arrhythmia and can lead to death from cardiogenic shock. But it is precisely this toxicity which, in bringing death, paradoxically permits the tree also to bring new life: Taxol, a drug based on extracts of yew, has antitumor properties and is used in chemotherapy for ovarian, lung, and breast cancers. The yew, then, is a tree which dissolves the boundaries of life and of death, and this is reflected in our myths and folklore. In the ancient Celtic world, the yew tree seems to have had extraordinary significance, and much of that significance lay in its ability to grant death when required. A passage in Caesar's *Gallic Wars* notes that Cativolcus, leader of the Eburones in Gaul, poisoned himself with yew rather than submit to Rome. Florus similarly notes that when the Cantabrian people of what is now Spain were under siege by Rome in 22 BCE, most of them took their lives by the sword, by fire — or by a poison extracted from the yew tree. In Shakespeare's *Macbeth*, the witches concoct a magical brew to conjure the souls of the dead, which includes "slips of yew, silvered in the moon's eclipse."

But the yew wasn't just seen as a tree of death: it was also associated with life, and with rebirth. Some of this is due to the tree's longevity; yew is the last on a list of oldest things in a passage from the fifteenth-century Irish manuscript, the *Book of Lismore*: "Three lifetimes of the

yew for the world from its beginning to its end." But it is
the regenerative nature of the yew which most lends itself to
these correspondences. Drooping branches of old yew trees
can root and form separate but linked new trunks wherever
they touch the ground, and which then spread out beyond
the tree as if it were slowly forging its own unique path
through the landscape. In this way, the tree is linked with
resurrection, and so it has become a symbol of the cycle of
death and rebirth.

I've been lucky to have known many remarkable trees,
but I've never before lived in close proximity to so many
yews. At first, I was overawed, and kept my distance; but
soon I fell under their spell. I felt a particular kinship with
that old Grandmother yew as I lingered for a while in the
valley of the shadow of Death. I soon took to sitting on the
old wooden bench next to her, reaching for her wisdom. I
wanted to know about birth and beginnings, but most of
all, I wanted to know about endings.

Iodhadh, a word which possibly refers to the yew tree, is
the Old Irish name of the twentieth and final letter of the
ancient runic Ogham alphabet — some of whose characters
appear to be associated with the names of trees. A few years
ago, my dear friend Moya, who lives in County Leitrim in
Ireland, gave me a yew stick carved with its Ogam symbol;
it is among that set of most treasured objects which I always
keep close to my desk. In this position in the alphabet, the
yew again represents not just the end but also the beginning,
completing the circle of life and death.

Death is a subject close to Moya's heart; she thinks of
Death, if not quite as a friend, then certainly as a treasured
companion. "I've apprenticed myself to Death for at least
thirty years," she tells me, "and probably even longer. My
first experience with death was nearly drowning when I
was eight or nine, and soon afterwards I learned that my

great-grandfather had been an undertaker. Apparently, he had the first motorized hearse in County Mayo! So maybe Death has been walking with my family line for generations." And somehow, ever since her days studying sociology at university, the subject of death has been ever-present in her work. "I always chose something death-related for my essays and research," she says. "Loss and bereavement, death rites, the sociology of death and dying…and it continued after I trained as a nurse. I worked in an employee assistance programme for the Department of Education, providing loss and bereavement support. And then there was my job in palliative care, working with the seriously ill and dying, after the specialist regional team created for me the post of nurse in complementary therapies. Alongside all this, my journey to the more 'ethereal' aspects of death deepened through shamanic work, my work with animals, and my own more personal journeying. This experiential work is what changed my relationship with death, deepening any 'learned' education about it." As we're talking, Moya mentions the "energy of Death" quite often, and I ask her if she could take a shot at defining what she means. "It's complicated!" she laughs "— but to me it incorporates all these qualities: honesty, truth, compassion, fearlessness, bravery, strength, a sense of being somehow unwavering."

More than anything, I'm curious about why, as a strong and healthy woman still in her forties, it's so important to her to actively work with death in this way. "By walking through life with Death by my side," she explains, "every breath, every step becomes sacred. It's as if each breath, and each step, is my last. In the sense that I'm always asking myself: If this were my last breath in this world, how would I choose to be? If I were to die right now, how would that be? Asking these questions instantly cuts through the trivia of everyday life. I'm lucky that I can mostly say it would be okay if I were to die right now. It's not that I want to, but it

would be okay. And if ever I can't say that, then it's a sign
for me that there's work to do — something that needs my
attention; something in me that needs some resolution to
come into ease. So death informs every living moment, and
with Death walking always by my side, every step becomes
meaningful."

There's no question that we need to look deeply into
our own relationship with death if we want to approach
the true nature of life — and if we want to fully live. As
Jungian psychologist Edgar Herzog suggested in his dated
but fascinating book *Psyche and Death*, "Only the man
who is prepared in his soul to pass through the Gate of
Death becomes a living human being."[109] We need to learn
(as wisdom traditions around the world insist) in some
sense to "die before we die." Unfortunately, here in the
West, we're held back by a culture which finds it difficult to
talk about, let alone accept the everyday reality of, death.
We see death as tragic, traumatic, something to be feared
or ignored until we're forced to face it in spite of our worst
night terrors. We can hardly even say the word — instead,
we use euphemisms: "gone to a better place," "passed
away," or even, bizarrely, "bought the farm" or "kicked the
bucket." But the more we try to push death away and see
it as the enemy of life, the more it swings back around to
consume us with fear. What we're really afraid of, perhaps,
is the unknown — but if we insist on pushing it to one side,
the more likely it is that the specter of the character we
still insist on calling the "Grim Reaper" will come to haunt
us. These days, pushing death to one side isn't a sensible
option. When you live in times in which it often feels like
everything is coming undone, the ability to tolerate endings
is more important than ever.

As part of her work, Moya runs workshops for people
who want to learn to "apprentice themselves" to Death.
"I feel that if we can do some preparation while we're still

living," she says, "it will influence our last journey — our dying. There are little deaths, losses, throughout our lives, and how we navigate them is an indication of how we'll navigate our dying." And that ability to navigate endings — to somehow make friends with the archetype of Death — is becoming a valuable skill, because the Covid-19 pandemic brought death closer for all of us. The statistics are ever-present, relentless; we obsess over the curve of a graph; we count cases, hospitalizations, deaths — and for most of us, who will never have lived through a war or another pandemic, death has come to dominate our lives in a way that we haven't ever faced before.

When I ask Moya what advice she'd give to people who want to begin exploring this work, she offers several suggestions. "The most important thing," she says, "is to be willing to welcome Death into your life, to invite Death to join you. It's about forming a relationship with Death. You can explore death in all kinds of ways — reading, writing, meditation, journeying practices, dancing, singing, educational programmes, exploring local death customs … I'd say, take every opportunity to deepen your knowledge. Look for things that will allow you to have an experience, as opposed to just acquiring theory. Welcome any form of death that appears. For example, if you come across a dead creature, tend to that being as if it were your own dead body. Wash it, lay it out, sing to it, wrap it, surround it with offerings, bury that body or build a funeral pyre. Sing, or weep; feel the loss of the death so that the life can be celebrated."

As she talks about these things, I'm reminded of the long, slow vanishing of our oldest cultural rituals around death. They were designed to bring us into an acceptance of, as well as a familiarity with it; they allowed us to acknowledge the grief of it for those left behind, while also celebrating the life of the dead individual. In the native traditions of these islands, those rituals were often bound up with women. In

Ireland, for example, the dead were traditionally mourned in a special ritual — the wake — at the center of which was another ritual, the keen: a kind of funeral lament. Keening hasn't entirely died out, but it had declined considerably by the latter part of the nineteenth century. This ancient practice has its roots in pre-Christian Ireland; one ancient text, *Cath Maige Tuired*, suggests that the act of keening was first practiced by the goddess Brigid while mourning the death of her son, Ruadán. The keen was performed over a corpse, almost always by professional keeners who would be hired for the occasion; these keeners were usually women, working alone or in small groups.[110] The function of the keening woman — the *bean chaointe*, in Irish — wasn't just to offer a necessary catharsis to the mourners; hers was also a spiritual role. She acted as a kind of midwife — but one who facilitated death, not birth. She helped the soul to find its place in the Otherworld, bearing it along on her wave of improvised music.[111] In this sense, she functioned as a kind of psychopomp: a beautiful word derived from the Greek, which means "soul guide."

In British and Irish mythology, old women are also associated with the coming of death; they are, after a fashion, its harbingers. Old Women who foreshadow the deaths of others include the *bean sí* (in English, the banshee) in Irish folklore, who wails, shrieks, or keens to announce the death of the member of a family with which she is associated. She's usually portrayed with long, unkempt hair; she wears a gray cloak over a green dress, and her eyes are red from continuous weeping. The *cyhyraeth* is a similar spirit in Welsh folklore, represented as a disembodied, moaning voice which sounds before a person's death. The legend of the *cyhyraeth* is sometimes conflated with tales of the *Gwrach-y-Rhibyn*, the Hag of the Mist, a hideously ugly old woman with a harpy-like appearance: disheveled hair, withered arms, leathery wings, long black teeth, and pale corpse-like features. At night, she approaches the window of someone who is about to die and calls their name. Other times, she is said to travel beside them, invisible, and to utter her cry when they approach a stream or a crossroads. Sometimes, like the *bean nighe* — the Washerwoman at the Ford in Scottish folklore — she is depicted as washing her hands there.

Today, like so much else of import, Death has come to be associated largely with masculine qualities; the Grim Reaper of popular imagination, for example, is incontrovertibly male. But in her marvelous debut novel *Mrs Death Misses Death*, poet Salena Godden personifies Death as a working-class Black woman — sometimes an old "homeless black beggar woman with knotty natty hair"; sometimes a "kind black lady"; sometimes a young, "shimmering" Nina Simone. This guise allows Mrs. Death — a surprisingly humorous woman who enjoys an evening spent watching TV, with a glass of red wine in her hand — to pass through the world incognito, because, as she points out, "Only she that is invisible can do the work of Death. And there is no person more silenced than the woman, talked over, walked over and ignored than the woman, the poor woman, the poor old woman, the poor old black woman, your servant bent over a mop, cleaning the floor of a hospital."

After an eternity spent unseen and unheard, Mrs. Death desperately wants to share her stories, and so she selects Wolf Willeford, an East London poet, to compile her memoir. It's a pretty rocky ride; Mrs. Death isn't your average surly skeleton. "When you die," she tells Wolf,

> it will not be how you think or when you expect.
> I do not come for you like a cleaner when it is
> handy and convenient for you. ... So take today
> and blow its mind; take this today and suck it
> dry. Take today and fill it with the best of you.

Take today and down it in one, take today like
a shot of petrol and set your day alight. Take
today and fuck it like the last fuck in Pompeii
as burning lava covers your home. Like the last
fuck before they switch off the light, shut the
curtains. Like the last fuck before they shut
down the machines, like the last fuck before
they drop the fucking bomb. Fuck it. Once and
for all. Fuck it tenderly and tell it you love it,
fuck it and hold it, fuck it and look it in the eye,
tell it you love it, but then fucking let it go.

~

It's not surprising, perhaps, that all through my treatment
and into the months of recovery beyond, I asked myself how
I would feel if the Hag of the Mist were to come and call my
name. Because walking through the valley of the shadow of
Death brings a vivid awareness that you might have little
time left in this world, and this knowledge brings everything
in your life into sharp focus. When you really understand,
perhaps for the first time — viscerally understand — that
your life might soon come to an end, continuing to hurtle
full tilt along a false path simply isn't an option. Death is a
fierce fuel for the alchemical fire; transformation isn't just
possible — it's inevitable.

The path that I was walking was nothing if not a path
of fire. Fire haunted me. I happened upon it everywhere: in
art, in writing, in stories — and, above all, in dreams. Just
a handful of weeks before my diagnosis, I'd had another of
those "big dreams" of which Jung wrote. It began when I
found myself locked in a small, dark cell, staring aghast at
my jailer: a hairless man, dressed in a belted, ocher gown.
He explained that I was going to be spending six months in
this jail. I had no idea why I was there, and declared that I

couldn't possibly take six months out of my busy life; surely
I would at least be able to go home during that time for
the occasional visit? Apparently, I would not. I must remain
here, he said, and then he gestured to a very small locker at
the side of my prison bed. *What will you bring with you*, he
asked, *to fill that little locker?* And I understood that I must
choose very carefully, and pack only what seemed to me to
be essential. What was it that I would need, I wondered in
the dream — not desire, but actually need? What was it that
would help me survive during those six months in prison,
and what was it that would nourish my soul? I turned away
from him, unsure, and noticed a candle on a wall shelf at
the other side of the bed. I held a match to its wick, and
it burst into radiant flame and burned brightly, hissing like
a gas-fueled blowtorch. Interesting, the jailer said: *a holy
flame. I wouldn't call it that*, I muttered, but he simply
smiled. The dream ended there, but I woke with feelings
both of foreboding and of possibility.

A holy flame: the transformative fire of alchemy. The holy
death which precedes a holy rebirth. A prophetic dream, for
sure. The first thing I had to consider, when I learned that
I was to undergo six months of intensive treatment, was
precisely that question of what I really needed to focus on
during what seemed incontrovertibly like a prison sentence.
This wasn't a question of choice; I simply wouldn't have
the energy to do everything I'd done before. I was going
to have to whittle away at my usually impossible schedule,
and seriously. What was it then, that I really wanted to do?
What was I doing because I was in the habit of doing it, or
because I felt I must; and what was it that actually gave me
joy? Who was I, in the end, after all? And after the fierce fire
of the cancer crucible had burned away all my superfluities,
what would then be left? Because if I understood anything
about this long upcoming passage through darkness, it
was that some things that needed to break in me had been

broken, and after the treatment had ended it would be time to put myself back together in a new way.

At such a time, everything insignificant simply falls by the wayside. The absolute necessity of forensically auditing your life must surely be the key benefit of a life-threatening illness. There's no room for a "not now"; no room for a "maybe later, when I have more time." You may never have more time; time has suddenly become startlingly finite. Time, like toilet rolls and pasta during the first days of the pandemic in spring 2020, has simply vanished from the shelves. That concentrates your mind, and it focuses your energies; there's no space for new goals and new agendas. And in this fallow time — in this ultimate place between stories — space is finally cleared for new growth.

The truth is, I didn't hesitate for a moment in brutally auditing my life; I didn't experience a single moment of resentment or dismay or doubt. All that I felt was relief. As if I'd finally been released from the asylum; finally been freed of everything that anyone could ever expect of me that would weigh me down. And so, over the course of treatment, unpleasant though it certainly was, this newfound freedom ensured that the underlying texture of every single day was joy. Joy at the chance to shed another skin; gratitude for the chance at another profound transformation. In the middle part of my treatment, I watched a recent movie, *Ordinary Love*. It stars Liam Neeson and Lesley Manville as an "ordinary couple" from Belfast who are faced with her sudden diagnosis of breast cancer and subsequent treatment. At the end of it all, Manville's character is sitting in a café with a friend. When her treatment first began, she tells him, she was afraid that it would change her. But now, several months on, she sees that it hasn't changed her at all — and she is glad about that.

It was one of the few times in my life when I really would have liked to break the TV and scream invectives at the screenwriter. Because these journeys through the valley of the shadow of Death are *supposed* to change us. That's what they're for. To get through several months of savage treatment for a disease that otherwise will kill you, without having learned a thing — that isn't an achievement, it's a failure. A failure of imagination, at the very least. The ability to give ourselves over to transformation, no matter how dark and daunting the pathway through it might be, is evidence that we are still growing; evidence that we are still living. Still living all the way up to the end. It's evidence that we're not done yet. It's necessary and right that we should be changed. During any descent into a feared and terrifying Underworld, we're required to eat of its fruit — even when we've been told it's forbidden.

And so, at the end of this brutal but restorative treatment, all washed up and wiped out, but burning with new insights, I am filled with a sense of acute clarity. I've learned what is important to me; I know what I have to do and how to do it. I've reacquainted myself with delight, with the pleasure of time and space to simply be. What survived the cull, and what I took with me into that six-month-long sentence, was simple enough: a fleecy leopard-skin dog coat to remind me of what love and loyalty is, the power of imagination, and the tools of my writing trade to translate my imaginings into words. I made time for myself, and time for family and friends; I ate good food and drank a little good wine. I spoke to trees and sang to crows, and rejoiced in every flower that bloomed in my garden with the coming of spring. Nothing else mattered, in the end, but these things; I allowed the rest to swiftly slide away.

The challenges and opportunities that I faced as a consequence of a life-threatening cancer diagnosis are really no different in their essence from the challenges that each of us faces as we approach elderhood. My journey through the valley of the shadow of Death was rather more acute, that's all. An illness like this leaves you with little choice but to transform, and expedites a transformation that might otherwise take years to complete — or perhaps might never happen at all.

Although the latest medical statistics suggest that as many as half of us will develop cancer at some point during our lives — mostly in our elder years — the same transformations are required of all of us as we approach elderhood, whether we are hurled headlong into them through illness or not. In the last part of our life, focus is everything. The years when we imagined we needed to be all things to all people are long gone, along with our dilettante days: the days of experimenting with this and that, of adopting and discarding different personas, of reinventing ourselves for every season of the year. Now, it's time to get serious. To let the inessential fall away, and focus on the essence of who we are. What is it that is left of us when Old Bone Mother comes along and strips that old, decaying flesh from our bones? Who is it that we are; what is it that we feel we are here to do? What do we imagine these final years of our lives are really for?

In our journey to become true elder women, we need — like all those fine heroes who are brave enough to kiss the Hag — to actively choose to embrace what most horrifies us. For many of us, those fears center around the dissolution of the aging body, the likelihood of serious illness, the inevitability of our final death. To grow old with hagitude is to see all this with clear and open eyes, and vow to carry on, nevertheless, in the face of it.

Hagitude. For me, fire-obsessed as I seem to have become, hagitude also encompasses the archetypal qualities of a dragon. In British myths and folktales, dragons live in caves or deep lakes — places that, traditionally, conceal entrances to the Otherworld. In these deep, dark places of the Earth, dragons are known to guard the most precious treasure. Fierce, protective, and gloriously herself, the dragon roars with the fire of transformation. This powerful winged creature — the quintessential bearer of the holy flame — represents, in alchemy, the process of renewal. Just as that ancient symbol, the ouroboros — the dragon or serpent which circles around to eat its own tail — represents the eternal cycle of death and rebirth, and shows us that the end of everything is already present in its beginning. The ouroboros can be seen in all its glory in an early alchemical text: the *Chrysopoeia* of Cleopatra the Alchemist, who we encountered in chapter 1.

In embracing our hagitude, kissing our Inner Hag — and whether we are forced to by illness or not — we must at the same time embrace the strange adventure of a life lived in the face of death. *In the midst of life we are in death* — the first line of a Gregorian chant known as "Antiphona pro Peccatis" or "de Morte." The first reference to it occurs in a written New Year's Eve religious service from the 1300s, though it's been suggested that the original source is from the year 903, in a battle song by Notker the Stammerer, a monk of the Abbey of Saint Gall. Thomas Cranmer's English-language version of the original Latin chant was incorporated into the burial service in the Book of Common Prayer.

Media vita in morte sumus. I came to realize, shortly into my treatment, that lymphoma wasn't my first experience of living life in the midst of death; in fact, I had actively chosen to live in this way once before — that time when, at thirty-eight years old, I decided to learn to fly to overcome a fear of flying. I couldn't have expressed my reasons for making that decision so clearly at the time, but as the years passed I came to understand that fear of death — fear of so many things — had been preventing me from being wholly alive. The only way I could imagine of breaking through everything that was holding me back, was to face Death and look her unflinchingly in the eye. I needed to learn what it was to burn, to risk, and finally to fully live. And so, two or three times a week for the best part of a year, that was precisely what I did. Every time I hoisted myself up into the narrow seat of that tiny tin can I was entrusting my life to, I genuinely believed I might possibly die. I was obsessed with small-plane accident statistics; it wasn't an entirely foolish belief. But more than anything in the world, I needed to know what I might become if only I could break through my fear. What would I risk to become that unknown thing? I would, I discovered, risk everything. Because "everything" is the only answer that counts.

During that year of dancing with Death in turbulent American skies, I felt more alive than I had ever felt before. I felt so clear, so vivid, so incandescent with joy that I feared I would burst into flame. By the end of it, standing on an arid New Mexico runway, clutching the flimsy pink slip of paper that I could now trade in for my pilot's license, I was utterly transformed. If I could do this, I firmly believed, I could do anything. And the first thing I did was finally to break free from the stultifying, soul-destroying corporate job that had represented safety for too many years, and I thoroughly reimagined my life.

Now, in order to fully live, in order to fully submit to the imminent flowering of my elderhood, it seemed that again I was going to have to test myself against Death. But more than this: now, I needed to befriend her. I remembered that when Nell had first been diagnosed with lymphoma, I told my friend Moya that I felt as if Death, uninvited, had walked through the door and sat down to eat at my table. Now, though, my job was to welcome Death in. To engage her in conversation, to come to know her properly for the first time. To pour her a glass of rich red wine and say,

Welcome, guest. Because this being human is a guest house, and Death the most honored guest of all.

We walk through the valley of the shadow of Death because we have no choice; we are required to go precisely to this place where we do not want to go. There is no map of this valley; there are no well-trodden paths. We make our own way through, hand in the hand of the shadowy being who walks by our side whether we invite her to or not. Look up: a red kite is flying overhead, and Old Bone Mother lurks in the shadows. Walk and breathe; breathe and walk until, finally, you discover you're no longer afraid.

As elders, our job is to die as eventually we came to live — always in the service of life. The nature of that service might be unique to each of us, but there is one common question that we all should ask ourselves, as we prepare to pass the baton of life to the generations that follow us. What is the legacy we each want to leave behind; what is it that we dream of passing on?

Virginia Woolf addresses this question in my favorite of her novels, *To the Lighthouse*. Mr. Ramsay wants his legacy to be a great book; Mrs. Ramsay wants hers to be a great dinner party. That might sound trivial, but in Woolf's eyes it isn't. At first, the dinner party that Mrs. Ramsay finally succeeds in constructing looks likely to become a disaster: four guests are late returning from the beach; Mr. Ramsay is rude to everyone; and one of the guests, Charles Tansley, bullies another — the artist Lily Briscoe. In the opening of the chapter which tells of the dinner party, the perspective shifts rapidly from one guest's perceptions of it to another's, offering the impression that each of them feels terribly distant from the others: "rough and isolated and lonely." But the group dynamic seems to shift as candles are lit, and as the darkness outside offers only a world in which "things wavered and vanished." Almost in spite of themselves, the guests find community in reacting against this sudden sense of uncertainty, and, for the remainder of the dinner, manage to create a collective meaning and order out of individual existences that seem, alone, to possess neither. By the end of the party, it's clear that Mrs. Ramsay has fully expressed her gift — a gift which Lily defines as a talent for creating social harmony that is almost artistic in nature. If Mrs. Ramsay is an artist, Lily reflects, then the dinner party must be her medium; the purpose of her art seems to be, as it is for Lily, to break down the barriers between people — to unite them and allow them to experience each other's essential nature in a brief moment of perfect understanding. In this sense, Mrs. Ramsay's dinner party is quite simply her masterpiece: the necessary and beautiful expression of the gift that is uniquely hers.

Some of the oldest spiritual traditions of Europe suggest that each of us is born with such a gift — what Plato referred to as a "genius," but which is often referred to today as a "calling." In his bestselling book *The Soul's Code: In Search of Character and Calling*, James Hillman declared: "Each person enters the world called." Each of us, in other words, came to the world — in this particular place, at this particular time — for a purpose. Calling, in the sense that Hillman defined it, has little to do with "fate" or "destiny," and — in my own view, at least — doesn't necessarily have anything to do with occupation. For many people, that sense of calling has very much more to do with ways of being in the world, rather than ways of doing.

Hillman's notion of calling can be traced back at least as far as the Classical Greek philosopher Plato, who expressed the idea in the "Myth of Er," a legend that concludes his book *The Republic*. In it, a man called Er dies in battle. He comes back to life again (handily) just as he's placed on his funeral pyre, and then tells the onlookers about his time in the afterlife. Er's story proposes that before each of us is

THE VALLEY OF THE SHADOW OF DEATH   291

born, we (as souls) select the new life that we will be born into, along with a purpose for us to fulfill, or a unique gift to be expressed, during the course of that lifetime. To help with this selection process, each soul must pass under the throne of the goddess Ananke (Necessity) — the mother of the Fates, and the one who, Plato said, helps establish what is necessary for each soul to do or to be when it enters the world. Nevertheless, the ultimate choices are made by the individual: "Your genius will not be allotted to you, but you choose your genius," the souls are told. After the soul's intentions have been agreed, it travels to the Plain of Oblivion where Lethe, the river of forgetfulness, flows; once it has drunk from its waters, it emerges into its new life irritatingly ignorant of its prebirth choices. We might roll our eyes, but that, it seems, is the whole point: the essence of the soul's journey is to uncover its purpose, to find and reveal its "genius" within the constraints set by Necessity, and to grow and transform along the way. The good news is that we don't do this entirely alone; the soul is accompanied into this life by a "daimon" — a spiritual companion (the equivalent, for example, of the "guardian angel" in some traditions) who acts as a kind of "carrier of our destiny," and constantly nudges us to fulfill it.

Hillman took up these ancient ideas, similarly suggesting that, before we are born, the soul chooses the pattern that it wants to live out, the lessons it wishes to learn, and the unique quality, "genius," or gift that it wants to bring into the world. And so each of us, according to this perspective, carries inside us an innate vision — a kind of concealed invisible potential — which we are meant to discover and express during the course of our lives. Hillman used many terms for this vision, but my favorite way of imagining it is as an acorn, because the acorn, like any seed, carries within it the image of, and the potential to become, the oak tree that it might eventually be — given the circumstances which would allow it to flourish. But there is, of course, no guarantee that it *will* flourish. All seeds need good soil in which to root and grow; the trick for each of us is to find the conditions in which our own unique acorn seed can thrive.

This image or potential which we carry inside — whatever we might imagine it to be — guides us through the course of our life, and presses us to remember what we're living for. Sooner or later, something tugs at us, and we're called to follow a particular path; what we must then do is be sure that we take the path which aligns our lives with our calling, rather than another which might seem to be the path of least resistance. But the paths we encounter as we walk through life will keep on trying to adjust themselves to our overall purpose or calling. And so, in other words, the journey which will ultimately lead us to fulfill our calling, reshapes itself in response to the choices we make. We are always going to encounter paths that align us with our calling; the world never gives up on us.

Although this all sounds rather fatalistic, Hillman is at great pains to assert his belief that expressing our calling is very much a potential, not a predetermined pattern. We move through life, he said, in continual, moving adjustments — not following some grand predestined design. It's also important to understand that here the journey really is all: most of us don't come to understand our calling until later in life, because uncovering it is a lifetime's work. And even after we've arrived at what we think is our destination, we're still not at the end of our quest — because the ways in which our calling manifests itself will continue to shift through the years. The purpose of life is continuous transformation; we're not here to turn to stone.

It's also important, when we look back on our journey through life, not to beat ourselves up for the times when hindsight allows us to understand that we took one or more paths which weren't aligned with our calling. It's in following those "wrong" paths that the deepest learning occurs. Nevertheless, by the time we reach the threshold of elderhood, time is running short. I believe that what Jung characterized as the purpose of the second half of life — the task of individuation — is actually the task of finally revealing our calling, of letting everything that is superfluous to that task fall away, and dedicating ourselves to the wholehearted expression of our "genius." Jung's ideas on individuation drew on the writings of Aristotle, who used the word *entelechy* to express the idea that there is a unique pattern, or seed, within the psyche of each living being. This has nothing to do with grandiosity, or a sense of being in some way "special"; it simply means that each of us is a unique expression of what it is to be human, and each of us has the opportunity in our lives to discover that uniqueness: our most authentic self. Jung described this as understanding the *Imago Dei*: the image of the Divine in us.

To accept the idea of calling doesn't require any specific religious beliefs; it is quite simply about learning to live our lives as if they mattered. It's about finding meaning. It is beautiful work which is not so much about doing and accomplishing as it is about developing and expressing a vision for your life. Because to express our calling is to allow ourselves to express a mode of being that is unique to us: one singular, exceptional facet of the creative life force of the universe — whatever you might conceive that to be.

To me, this idea of calling — the idea that we're ultimately driven to express our own unique gift or genius, come what may — feeds into my often-stated belief that we're not here to be safe, but to risk everything. We didn't come here for the purpose which much of Western society seems to want us to believe in: to accumulate sufficient wealth so that we can "retire" (from what? From life itself?) at the age of sixty or thereabouts, to a nice house in a nice safe neighborhood, to stop work and play golf or go on round-the-world cruises, and wait to die. That's not what our elder years are for, and nor are they for locking ourselves away in the seeming safety of ghettos or "retirement communities," abnegating responsibility for this too-challenged world which we helped create. It's not that we shouldn't hope for safety and pleasure in our lives — but these things shouldn't be our primary motivation. We're here to risk everything to fulfill our calling, to walk wholeheartedly along the path which leads us there, even if that path is difficult sometimes, and dangerous.

There are two key aspects to this work of expressing our calling; the first relates to our own individual soul journey through this life, to our necessary growth as a soul. What is it that we came here to learn? The second relates to our service to the world: What particular, unique gift do we bring to this world, at this time? How do we serve its evolution, and participate in its journey of becoming? It's important, when we reflect on calling, that we hold these two things in balance: first, service to ourselves, and our own soul journey — which is intimately entangled with the second: service to the soul of the world, and the unfolding journey of the cosmos. To do the work we came here to do, we have to say no to the cultural narrative which would render elder women invisible or write us off as irrelevant. But first, we have to take responsibility for ourselves and find a narrative to offer in its place — to uncover our own unique Inner Hag, and extend her fearlessly into the world instead.

~

After the ritual dismembering which occurs during our initiation into this new phase of our lives, the work of re-membering begins. How do we begin this process; where do we find the clues which will guide us in putting ourselves back together? My own "little death" enabled me to discover what it was that I really loved, what the work was that I really wanted to do. But discovering who we are, at the core of us, is about more than just discovering the work which brings us genuine joy. How, then, do we catch a glimpse of the truth of who we are? How do we construct an image of the elder that we're destined to become? — the elder woman who represents the kernel of our gift, our genius? How do we mature into our own unique brand of hagitude?

For me, the greatest clues of all can always be found in stories, and I hope that the stories I've presented throughout this book will offer some helpful places to begin. Which of those archetypal expressions of female elderhood did you most resonate with? Which of those rooms in the House of Elders do you feel most called to occupy? Baba Yaga's shapeshifting hut in the woods, with its man-size oven dominating a kitchen haunted by disembodied hands? Or the Henwife's cozy parlor, with cake on the table and a steaming mug of tea ready and waiting for the troubled young woman who comes to ask her advice?

Most of us will find that we relate to more than one of the archetypal old women who appear among the pages of this book, but the chances are that just one of them will most clearly reflect the essence of our individual calling. I am drawn in one way or another to several of these archetypes: to the truth-telling, bullshit-detecting Loathly Lady; to the Dangerous Old Woman who presents us with life-and-death choices to test our mettle…But it is the Wise Old Woman — the solitary old woman with deep vision who acts as a conduit between this world and the imaginal — who tugs at my heart more and more as I grow older. In that respect, I'm circling back around to the stories I loved most as a child: the stories in which she appeared. The solitary, mysterious old woman who can nevertheless always be found when she's needed. She's been with me pretty consistently through this last, most challenging of

years. Her candlelit room in the House of Elders is furnished
with skulls and bones, littered with feathers and rocks and
shells. There's a fox skin draped over the back of a chair, and
neatly tied bundles of homegrown mugwort hang drying over
the chimney breast which embraces her perpetual fire.

We can also find clues in the poems that break our
hearts or bring us joy; in the works of art that capture our
imagination and transport us into another world — and in
the objects we scatter through our houses: the things we
collect that somehow reflect us. So I find myself returning
now to those found objects of mine, thinking of the way
I am gathering them around me, as if — in the words of
the late Jungian analyst Marion Woodman — I'm gathering
together the prodigal parts of myself and welcoming them
home.[112] Somehow, these ordinary objects help me to make
sense of the muddle; when I look at them I see patterns
and connections that in some deep way go beyond words,
somehow make sense of me. So I'm thinking about the
objects I consider in some way to be sacred; about the things
that I might wish to take with me when I die. I am thinking,
I suppose, about grave goods.

The Hallstatt culture was the predominant Western and
Central European culture of the late Bronze Age (from the
twelfth to the eighth century BCE) and the early Iron Age
(from the eighth to the sixth century BCE). During this
time, members of its nobility were buried in mounds, along
with certain objects which were believed to have utility or
value in the afterlife. Noblemen were buried with funerary
carts, wagons, and chariots; the Lady of Vix was buried
with a torque, a necklace of amber, bronze bracelets, and
anklets. During the La Tène period, which developed and
flourished during the late Iron Age (from about 450 BCE to
the Roman conquest in the first century BCE), warriors were
buried with their armor, swords, and spears. Grave goods at
this time were often of Roman origin and included lamps,

coins — which were mostly placed in the mouth — phallic amulets, and clay figures of Venus. There was also a custom of providing the dead with food and drink, along with drinking and eating vessels, and related objects like cauldrons; animal bones were often included too.

Of all the objects which I've gathered around me in my house, I am wondering which ones I would want to carry with me into the next life. Which of them represent what I love most about this world and my place in it? My fox skull, certainly; fox is one of those creatures whose presence brings me utter joy. Beautiful, clever, playful, feisty fox. Nell's leopard-skin coat, for what would humans be without the company of dogs? Who else can remind us so perfectly of our own animal nature; who else will love us when everyone else has drifted away? The feather of a gray heron, in memory of the powerful, shapeshifting hags of my tradition. A hag stone, to peer back into this world from the Otherworld. A mermaid's purse to remind me of the north-eastern sea I grew up by, and the wild western shores I've inhabited for so many years of my adult life. The tiny box of bat bones with its transparent lid, as a symbol of rebirth. The beautiful, dead but still vibrantly yellow carcass of a brimstone moth, a symbol of the soul. The seagull's wing, found on a beach at Achill Island in the far west of Ireland, as a reminder that once, against all odds, I learned to fly. And if I could choose my own shroud, I would for sure be buried inside a wolfskin. With a sprig of rosemary; that's for remembrance.

My friend Caro came to the idea of grave goods ahead of me. Caro makes drawings and paintings from wild and ancient materials such as ocher paint, oak gall ink, and handmade charcoal. She also makes objects, which can be years in the making and honing. "For the last seven years," she says, "I've been making a series of objects that, if I'm lucky enough to have a say in my ultimate end, will be buried with me and so returned to earth when I die. They include a bronze sword, deerskin clothes, oak-gall-ink-inscribed shoes, a foraged-materials apple basket, knives, cups, footwear, jewelry, and ritual items. There's a small hidden box of yew seeds. And all of it to be contained in a wicker coffin, with a woolen shroud. Everything is made from natural materials. Every few months I add something to the mix, and it's an ongoing work that I expect to last the rest of my life. The items I've included here reflect my love of earth, my life in nature, in martial arts, and drawing. To accept these materials from the land, to transform them with delight and some skill, and eventually return them to earth, feels like a true expression of my gratitude."

There was no sudden decision to start making these grave goods, she tells me. "A couple of years into accruing these objects around me I suddenly realized what they were: not some sideline to my art practice, but a major part of the work. What got me started with this project was bringing together drawing, making objects, and gathering wild materials. There's no consistency in the era of these objects, but instead the forms follow the materials and my inclinations. Some things seem Bronze Age, others Stone Age, some almost modern. One day some future archaeologists will have a fun puzzle to unravel! I think that humor is vital to engaging with one's aging and mortality yet remaining joyful. The punch line to everyone's life is the same: we die. So, the task is, how do I tell this joke well, weave this story richly, fully live this life with all its sudden plot twists, and keep both my wits intact and my spirit raised? It seemed to me that my hands had the answer when they were handling wild goods found in the land. So, I go along with the wisdom hidden in my fingertips, which is always truer than any idea my mind cooks up."

Grave goods, of course, assume the existence of a grave, and I do admit to having something of a penchant for graveyards. During the years I lived in London as a PhD student, I briefly lived near Highgate cemetery; my landlady had a connection there, and so I was allowed a brief unguided sojourn among its wonders. Nearly forty years on, I can still feel the atmosphere of the place: its tree-lined paths, its old tombs, stone angels, and statues royally robed in moss and ivy. I wasn't at all interested in the much-visited grave of Karl Marx, but I'd made a point of researching where to find those of Christina Rossetti, George Eliot, and Elizabeth Siddal — women I admired for many different reasons. At the risk of stating the obvious, in a graveyard there's no ignoring Death; Death is precisely what it's about. They are liminal places, on the cusp of this world and the next; they're also places of ritual leave-taking. I love the fact of their existence; I love the sense of continuity, of communal history, of shared sorrow.

But as much as I love graveyards, I'm not sure that full-up burial is for me. In this chronically overcrowded world, cremation seems like a more suitable option. One final foray into the crucible; one last calcination. The ultimate in transformations; the greatest alchemical work of all. Would my collection of grave goods burn along with me? I don't think I could bear the thought of it. I'll plan for them to be buried with my ashes; it's a practice with a strong and ancient pedigree. Perhaps, when dust returns to dust and those ashes are offered back to this beautiful, animate earth, Old Bone Woman will visit again. Perhaps, accompanied by her entourage of skeletons, and guarded by her two silent monsters, she'll sleep on them — and birth me again into some new adventure; deliver me, squalling, into some other world.

A curious thing happened to me while I was writing this chapter about death. I realized that if I could go back to the beginning, whenever it might have begun, and obliterate my lymphoma before it properly took hold — I wouldn't choose to do it. Something about it has felt necessary, and the gifts it has offered have been too important to carelessly cast aside. It's part of my story now; it's part of who I am, and it's foundational in creating the elder I'm becoming. Would I feel differently if the lump on my neck hadn't vanished completely after two of the six cycles of chemotherapy, if I hadn't been told at the beginning that wiping it out was the most likely outcome? Perhaps. Though I don't yet know where this story will end, and, as in the finest and truest of stories, there are no easy guarantees; lymphomas can recur, and even though I'm in remission, the next couple of years will be critical. But Death has become my friend now; I've listened to her voice and felt the soft touch of her hand. When it's time to go home, I'll follow her there with few regrets.

By the time we get to our elder years, we've all experienced little deaths. The deaths of people we love and of the people we used to be — each of them dying so that the next new self can be born. We can't move forward without these endings, these necessary acts of letting go. We are all dying from the moment we're hurled headfirst and screaming into this world; we're always already slipping away. As the late Irish poet Eavan Boland writes in her remarkable poem "Anna Liffey":

> The body is a source. Nothing more.
> There is a time for it. There is a certainty
> About the way it seeks its own dissolution.
> Consider rivers.
> They are always en route to
> Their own nothingness. From the first moment
> They are going home.[113]

ACKNOWLEDGMENTS

I'm grateful as always to the inimitable Hannah MacDonald for her enthusiasm for this fourth book with September Publishing. I'm particularly grateful for her support and patience when my life took a few unexpected turns and this book ended up being over a year late.

Natalie Eslick's beautiful illustrations have perfectly captured my vision for the archetypal elder women who people these pages, and I'm deeply grateful for her care and commitment to the process over the two and a half years we've been talking about it all. Thank you, too, to all the women who donated their stories to *Hagitude*, to Jane Galer for reading and commenting on some of the trickier bits, and to Ceaití for allowing me to include her beautiful poem.

I'm grateful to the friends who saw me through the difficult stages of my journey with lymphoma, which both interrupted and fertilized the writing of this book, and who sent love and care packages. Angela Piears and Moya McGinley, you are the very best: the hags of all hags. Love and thanks also to Sarah Baylis, Caroline Ross, Kate Norbury, and to Cath van der Linden for "poetry as a railing." And all the too-many-to-mention other friends, readers, and students who kept me going with encouraging emails and kind thoughts. Thanks to Ruthie Kølle for holding the fort with all her usual heart, and Crystal Adkins for stepping in to help. Joe Landwehr, wood-wizard of the Ozarks, as always provided much-needed perspective and insight. And of course, I'm grateful to the hematology and chemotherapy teams at Aberystwyth's Bronglais Hospital for their fine care and for keeping it all going in the face of an impossible pandemic.

Other major supporters during the challenging last months of writing this book have included our elder and decidedly haggish border collie dog Nell, who paved the way and lent me her magical leopard-skin coat. The trees who listened so attentively — especially the Entwife, the Dragon Oak, and the Old Lady Yew. Maeve, the Kitten of the Apocalypse, who presided over the last six weeks of writing and made it all so very… interesting.

More than ever and above all, I'm grateful to my husband, David. For never flinching. For accomplishing all the necessary missions and a couple we didn't see coming. For the roses.

REFERENCES

All web links, unless indicated, were last accessed in February 2022.

1 "The Hag's Call" by Ceaití Ní Bheildiúin reprinted with kind permission of the author. The poem was originally written in Irish; that version, "Glaoch na Caillí," can be viewed at: https://www.connotationpress.com/featured-guest-editor /december-2011/1150-ceaiti-ni-bheildiuin-poetry.

2 https://www.theguardian.com/society/2019/aug/19/over-a -third-of-britons-admit-ageist-behaviour-in-new-study.

3 Carl Jung, *Modern Man in Search of a Soul.* Psychology Press (2001), p. 112.

4 https://www.newstatesman.com/lifestyle/2015/08/there-wont -be-blood-suzanne-moore-menopause.

5 Germaine Greer, *The Change: Women, Aging, and Menopause,* revised edition. Bloomsbury (2018).

6 https://www.theguardian.com/lifeandstyle/2019/may/11 /women-and-minorities-claiming-right-to-rage.

7 Rebecca Traister, *Good and Mad: The Revolutionary Power of Women's Anger.* Simon and Schuster (2018).

8 A. Freud, A. Strachey, A. Tyson, S. Freud, and F. Freud, *The Standard Edition of the Complete Psychological Works of Sigmund Freud, Vol. 12 (1911–1913).* Edited by James Strachey. Vintage (2001) p. 323.

9 R. Wilson and T. Wilson, "The Fate of the Non-treated Menopausal Woman: A Plea for the Maintenance of Adequate Oestrogen from Puberty to the Grave." *Journal of the American Geriatric Society* 11(1) (1963): pp. 1–12.

10 Robert Wilson, *Feminine Forever.* W. H. Allen (1966).

11 David Reuben, *Everything You Always Wanted to Know About Sex but Were Afraid to Ask.* McKay (1969).

12 Ursula K. Le Guin. "The Space Crone," in R. Formanek (ed.), *The Meanings of Menopause: Historical, Medical, and Cultural Perspectives.* Analytic Press (1990), p. xxiii.

13 http://www.profam.co.uk/how-it-works (Accessed 5 January 2021).

14 Friedrich Nietzsche, *Thus Spake Zarathustra.* Ernst Schmeitzner (1883).

15   Hua Ching Ni, *Complete Works of Lao Tzu*. Sevenstar
      Communications (1995).

16   Sharon Blackie, *If Women Rose Rooted*. September Publishing
      (2016), p. 329.

17   https://www.youtube.com/watch?v=dlmCvMRIZqw.

18   Anita Brookner, *A Start in Life*. Cape (1981).

19   Doris Lessing, *The Summer Before the Dark*. Bantam (1973).

20   Billy Gray, "'Lucky the Culture Where the Old Can Talk to the
      Young and the Young Can Talk to the Old': A Conversation
      with Doris Lessing." *Doris Lessing Studies* 24 (2004), pp.
      23–30.

21   Sylvia Townsend Warner, *Lolly Willowes*. Chatto & Windus
      (1926).

22   In: Bonnie J. Horrigan, *Red Moon Passage: The Power and
      Wisdom of Menopause*. Harmony Books (1996), p. 112.

23   C. G. Jung, *The Archetypes and the Collective Unconscious*.
      Translated by R. F. C. Hull. Pantheon Books (1959).

24   Toni Wolff, *Structural Forms of the Feminine Psyche*. Translated
      by P. Watzlawik. C. G. Jung Institute (1956.).

25   Hildegard of Bingen, *Meditations with Hildegard of Bingen*, by
      Gabriele Uhlein. Bear & Co. (1982); Joseph Baird and Radd K.
      Ehrman, *The Personal Correspondence of Hildegard of Bingen*.
      Three volumes. Oxford University Press (2006).

26   Ibid.

27   Ibid.

28   Plato, *Timaeus*.

29   Carl Jung, "Two Essays on Analytical Psychology," CW 7.
      Princeton University Press (1966).

30   Carl Jung, *Memories, Dreams, Reflections*. Vintage Books
      (1965).

31   Carl Jung, *Psyche and Symbol: A Selection from the Writings
      of C. G. Jung*. Edited by V. S. De Laszlo. Doubleday (1958),
      p. 334.

32   Dawna Markova, *I Will Not Die an Unlived Life: Reclaiming
      Purpose and Passion*. Conari Press (2000).

33   William James, *The Varieties of Religious Experience: A Study
      in Human Nature*. Longmans, Green & Co. (1902).

34   For a full discussion, see Ronald Hutton, *The Witch*. Yale
      University Press (2017).

35   L. J. Trotter, *The Witch of the Middle Ages, from the French of
      J. Michelet*. Simpkin, Marshall and Co. (1863).

36   Ovid, *Metamorphoses*. Translated by Brookes More, from the
      Cornhill edition of 1922.

37   https://www.heraldscotland.com/news/18833570.spell-wild
      -alice-tarbuck-witches-magic.

38   https://www.theguardian.com/books/2021/feb/09/mary-beard
      -witch-tweets-reflect-society-fear-older-women.

39   https://www.cosmopolitan.com/lifestyle/a22886013/witches
      -instagram-social-media-influencer; https://www.marieclaire
      .co.uk/life/witches-taking-over-instagram-672333.

40   J. K. Rowling, *Harry Potter and the Philosopher's Stone.*
      Bloomsbury (1997).

41   Whitley Stokes (ed. and trans.), "The Death of Crimthann, Son of
      Fidach, and the Adventures of the Sons of Eochaid Mugmedón."
      Revue Celtique 24 (1903), pp. 172–207.

42   See Jeanette King, *Discourses of Ageing in Fiction and Feminism:
      The Invisible Woman.* Palgrave Macmillan (2021).

43   In Lara Feigel, *Free Woman: Life, Liberation, and Doris Lessing.*
      Bloomsbury (2018).

44   Sharon Blackie, *The Long Delirious Burning Blue.* Riverwitch
      Press (2008).

45   David Whyte, from "All the True Vows," in *The House of
      Belonging.* Many Rivers Press (1997).

46   For more on the post-heroic journey, see Sharon Blackie, *The
      Enchanted Life.* September Publishing (2018).

47   Carol Shields, *Happenstance.* World Editions (2021).

48   Kuno Meyer, "An Old Irish Prayer for Long Life," in Oliver
      Elton (ed.), *A Miscellany Presented to John Macdonald Mackay,
      LL.D., July, 1914.* pp. 226–32.

49   Oein DeBhairduin, *Why the Moon Travels.* Skein Press (2020).

50   Ursula K. Le Guin, *No Time to Spare: Thinking About What
      Matters.* Houghton Mifflin Harcourt (2017).

51   https://www.theguardian.com/books/2006/jun/18/biography
      .features.

52   https://www.theguardian.com/artanddesign/2021/jul/04/paula
      -rego-tate-britain-exhibition-interview.

53   Betty Friedan, *The Fountain of Age.* Simon & Schuster (1993).

54   Diana I. Tamir, Andrew B. Bricker, David Dodell-Feder, and
      Jason P. Mitchell, "Reading Fiction and Reading Minds: The
      Role of Simulation in the Default Network." *Social Cognitive
      and Affective Neuroscience* 11(2) (2016), pp. 215–24.

55   Eleanor Hull, "Legends and Traditions of the Cailleach Bheara or
      Old Woman (Hag) of Beare." *Folklore* 38 (1927), pp. 225–54.

56   Máire Mac Neill, *The Festival of Lughnasa.* Comhairle
      Bhéaloideas Éireann (2008).

57   In Michael Newton, *Warriors of the Word.* Birlinn (2009).

58   J. G. McKay, "The Deer-Cult and the Deer-Goddess Cult of the
      Ancient Caledonians." *Folklore* 43 (1932), pp. 144–74.

59   Carl Jung, *Memories, Dreams, Reflections*. Random House
      (1965), pp. 358–59.

60   Joanna Macy, in Stephanie Kaza, *A Wild Love for the World:
      Joanna Macy and the Work of Our Time*. Shambhala (2020).

61   Carl Jung, *Psychology and Religion: West and East, CW* 11.
      Princeton University Press (1969).

62   See https://gateway-women.com.

63   See https://www.theguardian.com/commentisfree/2021/jul/31
      /fox-news-jd-vance-childless-left-week-in-patriarchy.

64   See https://www.theguardian.com/politics/2016/jul/09/andrea
      -leadsom-told-to-apologise.

65   Jamie Sams, in Bonnie J. Horrigan, *Red Moon Passage*. Thorsons
      (1997).

66   Leslie Marmon Silko, *Storyteller*. New York: Seaver Books,
      (1980), p. 247.

67   J. H. Delargy. "The Gaelic Story-Teller. With Some Notes on
      Gaelic Folk-Tales." *Proceedings of the British Academy* 31(177)
      (1945).

68   Clodagh Brennan Harvey, "Some Irish Women Storytellers and
      Reflections on the Role of Women in the Storytelling Tradition."
      Western Folklore 48(2) (1989), pp. 109–28.

69   John Heath, "Women's Work: Female Transmission of
      Mythical Narrative." *Transactions of the American Philological
      Association* 141(1) (spring 2011), pp. 69–104.

70   René Guénon, *Symbols of Sacred Science*. Translated by Alvin D.
      Fohr. Sophia Perennis (2004).

71   Claude Cahun, *Disavowals: Or Cancelled Confessions*. The MIT
      Press (2008).

72   Jeffrey H. Jackson, *Paper Bullets*. Algonquin (2020).

73   Richard Goswiller, *Revelation*, Pacific Study Series, Melbourne
      (1987).

74   https://the-mythic-imagination.mn.co.

75   Shon Faye, *The Transgender Issue*. Penguin (2021).

76   https://mermaidsuk.org.uk/wp-content/uploads/2021/09/260221
      -CYP-Mental-Health-Inquiry-Mermaids.pdf.

77   https://kathleenstock.substack.com/p/pride?s=r.

78   https://www.theguardian.com/uk-news/2021/dec/05/kathleen
      -stock-interview-university-sussex-transgender-headlines-2021.

79   See https://unherd.com/2022/06/i-was-hounded-out-of-school
      -for-transphobia for an interview with the schoolgirl.

80   See, for example, https://www.scotsman.com/news/opinion
      /columnists/young-womens-cruel-ageism-towards-old-lady
      -feminists-leaves-us-easy-prey-for-sexism-and-misogyny-susan
      -dalgety-3320203. Extract reproduced by kind permission of the
      author.

81   https://harpers.org/a-letter-on-justice-and-open-debate.

82   For a different perspective on "the conundrum of *Conundrum*"
      from a contemporary trans woman, see https://www.theparis
      review.org/blog/2021/01/29/the-conundrum-of-conundrum/.

83   Jan Morris, *Conundrum*. Faber & Faber (1974).

84   See https://www.britannica.com/topic/philosophy-of-art
      /Art-as-a-means-to-truth-or-knowledge.

85   https://languages.oup.com/word-of-the-year/2016.

86   Andree Kahn Blumstein, "The Structure and Function of the
      Cundrie Episodes in Wolfram's Parzival." *The German Quarterly*
      51(2) (1978), pp. 160–69.

87   https://en.wikipedia.org/wiki/Three_Billboards_Outside
      _Ebbing,_Missouri.

88   https://raginggrannies.org.

89   Nancy Schmitz, "An Irish Wise Woman: Fact and Legend."
      Journal of the Folklore Institute 14(3) (1977), pp. 169–79.

90   For more on the *bean feasa*, see Gearoid Ó Crualaoich, *The Book
      of the Cailleach*. Cork University Press (1983).

91   Emma Wilby, *Cunning Folk and Familiar Spirits*. Sussex Academic
      Press (2005).

92   See http://www.orkneyjar.com/folklore/witchcraft/spaewife.htm.

93   M. Winterbottom and R. M. Ogilvie (eds.), *Oxford Classical
      Texts: Cornelii Taciti: Opera Minora*. Oxford University Press
      (1975).

94   H. L. Jones (ed.), *The Geography of Strabo*. Harvard University
      Press (1924).

95   In Michael Scott, *Delphi*. Princeton University Press (2014).

96   Ibid.

97   Manda Scott, *Dreaming the Eagle* (2003), *Dreaming the Bull*
      (2004), *Dreaming the Hound* (2005), *Dreaming the Serpent
      Spear* (2006). Random House.

98   See http://accidentalgods.life.

99   Taisia Kitaiskaia, *Ask Baba Yaga: Otherworldly Advice for
      Everyday Troubles*. Andrew McMeel (2017); Taisia Kitaiskaia,
      Poetic Remedies for Troubled Times: From Ask Baba Yaga.
      Andrew McMeel (2020).

100 https://www.bustle.com/p/6-pieces-of-witchy-love-advice-from
-taisia-kitaiskaias-ask-baba-yaga-2345248.

101 https://lithub.com/baba-yaga-will-answer-your-questions-about
-life-love-and-belonging.

102 James Nowak, "Between Home and Hell." https://dark-mountain
.net/between-home-and-hell (December 21, 2018).

103 Sharon Blackie, *The Enchanted Life*. September Publishing
(2018).

104 "Samojedische Märchen," in Matthias Alexander Castrén,
Nordische Reisen und Forschungen (1857), pp. 157–64. I'm
grateful to Katrin Siek for translating the full story for me
from the German of Anton Schiefner, who in turn translated it
from the original Swedish. In its entirety, it might be one of the
strangest stories I've ever read.

105 Coleman Barks, *The Essential Rumi*. HarperCollins (2004).

106 See Barbara Freitag, *Sheela-na-gigs: Unravelling an Enigma*.
Routledge (2004).

107 Joseph M. McPherson, *Primitive Beliefs in the North-east of
Scotland*. Longman, Green & Co. (1929).

108 Marija Gimbutas, *The Language of the Goddess*. HarperCollins
(1989).

109 Edgar Herzog, *Psyche and Death: Death-Demons in Folklore,
Myths and Modern Dreams*. Spring Publications (2000), p. 209.

110 A. Partridge, "Wild Men and Wailing Women." *Eigse* xviii
(1980–81), pp. 25–37.

111 Mary Theresa McLaughlin, *Songs between Worlds: Enchantment
and Entrapment in the Irish Otherworld Song Tradition*.
Thesis submitted to the University of Limerick in fulfillment
of the requirements for the Degree of Doctor of Philosophy
(2018); Breandán Ó Madagáin, *Caointe Agus Seancheolta
Eile — Keening and Other Old Irish Musics*. Clo Iar-Chonnachta
Teo (2005).

112 Marion Woodman, *Bone*. Penguin (2001).

113 Eavan Boland, "Anna Liffey," in *In a Time of Violence*. Carcanet
Press (1994). Reprinted with the kind permission of Carcanet
Press, Manchester, UK, and W. W. Norton & Company, Inc.,
USA.

ABOUT THE AUTHOR

Dr. Sharon Blackie is an award-winning writer and an internationally recognized teacher whose work sits at the interface of psychology, mythology, and ecology. Her highly acclaimed books, courses, lectures, and workshops are focused on the development of the mythic imagination and on the relevance of myth, fairy tales, and folk traditions to the personal, social, and environmental problems we face today. Sharon has written five books of fiction and nonfiction, including the ecofeminist bestseller *If Women Rose Rooted*, and her work has been translated into multiple languages. Her writing has also appeared in several international media outlets, among them the *Guardian*, the *Irish Times*, and the *Scotsman*. Sharon lives on a small farm in the Cambrian mountains of Mid Wales with her husband and dogs.

www.hagitude.org
www.sharonblackie.net

NEW WORLD LIBRARY is dedicated to publishing books and other media that inspire and challenge us to improve the quality of our lives and the world.

We are a socially and environmentally aware company. We recognize that we have an ethical responsibility to our readers, our authors, our staff members, and our planet.

We serve our readers by creating the finest publications possible on personal growth, creativity, spirituality, wellness, and other areas of emerging importance. We serve our authors by working with them to produce and promote quality books that reach a wide audience. We serve New World Library employees with generous benefits, significant profit sharing, and constant encouragement to pursue their most expansive dreams.

Whenever possible, we print our books with soy-based ink on 100 percent postconsumer-waste recycled paper. We power our offices with solar energy and contribute to nonprofit organizations working to make the world a better place for us all.

Our products are available wherever books are sold. Visit our website to download our catalog, subscribe to our e-newsletter, read our blog, and link to authors' websites, videos, and podcasts.

customerservice@newworldlibrary.com
Phone: 415-884-2100 or 800-972-6657
Orders: Ext. 110 • Catalog requests: Ext. 110
Fax: 415-884-2199

www.newworldlibrary.com